ORIGINAL
PORSCHE 911
1964-1998

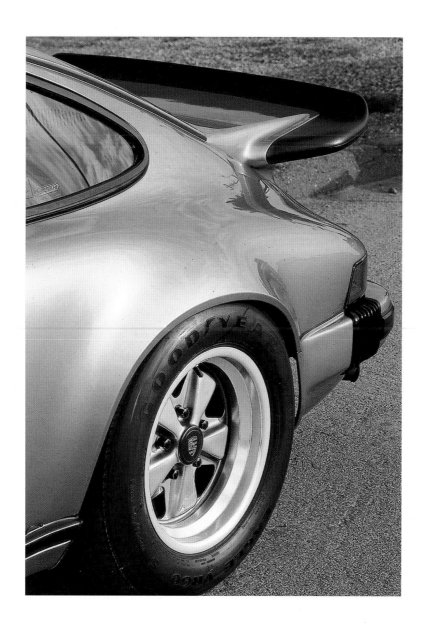

ORIGINAL
PORSCHE 911
1964 - 1998

The Definitive Guide to Mechanical Systems, Specifications and History

PETER MORGAN

Photography by John Colley, with David Fetherston,
Dieter Rebmann and Ian Kuah

© 2016 Quarto Publishing Group USA Inc.
Text © 2016, 2009, 1998, 1995 Peter Morgan

This edition published in 2016. Previous edition published in 2009 by Motorbooks, an imprint of Quarto Publishing Group USA Inc., 400 First Avenue North, Suite 400, Minneapolis, MN 55401 USA. Telephone: (612) 344-8100 Fax: (612) 344-8692

quartoknows.com
Visit our blogs at quartoknows.com

Motorbooks titles are also available at discounts in bulk quantity for industrial or sales-promotional use. For details contact the Special Sales Manager at Quarto Publishing Group USA Inc., 400 First Avenue North, Suite 400, Minneapolis, MN 55401 USA.

10 9 8 7 6 5 4 3 2 1

ISBN: 978-0-7603-5209-0

Acquiring Editor: Zack Miller
Project Manager: Jordan Wiklund
Art Director: Brad Springer
Cover Designer: Jay Smith–Juicebox Designs

Printed in China

Front and back cover images: © Michael Alan Ross

On the frontispiece: By 1973, the performance of the production 911 had reached a peak. This German-registered 2.4T shows off the lip spoiler introduced with the previous year's S model and optional for the T and E. For 1973 models the finish for the horn grilles and the trim around the driving lights changed from bright plated to black.

On the title page: 1974 2.8 Carrera.

Contents

Introduction

With a continuous production run of more than 50 years, the Porsche 911 has developed, evolved, evaded execution, matured, and been transformed in a style that no other automobile has ever experienced. It is an industry phenomenon, and the fascination with this evergreen sports car is still capturing new fans today as much as it did after its launch in 1963.

One of the 911's most fascinating aspects is the way its specification has not just evolved over generations but has often seen complete re-engineering to achieve ever improving performance, reliability, comfort, and, of course, profitability for its maker.

A grouping of faster 911s. In the foreground is a 1991 Carrera 2 RS, to the right a 1973 Carrera RS, and in the background a 1987 Carrera Club Sport.

The first edition of the book *Original Porsche 911* was published in 1993 with the objective of providing a quality reference for enthusiasts not only to identify the differences between the distinct generations of 911, but also to show the variances between similar models of the same type. A second edition followed in 1998, with the addition of the 993 series. It has become accepted as a standard reference on the model and has appeared in at least seven languages, further proof of the enduring love enthusiasts have for this sometimes quirky, but always exciting, rear-engine sports car..

With the introduction of the "new generation" water-cooled 911s in 1997, the previous models became near-instant classics. The air-cooled 911 has come to represent the best of Porsche, and enthusiasm for the models has increased spectacularly. With the unmatched charisma of competition success, old-school quality and reliability standards, and, most importantly, that instantly recognizable profile, these 911s are now the most sought-after classics in the world—be it a pioneering 1960s 2.0-liter or a relatively luxurious 993 Turbo S.

The key to this book's ongoing popularity is the remarkable access I had to Porsche's marketing and archived production records back in the early and mid-1990s. Such access is no longer possible in the super-corporate Porsche of today. Back then one could simply ring up the relevant staffer who possessed the information and sit down at a spare desk to trawl his often dusty files. Researching at Porsche in those days was an unforgettable experience, not least because of the remarkable enthusiasm that glued the business together.

"The styling cues of the 911 are in graphic and form—the shut lines of the bonnet, the doors, the engine lid, the drip rails, and obviously the side windows."
—Porsche designer Harm Lagaay

I'm flattered that this data has been much copied since and that this book remains a valid chronology of the air-cooled 911's production. Despite some gaps (in the early days of 911 production, in particular, when old, handwritten production information was sometimes lost), *Original Porsche 911* remains a record of the best information available at that time, which for Porsche was just before everything—including the 911—changed.

In this revised edition, I have updated some of the known errors in the earlier texts. It's always been a fundamental objective of *Original Porsche 911* to provide a reliable reference for all enthusiasts. If you see any obvious mistakes after reading this edition, please do get in touch.

I have played around with karts and cars since my early teens, but my first 911 experience didn't come until my mid-20s. Back in 1976, my head was turned by the wonderful sound of a contemporary Carrera as it rasped by in a busy main street.

Turbos are often described in superlatives. These views show the spectacular 360-brake-horsepower version of 993 (top) and its 408-brake-horsepower successor of 1995 (above). The latter view shows the profile that every schoolchild knows simply as "the Porsche."

I bought my first Porsche in 1978. It was a 1973 911T, and while I took to driving it with the windows down so I could hear that wonderful sound, I came to appreciate the car's surprising performance and what not to do when you find yourself going into a corner too fast. There were other downsides, of course. In our damp United Kingdom climate, the thing rusted like you wouldn't believe. Nevertheless, as one model after another found its way into my workshop, I came to appreciate the reliability of that six-cylinder engine and, despite the corrosion, the exquisite build quality of the body.

One 911 has stayed with me longer than any of the others: My 1972 911S has become the benchmark by which I judge all the modern reincarnations. The early 911s demand a period of learning from any driver before their full capabilities can be mastered, a fact that makes them completely unacceptable as user-friendly sports cars of the modern age. But their inherent agility, lightness of touch, and instant responsiveness are the key to the enduring 911 legend and remain the ultimate goal for the new generations to aim for.

The air-cooled 911s built from 1964 to 1998 have not changed, but our perception of them has transformed completely. It is sad that we no longer see most of the special 911s built during these years, as they are hidden away like art treasures. Many cars that survived decades of everyday use and, of course, motorsport have been "restored" to better-than-new condition. Often this is undertaken solely because of their potential financial value. This was never the use that Ferry Porsche and his team of engineers and craftsmen would have intended—even though they would have been in awe of the quality of many of these restorations. Many of the inquiries I get today are focused not on authenticity detail or relative performance but on identifying what is real or fake and what a car is worth. Nevertheless, the upside is that all air-cooled 911s are now desirable, not just the specials, and at least that has introduced a ladder of affordability into the market.

In technological terms, the air-cooled 911 was indeed a triumph of development over design. It's easy to compare a 1966 911S with a 1998 Carrera 4S. One may have more tech than the other, but the two cars have the same idiosyncrasies

Four cars show the evolution through the ages in a splendid photograph by Dieter Rebmann: 1964 911 (bottom left), 1973 911T 2.4 (bottom right), 1984 Carrera 3.2 (top left), and 1993 Carrera 4 (top right).

Owners of Featured Cars

In the United Kingdom:
Richard Baker (1965 911), David Cocker (1967 911S), Patrick Amos (1971 911 T 2.2), Mark Waring (1971 911S 2.2 and 1973 Carrera RS Touring), Anthony Minshull (1972 911T 2.4 U.S.), Nancy MacLean (1973 911T 2.4 Sportomatic), Dave Gray 1973 911E 2.4), the late Tony Knapp (1975 911 Carrera 2.7), Peter Hatfield (1977 911 Carrera Sport 3.0), Sue Baker (1979 911SC Targa Sportomatic), Peter Foskett (1982 911SC Sport), Andy Frost (1984 911 Carrera 3.2), Terry Davison (1987 911 Carrera 3.2 Cabrio Turbo-Look), John Colley (1987 911 Club Sport), Roger Vynne (1988 911 Anniversary), Mike Flannery (1989 911 Speedster), Ian King (1990 Carrera 4 Targa), Mike King (1991 Carrera 2 Tiptronic), Alan Stein (1976 911 Turbo), and Robin Duckitt (1989 911 Turbo).

In the United States:
Ernie Wilberg (1967 911S), Terry Zaccone (1968 911L Targa), Joe Hartman (1974 911 Carrera 2.7), Brian Carleton (1980 911SC Weissach), Jim Boyden (1986 911 Turbo), and Carlsen Motor Cars Inc. (1993 Carrera 2 RS America).

and driving charisma. They are 911s linked by a common passion—and that isn't a passion about their respective financial desirability. It is a passion to produce a sports car that delivers driving in its finest form.

Porsche's former chief designer and head of the Weissach Styling Department Harm Lagaay once said that 911 is not just a number. It represents a car concept—a package of engineering and styling—that is eternal. "No matter how many changes the car goes through," Lagaay says, "the philosophy of the car, namely the way it drives, the seating arrangement, the rear-engined drive, and so on, that is forever."

Those now-immortal three numbers, 911, have come to signify the benchmark by which every other sports car is measured. Just as it was 50-plus years ago, sports cars are still all about excitement and speed. This the 911 provides in abundance.

In this revised *Original Porsche 911*, I try to answer all the specification questions that I asked myself over the years. I had to leave out a lot, but it is down at the cotton-bud level of detail (to use a concours analogy) that the sifting has occurred. Option lists are an example: I have not been able to include the full worldwide option list for every year, especially where models are similar, but the lists presented give a feel for what is right and what is not.

The subject of specifications and their accuracy on the earlier models makes dedicated enthusiasts become emotional, but I would suggest that maybe we should not get so serious about this. In the 1960s and early 1970s, Porsche's attitude toward new component introduction was simple. The spirit of control was there in the form of the program changes from year to year, but on a detail level this pattern was often broken. When a new part or modification was considered, the engineers would first try to break it, say by thrashing a car around the Nürburgring or on a drive down to Sicily for the Targa Florio. Parts that survived usually found their way into production fairly quickly, so it was quite normal to see changes being rolled into production at any time of year as new stock became available. In those days the options list was fairly limited, but today the story is quite different. Part of the task of buying a recent 911 is to determine what factory options it has fitted and whether these options affect the value to a greater or lesser extent.

It is important to keep these thoughts in perspective. The differences make any prospective 911 more interesting. This guide cannot help you tell an original car from a rebuilt or customized one, but I hope it will give you the information to understand the original factory specifications from year to year.

This book is the result of a significant amount of personal research, but I could not have produced it without talking to a large number of people. Among those at Porsche in Stuttgart, I must mention Klaus Parr and his successor in the Porsche archive, Dieter Landenberger, plus Dieter's ever helpful associates Jens Torner and Dieter Gross. The original text could not have been produced without the enthusiastic help of the late Olaf Lang. Both Porsche Cars Great Britain and Porsche Cars North America opened essential doors in the research for the book. For this revised edition, I updated the early 911 data with the help of Allen Henderson.

I compliment John Colley on his superb photography of cars for this update. In the original text, in addition to Colley, David Fetherston, Dieter Rebmann, and Ian Kuah provided equally accomplished camera work from the United States and Germany. More shots were supplied by the late Jerry Sloniger and myself. We chose our cars carefully, and I thank all the owners who persevered with us in the task. Their names are listed in the accompanying panel.

Peter Morgan of Marlborough, England

The 2-Liter 911 (1963–1969)

The cry was heard after the prototype 901 was revealed at the Frankfurt Motor Show on September 12, 1963: "It's not a real Porsche." By that time, the company had built up a solid reputation based around the 356, a car that achieved its performance through fundamentally lightweight design and simplicity. For some people, therefore, the company had lost its way with the 901 by building a bigger, more powerful and more luxurious car. Porsche's first entirely new model since the 356 had been launched in 1948, the new concept was happily accepted by the majority as a major step forward, and customers clamored for a production version.

But the Frankfurt car, the result of a concentrated and tortuous development program that had started in earnest in 1959, was a one-off. It would be toward the end of 1964 before the company was ready to put the 901 into full production at its factory in Zuffenhausen, Stuttgart. In October 1964, the 901 became the 911 in response to Peugeot's trademark objections, and so the most famous three numbers in the sports car world were coined.

The small styling team, under the guidance of Dr. Ferry Porsche's son Butzi, developed a compact 2+2 shape that would prove to have a timeless profile. Combined with the rear engine location and a smooth aerodynamic profile, the 2+2 accommodation is the essence of the 911. The new car was unmistakably a Porsche, capturing

Evolution Outline

September 1963: Porsche presents the 901 prototype at the Frankfurt Motor Show.
August 1964: The 911 is introduced with two triple-choke Solex carburetors, 130 brake horsepower, and a five-speed gearbox.
March 1966: Weber carburetors replace Solex carburetors.
October 1966: The 911S with 160-brake horsepower and Fuchs wheels is introduced.
December 1966: The Targa begins production (with soft rear window), and a four-speed Sportomatic option is launched.
August 1967: The 911T is launched with 110-brake horsepower (replaces four-cylinder 912), the 911L is launched with 130-brake horsepower (replaces 911), and dual-circuit brakes are introduced.
August 1968: The 911E is launched with 140-brake horsepower (replaces the 911L), the 911S (170-brake horsepower) receives mechanical fuel injection, a glass rear window is added to the Targa, and the 911E and 911S have CD ignition.

The clean lines of the Porsche factory's own 1964 911 coupe. The first 911s had minimal flaring to their wings, giving the cars a clean aerodynamic shape. Evident in this view is the Durant driver's door mirror of 356 vintage.

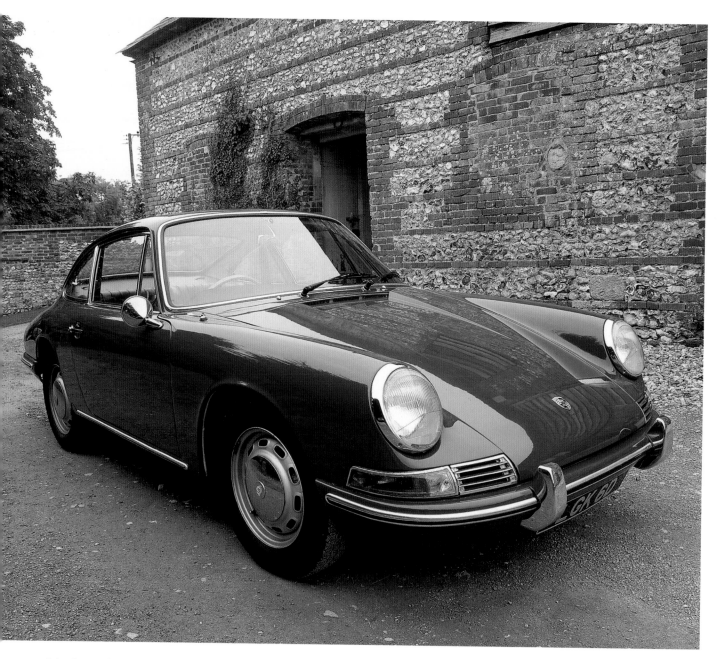

A timeless profile that is unmistakably a Porsche, as shown on Richard Baker's 965 model (above). Painted slate gray and fitted with steel wheels, this car was the fifth right-hand-drive 911 imported into the U.K. This view (opposite) of Ernie Wilberg's 1967 S shows the classic 911 roofline and the graceful double curve of the rear wing line.

accents from previous prototypes and from the 356 line, but it was also fresh. The windshield was more steeply raked than on the 356, and there was a larger glass area, but probably the single most distinctive styling feature was the gradual, yet continuous, curve of the roof from the top of the windshield to the rear bumper. It gave the car its excellent aerodynamic penetration and was at the same time attractive. The attention to detail was carried over to the interior, and several features, such as the grouping of the five large circular instrument dials, have endured throughout the course of 911 production.

The 2-liter cars were subject to a massive development effort after launch. The best of the bunch are probably the 1967 models (with their elegant simplicity, especially in the United States before emissions laws arrived) and the 1969 models (on which handling and braking were close to their best).

Bodyshell

The 911 bodyshells carry alphabetic designators, which make the differences easier to categorize. The first models formed the A-program, covering the cars from the start of production in August 1964 to July 1967. The chassis number of the earliest cars was carried on the left-hand door pillar, but by the start of proper A-program production a second chassis plate was carried on the lock plate at the front of the luggage compartment. The full chassis number was stamped on the bodyshell structure in the luggage compartment, on the left side to the rear of the fuel tank. The last four digits of the chassis number were also found on the doors (beneath the interior trim, under the opening vent) and on the bonnet and engine lid. This was a factory aid to ensure correct fit during assembly.

The layout of the 911 bodyshell was based around the rear engine location and the requirement to provide comfortable 2+2 accommodation for the occupants. Because the new Porsche was a luxury GT, it had to have satisfactory space for luggage too. With these major compartments defined, together with the essential wind-cheating profile and an ancestry traceable to the 356, the 911 shape began to evolve into its unmistakable form.

The basic bodyshell was a unitary design (with no separate chassis) with much of its strength coming from a stiffened floorpan, large box section sills (or rockers), and a stressed roof. Sheet metal box sections gave support for the engine and rear suspension. Bodyshell stiffness at the front derived from the assembly of the sheet panels, especially the sculpted inner wings and the front crossmember supporting the front of the fuel tank.

Compared with the 356, the new 911, surprisingly, was 61 millimeters (2.4 inches) narrower externally (but with more interior width) and 152 millimeters (6.0 inches) longer. The wheelbase was 111 millimeters (4.4 inches) more at 2,211 millimeters (87.0 inches), aimed at giving the 911 a more comfortable ride. Compared with other sports cars of the time, the 911 was still a short-wheelbase design, the E-type Jaguar, for instance, having a wheelbase of 2,438 millimeters (96.0 inches). The 911, with its overhanging engine installation and relatively small distance between the wheel centers, would give the engineers considerable challenges over the years. It would be some time before "development triumphed over design."

The earliest 911s had a more efficient aerodynamic shape than any previous Porsche. It came in part from the narrower body and from attention to detail,

Despite its lowered suspension and wider tires, this 1968 911L Targa is a remarkably original car because Terry Zaccone has owned it since new and has covered 320,000 miles. The car has made more than 2,500 race starts. Note the U.S.-specification sealed-beam headlamps with their large chromed surrounds, the 1968-only side reflectors, and the "new" Durant external mirror.

like integrating the front and rear bumpers into the body shape. The original 901 was even better aerodynamically than the Abarth Carrera racer that was considered state-of-the-art at the time. Of course, as the years passed, the slippery shape grew more and more external bits and pieces, such as bumper over-riders, external mirrors, wider wheel arches, and even spoilers. I shall leave it to you to decide whether or not the engineers got the appearance right the first time.

An open version of the basic coupe was announced in September 1965, and Porsche conceived for it another term that has become an industry standard. The open-topped Targa went into production in December 1966 and featured a folding roof that stowed in the front compartment or behind the front seats. A zippered convertible-type plastic window covered the rear area on the first cars, giving a rather cheapened look for such a luxury GT model. The word *targa* is Italian for *shield*, and this is appropriate for the function of the brushed-finish stainless-steel roll hoop, but Porsche fans always refer to the factory racing success in the Targa Florio, the legendary Sicilian road race. This grueling event was won more times postwar by Porsche than by any other marque, and the Porsche marketing people loved the association.

The Targa model was not a true convertible but featured the first production roll-over bar. The roll-over bar, a wide-section hoop to which a removable roof section could be attached, acted as a stiffener for the chassis, which would otherwise have been weakened by the loss of the coupe's roof. In producing a convertible, the engineers wanted to avoid the usually significant weight increase that comes from additional chassis stiffening. They partially achieved their aim because the lower body panels and undertray are identical to the coupe's, the rigidity coming in part from the roll hoop. The reality was that Targas came out some 50 kilograms (110 pounds) heavier than the coupe. Targas would never be as rigid—and the early ones without the glass rear window were even more flexible—but the trade-off in handling was more than balanced by the attraction of open-air motoring.

The Targa was heavily marketed in the United States, brochures showing the various Targa configurations (top on or off, rear window in or out) described with attractive names like Spyder, BelAir, and Voyage. This model was truly versatile.

The development years immediately after the 911's launch were spent improving what *Road & Track* magazine termed as the car's "animal oversteer." This accusation had been leveled at the earlier 356, but with the 911 it went deeper. In his book *911 Story*, Paul Frère recounts that the problems stemmed from the fact that the early press cars were assembled by very experienced technicians and so had few handling defects. When the 911 went into production, the impossibly fine setup tolerances specified could not be held, and as a result some cars handled "like real beasts." *Autocar* magazine was more restrained—and very British!—in saying that the car needed care in the wet. Even the factory's own sales brochure suggested that the 911 "was not a car for the novice." The problem was seen at its worst if you lifted the accelerator when cornering hard. The result would more often than not be a view of the world rotating around the car.

This Belgian-registered 1967 Targa—actually a four-cylinder 912—shows off its satin-finish roll-over hoop at the style of Targa driving. The zippered rear window of early Targas may not have looked too permanent when in place, but it allowed virtually open Porsche motoring when removed.

Porsche's engineers needed to find more latitude in the handling, and their attention focused on the rear-biased weight distribution and the relatively short wheelbase. The first, fairly crude, attempt to improve stability came in 1966, when 11-kilogram (24.3-pound) weights were added into the extreme ends of the front valence, a modification the engineers were not particularly proud of.

The A-program models from August 1967 did not fundamentally address, in chassis terms, the handling issues inherent in the original models, so it was the B-program models, launched for the 1969 model year, that produced the first big improvement. The wheelbase was increased by 57 millimeters (2.2 inches) to 2,268 millimeters (89.3 inches), which had the effect of shortening the engine overhang and reducing the "dumbbell" effect in cornering. With a reduction in the weight of the engine casing included, the front/rear weight distribution became slightly less biased to the rear when it changed from 41.5/58.5 to 43/57, and handling was significantly improved.

The earliest style of horn grille was made of chrome-plated brass and mounted with four screws (above), but a cheaper design for the 1967 model year was secured by only two screws (below). Both cars have the European-specification Bosch asymmetric (nonsealed-beam) headlights used until the end of the 1967 model year, but the bumper styles differ because the later car, without over-riders, has the wide rubber insert that was a new feature of the S.

The wheelbase extension was achieved simply by moving the rear wheels backward in the bodyshell, without moving the engine and gearbox. This resulted in slightly angled driveshafts, but this aspect was not considered to affect the durability of these components. Externally, the longer wheelbase cars can be identified by the larger distance between the rear wheel arch opening (at its front edge) and the cover over the rear torsion bar. The B-program cars also introduced the first slight flaring of the rear wheel arches.

Body Trim and Fittings

As was the fashion of the time, the window fittings and other trim of the launch cars used chrome as far as possible. This included the wipers, which parked on the right side of the screen irrespective of the market. It was not until August 1967 that black wipers, which parked on the left-hand side of the screen on left-hand-drive models, were introduced.

The horn grilles, next to the indicators and either side of the front luggage compartment lid, were changed in mid-1966 from the original chrome-plated brass examples, which were secured with four screws, to a cheaper design

The original style of tail badging had a gold-anodized finish for the linked-lettering Porsche script and the angled 911 designation.

The first 911s used a simple push-button external door handle. The tooling for this door handle was changed for the 1967 model year, the later version having slightly more radius in the curvature around the button. A new handle, which protected the button and prevented the door from being accidentally opened, was introduced for 1968.

This 1967 911S (with the early style of push-button door handle) shows off its opening rear side window. The plated-finish rear wiper was an option.

that used only two mounting screws. Optionally, owners could also specify additional spotlights that mounted through special horn grilles. For 1969, the horn grilles changed again, to a narrower design that made room for enlarged indicator/sidelight assemblies.

For the 1967 model year, the chromed over-riders were revised and received a rubber trim. The pencil-thin rubbing strips along the edges of the bumper valences and on the trim under the doors were initially similar to those used on the 356C, but for 1967 the new 911S was launched with a wide rubbing strip. It was only an option on the same year's regular 911 U.S. models. The 1968 911S sill trim consisted of a wider vinyl strip fitted to a much larger anodized aluminum extrusion, which covered the whole sill area under the doors, from wheel arch to wheel arch (and over the torsion bar covers). When the B-program cars extended the wheelbase, this extrusion was lengthened and the new trim was also fitted to the new 911E model. A year earlier, for the A-program models, the gold-anodized script on the rear engine cover also changed, from the previous linked lettering and angled 911 designation, to more spaced-out lettering with the model type positioned just below the grille.

This detail of a 1968 Targa shows the "soft-window" rear screen stowed and the tonneau in place. The position of the interior light in the roll-over hoop and the gold-anodized Targa script can be seen.

Rear view of an Austrian 911 (above) shows the complexity of the hand-assembled engine lid grille of the 2-liter cars. The manufacturing cost of the grille was later reduced by using pressed bars and welded construction. The 1967 911S (above right) shows the rubber trim introduced on the rear over-riders for this model year. These items were previously in plain chrome. This model year was the last when the engine cover featured a distinctive central body rib under the grille.

An electric sunroof was available as an option on the coupe from the beginning. There were external water drain slots above the top of the rear three-quarter windows on early cars, but the design was cleaned up at the start of the B-program by running the drains down into the inside of the rear wheel arch.

Two other trim details—door handles and exterior mirrors—help the diligent 911 spotter to identify the early cars. The first 911s had simple outside door handles with pushbuttons that stood proud of the handle. A tooling change to the handle casting in 1967 was so minor that you have to inspect both handles side by side to see the slightly more rounded corners of the later version. The prominent pushbuttons were changed to a recessed type for 1968, and these handles became more wedge-shaped.

The external door mirror was an option. It started out as the same Durant-manufactured type used on the 356C, with a cone-shaped backing to the mirror. The new 911S was given a Durant mirror with a larger flange holding the glass in place, and this became standard across the range in 1968. The story does not stop there, however, as other mirrors were available as options. These included simple rectangular mirrors in 1967 (which became mandatory in some countries later due to the larger glass area) and the sporty Talbot mirrors as used on the racing cars of the time.

By the start of 1968 a new Targa version was offered with a significant improvement. A large, curved, glass rear window replaced the soft convertible type and was a more practical proposition for owners who wanted open-top motoring with civilized 2+2 accommodation. The glass rear window remained available as an option until 1971, after which it became standard in all markets. For the 1969 model year, Targa ventilation was improved further when air extractor slots were included at the sides of the stainless-steel hoop (and unlike the coupe, the Targa's front quarter windows could still be opened).

Interior Trim

To talk seats and Porsche at the same time is to talk Recaro. There is a history lesson behind this that goes back to the war years, when the original Reutter father and son were killed. The company was managed on behalf of the remaining family after the war and Reutter prospered, especially when it signed a deal in 1951

The engine lid release on the 911 is to be found on the left-hand B pillar. This feature is not so convenient for right-hand drive.

This 1965 car shows a typical early interior with leatherette seat coverings, a perforated pattern to the pleated seat panels, and a chromed finish for the backrest support frame.

Folding rear seats have always been a feature of the 911, the 1965–66 models uniquely having a small leather surround to the seat cushion. The seat belts are a later fitting.

with Zuffenhausen neighbors Porsche to build bodies and supply seats for the new 356 model. Eventually, Reutter came to the point at which it had to decide on a major investment program to cope with the ever-increasing volume of bodyshell business from Porsche. The investment would have been large and the family backed away, deciding to sell the coach-building factory in Zuffenhausen to Porsche in 1963. The main Reutter factory remaining in Stuttgart became the hub of a new seat-manufacturing business named Recaro.

The first Porsche-designed 911 seats were simple affairs developed from the 356 experience. They incorporated adjustment only for fore and aft position and seat backrest incline, with the combined seat recline and locking lever at the door-side base of the back. The mechanism for these seats extended across the base of the seat back to operate on the inside seat back support. The seat back supports were chromed, changing progressively from the 1967 introduction of the reclining Recaro sports seat to a black-painted finish. Seat tilt lock levers were incorporated into the top of the seat back support from 1969. Early production 911s came with basketweave vinyl seat inserts as standard in a

Some of the interesting features inside a 1965 model: The lever ahead of the gear lever (above) is the heater control, and the warm air outlet at the front of the side member can be seen. The early 911 logo and period Blaupunkt Bremen radio have an elegant simplicity. The early style of door panel was simple (below). A button to open the door was fitted to the front of the armrest, which on the driver's side had no pull handle. A small door compartment was unique to the 1968 model (bottom), and there was generally an improved finish to the door trim. The loudspeaker is a later addition.

range of just four colors, although hound's-tooth material was an option. Leather was available to special order from the beginning, or from 1965 as an option.

No head restraints were fitted as standard to the original cars, but these could be specified as an option, the 1965–1967 models using 356 items. These attached on the rear of the seat back; whereas, the later restraints were mounted on bayonet-type legs that entered through the top of the seat back. The early 356 restraints were only adjustable for height, but the later ones could be angled forward or backward as well.

Sports seats were available from 1965, and the history of these on the early cars is one of essentially adding more and more comfort. To start with there were the Recaro or "Ferrari" types. The Ferrari was little more than a padded bucket with only reach adjustment and no head restraint, and it is believed this seat was discontinued after 1966. The Recaro was a more comfortable, but nonreclining, seat with high side supports and an integral head restraint. From 1967 Recaro developed its version to include reclining, and it came in all the materials available for the standard seats. By 1969, it was an even more luxurious affair with height and pitch adjustment.

The rear seats featured fold-down backs. When they were down, the parcel shelf that resulted provided a useful extra area for luggage, and the area under the shelf provided concealed storage spaces on the seats themselves. The seat backs were held upright by leather straps that attached to the rear wall by popper studs. The rear seat backs on the Targa were shorter than those used on the coupe. An interesting feature offered to Targa owners from 1967 (but discontinued after 1971) was a security box, formed by a rear parcel shelf that replaced the folding seat sections and offered two lockable compartments below. The same year, 1967, also saw the first attempt at installing air conditioning in the 911 for the U.S. market.

The door trims on the first 911s featured an armrest (with the door opening button at its front edge) below which was a pleated soft fabric pocket for maps. The passenger door had a pull handle, but the handle was omitted from the driver's door because it would restrict movement. The door panels changed in detail through to the 1968 models, when, after a unique 1968 pattern door featuring a rigid pocket under the armrest, the design adopted the shape seen to the end of the 2.4 models. This used a rigid forward pocket and an opening compartment under an extended armrest, which now had a flush-fitting (and safer) door handle mechanism in its side face.

The interior of this European-specification 1968 model year 911S shows off the hound's-tooth inlays on its leatherette seats. This car has two interesting features: There is only one head restraint (on the passenger side), and no radio is fitted. Compared with earlier cars, the heater control has moved from ahead of the gear lever to a new position, out of sight here, alongside the handbrake.

The 911 began life with a velour interior carpet, which later became the more luxurious option for the higher-spec cars like the E and S. From 1967, a cheaper material termed Perlon (with an appearance like felt) was introduced for the basic models (the 911 and the later 911 T). Until approximately the start of the 1968 model year, you could have any carpet color as long as it was dark gray.

Increased safety standards demanded that the original internal mirror, mounted centrally to the front roof section by three screws, was changed to a break-away type for 1968. That year only the mounting stayed on the roof section, but the following year the mirror was mounted directly onto the windshield glass by an adhesive pad. Few drivers of these particular models have not come out to their cars to find the interior mirror sitting on the floor of the car.

Heating, never a strong Porsche feature in the early days, was provided by ducting fresh air from around the exhaust system and piping it forward through silencers in each of the sills. A mixer provided after each of the two exhaust-mounted heat exchangers allowed the driver to control the amount of hot air ducted forward to the passenger compartment or dumped to the outside. The problem with an air-cooled engine, however, is that heater output is dependent on engine speed. High engine speed meant lots of heat, but low engine speed (in town traffic for instance) meant little warmth for the occupants. It was for this reason that a small fuel-driven heater was standard on the first cars and an option on A-program and later left-hand-drive cars to 1973. These supplementary heaters were fitted into a small cavity behind the fuel tank and were manufactured by Eberspacher. The fuel heater took air from a vent in front of the rear seats and generated hot air for defrosting.

Cabin fresh air ventilation was achieved by allowing air to enter through a small inlet carefully placed in the high-pressure area just in front of the windshield and expelling it through a line of almost concealed vents in the roofline above the rear window. An option to the full heater on the A-program cars was an electric fan, which assisted circulation of cabin air. Heater output was controlled by a lever mounted just ahead of the gear lever. The 1967 cars had an additional duct that directed hot air onto the rear window for demisting, while B-program models offered an optional electric rear window demister in place of the earlier ducted warm air solution. The floor-mounted lever (just ahead of the gear lever) controlling the heater output was moved to the right-hand side of the handbrake lever on the 1968 cars. The new model's heat could be separately ducted to the windshield and the occupant's feet. Output was further enhanced by a three-speed fan under the dash.

Dashboard and Instruments

The dashboard of the 911 is dominated by the familiar flattened oval instrument housing containing five large dials. A classic Butzi Porsche detail, the layout was a case of "if it's right, leave it alone," so the dial area has remained largely unchanged in basic form for more than 30 years and has always been the same for left-hand and right-hand drive.

The five black-faced dials reduce in size either side of the large central rev counter, which on early cars was red-lined at 7,000 rpm with a maximum of 8,000 rpm. To the right of the rev counter are a 250-kilometer-per-hour, or 150-mile-per-hour, speedometer and (at the end) a clock. To the left of the rev counter are the combined oil temperature and oil pressure gauges, and to the left again another combination gauge showing fuel level and (uniquely) oil tank level. In the 1965 *Hints to Drivers* handbook, this last gauge was described as follows: "The small combination dial on the far left of the panel indicates fuel level and has a red warning light which is illuminated when the fuel level drops to 6 liters (1.6 U.S. gallons). The same dial incorporates the oil level—there are in fact 9 liters of oil circulating in the lubricating system. The gauge only shows oil in the tank when the engine is idling. The method is much neater and does away with dirty hands." Until 1973, this clever combination gauge was labeled in one language only, with the oil level always denoted by the German word *oel*.

The early 2-liter cars have an elegant simplicity in their instrumentation. The pre-1968 models had chrome rims on the five main dials that, combined with the green lettering and wood veneer lower dash trim of the 1965 and 1966 cars, demonstrate automobile fashion of the time. From 1968 the dial rims became black, with white lettering on the black instrument background. For 1967 and 1968, brushed aluminum replaced the wood (no doubt inspired by contemporary racing car style) for the lower dash area on all models except the S. The 1967 S had the heavy basketweave finish on the lower dash that would become used

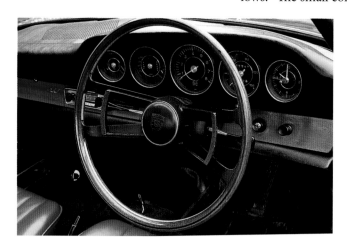

Right from the start, the dashboard featured the 911 trademark of five dials reducing in size either side of a central rev counter. The colors of the wood veneer (used for the 1965–66 model years) and the green features on the dials (1965–67 model years) complement each other and are accented by chrome bezels.

across the 911 range from 1969. The dash contained an opening on its top deck for the single speaker radio. The holes for this opening were integrated into the dash top until 1969, but thereafter the speaker opening could be accessed by a separate panel.

There were many variations to the detail of the main gauges from year to year and model to model, including warning lights for the fuel, oil (on models where no level gauge was offered), charging failure, and handbrake application. For the B-program, the turn signal and headlight main beam indicators were located on the rev counter. As the engine was developed, the peak revolutions red marking on the rev counter changed according to specification. The speedometer had a trip odometer for specific distance measurement.

The instrument layout generally has received considerable flack over the years, one British journalist describing the switch gear as looking like a packet of boiled sweets thrown haphazardly over the dashboard! But most 911 drivers will tell you that once you know your way around, the switches are just fine. On the earliest models there were relatively few controls to find, but when accessories were fitted, ergonomics did become questionable. There were two areas where accessory switches could be clustered on the lower dash to either side of the steering wheel.

The light switch was down by the driver's door side of the steering wheel, just to the outside of the ignition. Above that under the instrument cluster was the optional sunroof rocker switch. On the passenger side of the steering wheel, under the "inboard" dials, was the fresh air control lever, and under this on the dash panel was the switch for the cigarette lighter. Other switches were grouped to the passenger side of the ashtray, above the radio if one was fitted. These might include switches for auxiliary driving or foglights, the petrol heater switch, and the hazard flasher switch (which found its way over next to the ignition switch from 1970). Until 1968, these switches usually had a small indicator light at their center to denote operation. From 1968, the switch knobs for the American and certain other export markets changed to larger rubber-rimmed affairs, with

The dashboard began to change for the 1967 model year. The S was given a leather-rimmed steering wheel and basketweave vinyl trim on the lower dash area, but the green instrument markings remained. Note also the new glove compartment lid with "square" 911S lettering.

The markings of the dials changed from green to white for the 1968 model year, and chrome trim virtually disappeared from the dashboard. Interesting details include the large switch under the clock for the optional sunroof and the heavy grain lower dash that was also new for the 1968 model year.

symbols denoting function at their centers. The lever controlling the intake of fresh air from ahead of the windshield was replaced in 1969 by a new heating and ventilation control in the lower dash where the ashtray had previously been sited (the ashtray moved into the central knee guard area of the dash). The hazard flasher moved next to the ignition switch in 1969 and from 1970 was changed to a red pushbutton.

Until 1971, the model designation was mounted on the glove compartment lid. This script was originally an italic "911," but evolved to a block capital style for the 1967 911S. The lid itself started life with a wood inlay and a small central pull handle and separate lock, but in 1967, the handle was integrated into the whole of the top edge of the lid, with the lock slightly offset toward the driver.

The steering wheel is something that many people get completely wrong when restoring a car. As with the road wheels, it is relatively easy to switch steering wheels as part of a customizing exercise, so it is important for the seeker of the original 911 to know what is right for the car. All steering wheels were of 400 millimeters (15.6 inches) diameter. The first 911s had wood-rimmed wheels, believed to have been made by VDM, with four black-painted spokes arranged in what *Car and Driver* described as a "shallow X." This characteristic pattern, another feature of the 911 to have lasted through the years, offers good instrument visibility and a place to rest your thumbs. The appearance of the wheel was updated after about a year's production, the spokes being coated in black plastic, presumably for better wear. From 1966, you could specify a horn "butterfly"—so-called because of its winged shape similar to the wheel spokes—that replaced the previous central horn contact mounted in the boss; the first horn butterflies had a bright finish to the rim of the hub boss. A black plastic-rimmed (or hard rubber) steering wheel was also available and was standard on the four-cylinder 912.

A leather-rimmed wheel with leather thumb rests at the ends of the spokes was standard on the 911S from 1967 and optional on the other models. This wheel, which used a heavier design of horn butterfly that covered the wheel spokes completely, also became standard on the E from 1969, the year in which the wood-rimmed wheel disappeared altogether. It was also at this time that the two stalks behind the steering wheel were given a black look, the previous style of chromed stalk with a molded top having been taken from the 356. The left-hand stalk was for indicators/headlamps and main/dipped beam, and the right-hand one was for the windshield wipers. A feature of the 911 was that there was a three-speed wiper system and an electric wash/wipe.

Luggage Compartment

It is difficult to get excited over things like luggage compartments on a car like the 911, but great care went into the compartment design to make sure that two people could pack enough belongings for a week's vacation. The shaped fuel tank of 62 liters (13.64 Imperial gallons, 16.38 U.S. gallons), including a reserve of 6 liters (1.32 Imperial gallons, 1.59 U.S. gallons), accommodated the spare wheel, with both of these set low between the longitudinally aligned torsion bar front suspension. This compact design resulted in a relatively large luggage volume. The washer bottle on the early cars does look like an afterthought, however, in its exposed position on the left-hand wing wall.

The first 911s benefited from the same square-weave carpeting in the front area as was used inside the car. Unfortunately, this was replaced for the start of the

The 1968 S had a soft-grain finish to its tool bag, but from 1969 the tool bag vinyl changed to a basketweave. The chassis number plate is seen to the left of the latch, with the windshield washer filler on the right. The battery at top right has the correct rubber strap and plastic cover.

1966 model year by a cheaper felt carpeting called Perlon. This initially came in three pieces (or more after the battery acid got to them!), but from 1969 a fourth piece covered the front area behind the latch panel. This carpeting was functional but not very robust.

The vehicle chassis number, a strip of stamped aluminum sheet riveted in place, can be found on the left-hand side of the front lid latch panel.

Engine

The new 911 needed an engine with the power of the existing four-cylinder, four-cam Carrera racing engine but without the noise and the complexity. But why the rear engine location when virtually every other manufacturer at the time was saying such a layout was obsolete?

The answer lies in a mixture of business risk and tradition. Porsche was a small company relative to the big names of the industry, and all its experience as a manufacturer of sports cars lay with the rear engine layout. The 911 was also the first production Porsche totally to make the break with the VW parts bin, so everything was new. Design innovation, therefore, had to be kept within known boundaries, which meant that for the engine the opposed-piston (or boxer) layout was a requirement.

The six-cylinder 901 engine (the engine kept the original type number until the 2.2-liter version came along) was an elegant and "leading-edge" production design in many respects, incorporating features that were usually only seen in motor racing at the time. These included dry sump lubrication, overhead camshafts, and hemispherical cylinder heads.

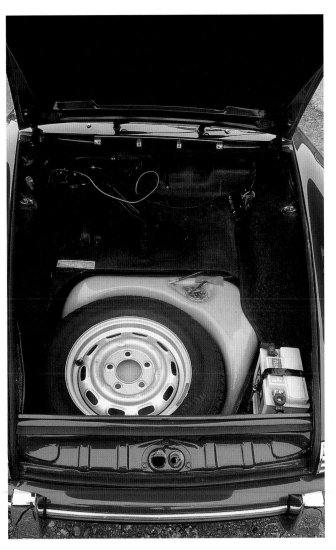

The luggage compartment, seen here on a 1965 model with the central piece of carpet removed, housed the spare wheel and the fuel tank, both of which were recessed between the front wheels to allow a useful volume on top for personal belongings. Note the fuse block fitted at the top right. The battery is attached by a later fitting, the original rubber strap and plastic cover no doubt having disappeared long ago.

The new engine was very over-square, with a short stroke of 66 millimeters (2.57 inches) and a bore of 80 millimeters (3.12 inches), giving a total capacity of 1,991cc (121.45 cubic inches). Firing order was 1-6-2-4-3-5. The individual cylinder heads, six in total, each contained one 35-millimeter (1.37-inch) exhaust valve and one 39-millimeter (1.52-inch) inlet valve, with a centrally mounted spark plug. The plug aperture was fitted with a Helicoil insert, so that if the thread should be stripped for any reason the Helicoil—a coiled wire that formed an internal screw thread—could be replaced, rather than having to scrap the head. From the start of production the exhaust valves were hollow and filled with sodium for better cooling. On each cylinder bank, these were actuated through rockers by a camshaft contained in an aluminum housing. Each bank of heads bolted to each of these camshaft housings, which in turn bolted down to each side of the crankcase.

The cylinder barrels of the first prototypes were cast iron, but the first production models used Biral, a trade name for the process of sleeving the cast-iron barrel with aluminum cooling fins. These fins and the cylinder heads were air-cooled by a vertically mounted axial-flow fan, which improved on the old radial-flow 356 unit by distributing the air more evenly to both banks of

The vertically mounted fan distributed cooling air to the cylinder barrels more evenly than the 356's axial unit. The Solex overflow carburetors seen on each side of the engine were difficult to tune correctly and gave the engine a significant flat spot around 2,500 rpm. The later label (mentioning the 911S/911L) on the fan housing is incorrect on this 1965 model.

cylinders. The alternator was mounted within this fan. Both fan and alternator were turned by a belt driven from the rear of the crankshaft at 1.3 times engine speed. The cooling airflow was ducted to the engine using a plastic-mounted shroud that covered the top part of the engine. Ducts in the shroud ensured that some of the air was directed to the barrels, the heads, the crankcase-mounted oil cooler, and, last, to the fresh air inlets of the exhaust-mounted heat exchangers. This latter air was heated by passing it over the exhaust pipes from each bank of cylinder heads. From there the amount of heated air passed to the cabin was controlled by driver-operated flap valves just downstream of each heat exchanger. The complex exhaust system, with two complicated heat exchangers (one per bank of cylinders) each leading to the rear-mounted silencer, meant significant cost when replacement was due.

The pistons were cast aluminum with two compression rings and one oil scraper ring. Steel connecting rods ran in main bearing shells of leadindium, the same material being used on the main bearings. The forged crankshaft, with seven main bearings, was fully counterbalanced. At its rear end, where there was an eighth bearing of smaller size, was a pinion that drove an intermediate shaft running at almost half engine speed—the ratio was 48 to 28—in order to avoid unnecessary wear or noise. The ratio from the intermediate shaft to the cams was 24 to 28 via duplex (two-row) timing chains and sprockets, and brought the cam speed to exactly half engine speed. The intermediate shaft also drove the crankcase-mounted oil scavenge and pressure pumps. With a dry sump system there is no oil sump to act as a reservoir, so a separate oil tank was mounted in the right-hand rear wheel arch.

The timing chains were tensioned by spring-loaded hydraulic tensioners fitted into the rear chain cases. These tensioners, one for each cylinder bank, would prove to be a 911 Achilles' heel over time. The tensioner was a mechanical spring, which forced a piston against the lever arm of an idler sprocket. This sprocket kept each timing chain in correct tension. The spring was encased in a small cup-shaped aluminum housing: The open top allowed engine oil to enter the assembly and, by a series of drilled holes in the piston, provided a simple form of hydraulic damping to the spring movement. These first tensioners were actually fairly reliable, but the oil could drain out of the tensioner in some situations. For instance, it was common practice to take the engine out if work was needed on the cylinders or heads, and then to turn the engine over to fit the heat exchangers. To overcome this drainage problem, a new sealed tensioner was introduced

The engine compartment of the 1967 S shows the coil ignition and the fuel pump mounted on the left-hand side. Emissions controls had yet seriously to restrict the 911's raw performance power output for the S leaping from the regular 130-brake horsepower to 160-brake horsepower.

The 911L model was unique to the United States and had a 130-brake horsepower engine that could be fitted with an exhaust air pump for emissions control.

for the 1968 model year. This unit required filling and bleeding of air after assembly, and now the tensioner problem became one of unexpected failure of the sealed unit. Owners were soon able to purchase tensioner guards, small clamps that fitted around the piston shaft that would prevent the piston from collapsing into the tensioner body and relaxing the all-important chain tension (which would, in turn, cause the cam sprockets to jump a tooth and potentially bring the valves into contact with the pistons).

The chain guide ramps were also targets for development. The effective, but complex, plastic-faced aluminum items were switched for soft black neoprene ones at the same time as the sealed tensioners were introduced. This change was accompanied by a cheaper idler arm, which did not have a bronze bushing. Studies would later show that this cost saving directly affected reliability.

By using a seven-bearing crankshaft, it was clear the designers were looking to future designs that would allow higher crankshaft speeds and more power. As Jerry Sloniger notes in an early text, "all were plain bearings. . . . Porsche had obviously had enough of roller bearing cranks," a reference to the highly complicated layout used on the four-cam Carrera 356 engines. The original 901/01 engine delivered 130-brake horsepower (DIN) at 6,100 rpm, running on 98 RON fuel. It was quite a screamer by contemporary standards and notable for its free-revving character, thanks to the rigid design of the overhead camshaft cylinder heads.

The first production 911S used Solex overflow carburetors, but although these functioned like an injection system, they needed to be kept in very close tune. The Solexes replaced the triple downdraught types fitted on the Frankfurt prototype. Unfortunately they gave the new engine a significant flat spot around 2,500 rpm, and two triple-choke Weber 40 IDA carburetors quickly became the standard fit for racing. On the road cars, no other solution could be found to the Solex problem, so from February 1966, with the introduction of the 901/05 engine, the Webers were used.

Using experience gained from racing, the engine announced in July 1966 for the new 911S was coded 901/02. As a side note, 911 production engine numbering generally does not appear to follow any logical pattern, but this is because all the special variants made during development and for racing were included in the numbering. On the 901/02, the pistons had higher crowns, and this lifted the compression ratio from 9:1 to 9.8:1. Increased valve overlap, bigger valves of 42 millimeters (1.64 inches) inlet and 38 millimeters (1.48 inches) exhaust, Weber 40 IDS carburetors, and a new gas-flowed exhaust system resulted in a power output of 160-brake horsepower at 6,600 rpm. Internally, the engine was stronger with nitrided connecting rods and forged pistons. The new exhausts were used on the 901/06 engine for the "Normal" cars, but their 10-brake horsepower power gain was eliminated by reducing the camshaft overlap, thereby slightly improving maximum torque. The weight of the 1965/66 engines (including the 911S unit) was given as 184 kilograms (406 pounds) in workshop documentation.

The 911T engine, the 901/03, was introduced in 1967. With 110-brake horsepower at 4,200 rpm, this less-stressed engine had cheaper cast-iron cylinders (as used on the prototypes) and a crankshaft without counterbalancing for the big end bearing carriers. The T used the same 42-millimeter (1.64-inch) inlet and 38-millimeter (1.48-inch) exhaust valves as the S, with the same porting. Unlike the S, however, the compression ratio was restricted to 8.6:1, with less overlap on the valve timing. The steel camshaft rockers used on the higher output engines were replaced by cast-iron items on the T, a modification that was incorporated across the range in 1968.

In July 1967, new engine variants were used for the T (901/13), the Normal (901/07), and the S (901/08) engines to coincide with the introduction of Sportomatic transmission. These differed mainly in the mounting flange for the new transmission. Two more 911L variants for the U.S. market had fittings for the unloved exhaust air pump (driven by a V-belt) on both manual (901/14) and Sportomatic (901/17) versions. Many a 1968 U.S. 911 had its air pump removed, which partly cured that model's tendency to oil its plugs and backfire. The U.S. market was starved of the T, E, and S models in 1968, with only the emissions-compliant Normal and L models being offered.

In August 1968, with the B-program models, Bosch mechanical fuel injection was fitted to the Normal and S models. This injection system, well proven by Porsche since it was first tried on the 1966 Carrera 6 racing cars, employed a six-plunger metering unit (using variable stroke pistons) pumping fuel through six equal-length pipes to injectors inserted directly into the inlet ports. The metering unit was controlled by a "space" cam, a three-dimensional position controller that governed the amount of fuel sprayed into each cylinder according to throttle position and engine revolutions. The amount of fuel injected was also controlled by a thermostat (permitting a richened mixture when the engine was not at normal working temperature), a barometric compensator, a cold-start enrichment solenoid, and an over-run fuel cut-off. The pump was driven from the nose of the left-hand camshaft by a small toothed belt. The adoption of this injection system also forced the replacement of the original Bendix fuel pump with a higher pressure roller-type unit. Overall, the new injection added about 10-brake horsepower to the maximum output of those engines it was fitted to. Interestingly, Frère noted that the injected cars seemed to be more fuel efficient at higher revolutions than the Weber-equipped models of the same basic engine.

The S also used the new Capacitative Discharge Ignition (CDI) system, which helped to keep the engine from oiling its plugs in traffic. CDI gave a fatter spark but still used low-tension contact breaker points. The S was also fitted with a second oil cooler mounted in front of the right-hand front wheel.

The new E model replaced the midrange Normal and L 911s. The E reverted to the valve timing of the 901/05 engine and a compression ratio of 9.1:1. It too had the new mechanical fuel injection in place of the Webers. The S now had 170-brake horsepower at 6,800 rpm and the E had 140-brake horsepower at 6,600 rpm.

The last major improvement introduced with all the B-program models

Beautiful triple-choke Weber carburetors adorn the 2-liter S engine. Another visual distinction of the S is the red cooling air duct over the engine.

was that the crankcase halves were cast from magnesium rather than aluminum. This saved about 10 kilograms (22 pounds).

The engine number for the classic 911s can be found stamped on the crankcase to the right of the cooling fan. Incidentally, you can tell a T, E, or S just by looking at the color of the cooling fan shroud in the engine compartment: the T was black or yellow, the E was green, and the S was red.

Transmission

The 911 was offered with a brand new five-speed gearbox (called the Type 901), driven from the front of the engine through a single diaphragm clutch. The gearbox, therefore, is sited under the central tunnel fanned between the rear seats.

The new 911 gearbox was designed for the higher torque of the six-cylinder engine, but retained Porsche's unique and effective synchronizing system developed through the life of the 356. This system, using a split ring and cone arrangement for each forward ratio, was further enhanced so that a gear could not be engaged until full synchronization had been achieved. The housing was a single cast-aluminum unit, which included at its rear an integral bell housing for the clutch and differential that attached directly to the front of the engine crankcase. With the left-hand driveshaft removed, a cover could be removed from the gearbox housing for access to the differential. The main gear set had two shafts, onto which the second to fifth gear clusters were mounted. The gear sets were inserted through the open front of the casing. Assembly was completed by fitting the end-cover (which carried first and reverse gears and the gear selector shaft) to the front of this casing. This layout gave a "dog-leg" gear shift pattern, with first over to the left and back, with reverse opposite. It was a good pattern for racing but hard work around town.

Ratios could be specified, but normally a standardized set was used except on cars destined for the United States, where generally the ratios for fourth and fifth were shorter. From launch the standard set was termed 901/0, but was updated in 1966 to 901/02. Special option sets covered myriad competition uses.

The 902 transmission was originally developed as a four-speed unit for the 912 and is similar to the 901, except that there is no forward gear in the end cover. It was used on the Normal or L version of the car until the new T model arrived for the 1968 model year.

The 905 was the Sportomatic transmission, launched in August 1967. This was a semi-automatic four-speed, giving manual operation but clutchless gear changing. The two-pedal cars had a hard time from those reared on the macho image of the sports car driver rowing up through the gears, but the cars proved popular, especially in the United States where up to 25 percent of 911s were Sportomatics. Developed with Fichtel and Sachs, the transmission had a hydraulic torque converter, a single vacuum-operated diaphragm clutch, and a conventional four-speed gearbox. The system used a lower crown wheel-and-pinion ratio of 7:27 instead of 7:31. The automatic clutch was only used for changing ratios and not for starting or stopping, which were the function of the torque converter. Micro switches at the base of the gear lever actuated the clutch as soon as the lever was moved by the driver: The switches operated a solenoid controlling a vacuum servo (connected to a vacuum reservoir purged by the engine intake), which in turn actuated the clutch release mechanism. It was a relatively simple but novel form of gear selection, not a full automatic, and it could ease the fatigue of town driving.

From the start of production the 911 was fitted with Nadella drive couplings at the differential end of the driveshafts. These featured a hinged link allowing axial movement of the driveshaft and prevented the lock-up sometimes seen with the cross joint. Unfortunately the Nadella joints also suffered from vibration. The need for a constant velocity coupling was addressed on the 1967 911S with the introduction of Lobro shafts using Rzeppa constant velocity joints. In larger and larger form, these latter joints have been used ever since.

Electrical Equipment and Lighting

A single 45-amp/hour 12-volt battery, mounted in front of the left wheel arch and beside the fuel tank, was used until 1968. A simple 360-watt generator provided electrical power on the prototypes, but production cars used a more powerful 490-watt/35-amp/hour unit. With the start of the B-program cars, two 36-amp/hour batteries were used in parallel, mounted in front of each wheel arch and accessed from the luggage compartment. Their position also helped the handling.

The development of the fuse board gives a good idea of the 911's electrical complexity during the early years. On the 1965–67 models there were just 12 fuses, mounted at the back of the luggage compartment's left side. In order, these covered stoplights; indicators; taillights; interior light, cigarette lighter, and clock; petrol/ electric heater (option); windshield wipers/washers; foglamps; license plate light; boot light; front sidelight (RH); front sidelight (LH); low beam (RH); low beam (LH); high beam (RH); high beam (LH). The number of fuses went up to a potential 21 in 1968 with added items such as electric windows, sliding roof, fresh air fan, starter solenoid, Sportomatic control, and rear window demister.

Bosch asymmetric headlights were fitted to most 911s from launch, in either left-hand drive or right-hand drive. These each had a single bulb with dual filaments rated at 45 watts (main) and 40 watts (dipped). Bosch took a step forward with the lighting of European-specification models for the 1968 model year when it introduced H1halogen bulbs, giving a 55-watt main beam that greatly improved night illumination. Yellow bulbs were used in France, while for the United States, Hella sealed-beam units were required. The sealed-beam lamp fitted to the first 911s was housed within a similar casing to the European (nonsealed-beam) headlamps. These units were rated at 50 watts (main) and 40 watts (dipped). The external glass was separate from the sealed-beam unit's front glass until 1968 when a new Hella sealed lamp gave American 911s a look all of their own, with a much more pronounced rim to the lamp. The H1 and later H4 European specification headlamps give much better illumination, and it is possible to upgrade from the sealed-beam units.

The 911 did much to enhance its reputation as a top grand tourer by offering sophisticated accessories. Worthy of particular mention are the electric sunroof (available as an option from the 1965 cars) and the electrically heated coupe rear window and window lifters (available from the start of the B-program in August 1968). The first optional air conditioners were fitted in 1967, but the B-program models saw a better installation with a system designed by Behr. That same year, 1968, the alternator was enlarged to 770 watts because the increased number of accessories had added to the battery charging requirement, and there was a higher-capacity fuel pump for the new mechanical fuel injection.

Optional Hella spotlights could be specified and fitted through special horn grilles.

The front suspension of this 1965 car shows the MacPherson strut and, behind it, the actuating lever for the 13-millimeter anti-roll bar—an early attempt to stiffen the front and delay the onset of oversteer. Brake discs were solid and at the front used the M-type cast-iron caliper.

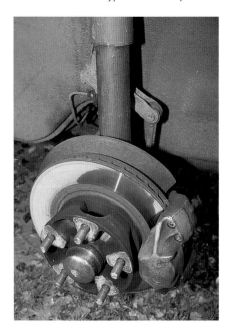

The front suspension of an early 911S shows off a red Koni strut and ventilated disc with the M-type cast-iron caliper. The A-program S model received a dual-circuit braking system, a safety factor that helped to cure the earlier tendency for the car to pull to one side under braking, and the B-program S was given light alloy S-type front calipers.

Suspension and Steering

At the front, the arrangement used was a MacPherson strut design. On each side, a telescopic shock absorber was mounted to a lower wishbone, itself actuating the 19-millimeter torsion bar. The torsion bar was mounted forward and longitudinally on the car's axis, allowing the fuel tank and the steering rack to be positioned lower between the wheels, increasing front luggage compartment space. The ZF rack-and-pinion steering system, quite advanced for the early 1960s, used a 1:16.5 ratio and a hydraulic damper.

Early cars had rather heavy steering, caused by the ingenious—and safety-conscious—column that contained two universal couplings to reach the centrally located rack. To initiate understeer from a car whose weight was notably rear biased, a 13-millimeter anti-roll bar was fitted to the early models, but by the start of the 1968 model year the early handling problems were much improved and the 911L used a softer 11-millimeter bar, while the T had no bar at all.

With the B-program, self-leveling hydropneumatic struts became standard on the E and optional on the T and the S, in conjunction with 14-inch wheels. These struts replaced the front torsion bars, and since they had a rising rate, no front anti-roll bar was used. From 1969, however, the self-leveling struts were no longer available for the S, because of their softer ride and thé 15-inch wheels fitted to this model. The cost of the ZF steering rack had also caught attention, so the Porsche-designed rack used on the 914 was transferred to the 911. This had a lighter casing than the ZF unit and a slightly increased ratio of 17.78:1.

Various rear suspension layouts were tested during the development of the prototypes, but production 911s used a novel trailing wishbone layout that had a spring arm connected directly to a transverse torsion bar and a tapered tube. This latter tube acted as a steady arm between the torsion bar housing and the wheel hubs. The geometry meant the rear wheels responded to bounce and rebound with minimal camber change. Open half shafts were used, with Nadella couplings accommodating the out-of-center shaft movements, while a telescopic shock absorber damped out the suspension travel. The first 911s used the same 23-millimeter rear torsion bar as the 356 Carrera 2. From 1967, a rear anti-roll bar was added and Koni shock absorbers were fitted to the S.

Brakes

From the start of production, the 911 followed the 356C by using disc brakes all round. Porsche had earned a reputation for building cars that stopped exceedingly well, but early 911s only achieved average comments from road testers. Unless the single-circuit system was set up correctly, the cars would pull to one side or brake unevenly.

Early prototypes started with small 235-millimeter (9.2-inch) front and 243-milimeter (9.5-inch) rear discs, but for series production these were replaced by the larger Ate solid discs and cast-iron calipers (made under license from Lockheed) used on the 356C. The 282-millimeter (11.1-inch) diameter front discs used the M-type caliper with a pad surface area of 52.5 square centimeters (8.14 square inches), while the 290-millimeter (11.2-inch) rear discs used the L-type caliper with a pad area of 40 square centimeters (6.20 square inches). The handbrake, independent of the disc system, was a novel arrangement that used the inner face of each rear disc hub as a brake drum. The S, introduced during 1966, used thicker ventilated brake discs, which increased the width of the track front and rear.

The 4.5Jx15 ventilated steel wheel (left) was mandatory until the classic Fuchs forged-alloy wheel arrived for the 1967 model year. In 1968, the width of the Fuchs wheel was increased to 5 1/2 J (right), giving the 911 a more purposeful look. The following year the rear wheel arches were flared slightly to accommodate new 6-inch rims.

The A-program cars introduced a twin-circuit braking system in August 1967, and the new 911L model had ventilated discs both front and rear that had been fitted to the S. These were also used on the E from the start of the B-program in 1968. The 1968 S used light-alloy S-type Ate calipers, which had been derived from the cast-iron M-type used on the front of all previous 911s. From 1968, the M-type calipers were fitted to the rear on all models as well, but with 38-millimeter (1.48-inch) pistons rather than the 48-millimeter (1.87-inch) used at the front.

Wheels and Tires

There were quite a few complaints about the skinny 165HR tires fitted to the 4.5Jx15 steel wheels of the original 911. And for 1967, the new S dismayed *Car and Driver* by still using 4.5-inch rims for its "flashy new wheels," and the magazine was none too complimentary about the Dunlop SP tires either. These new wheels, manufactured by the Fuchs Company, were the first of the classic five-spoke forged-alloy wheels that would become a Porsche trademark in later years. In 4.5-inch width, the alloys were 2.3 kilograms (5.1 pounds) lighter than their steel equivalents, and roundness was easier to control than with a stamped wheel. Clearly, the weight advantage of alloys was to increase as wheel rim width grew. So strong was the obsession to reduce unsprung weight that even the wheel nuts were light alloy and still are today.

It was not until August 1967 that 5.5-inch rims became available for the S, and the size grew again to 6 inches for the E and the S with the following year's B-program. Where hydropneumatic suspension was fitted, the ride was further improved by 51/2Jx14 Fuchs wheels, the 1-inch reduction in wheel diameter giving a deeper and more flexible tire wall. Dunlop tires were still the preferred fit for the T and E, the E with the new 185/70VR size. The S went one better and was offered with new Michelin XVRs, tires that significantly improved the cornering ability of the firmly sprung car.

The classic Fuchs forged-alloy wheel was introduced on the 1967 model year 911S, but the narrow rim width of 4.5 inches dismayed *Car and Driver* magazine. Note the restrained use of black paint on these early wheels and the elegance of the non-spoilered front profile.

Identification

Model year 0-program	Model	Engine	Gearbox	Chassis numbers	Engine numbers
1964	901 Coupe	901/01	901	Prototypes	Prototypes
1965	911 Coupe	901/01	901/0	300001–300235	900001–903600
1966	911 Coupe	901/01	902/01	3002361–305100	903601–907000
1967	911 Coupe[1]	901/05	901/01	305101–308522	911001–911190
	911 Coupe[2]	901/06	902/01	307351–308522	911001–911190
	911 Targa[3]	901/05	902/01	500001–500718	911191–912050
	911S Coupe[4]	901/02	901/02	305101S–308523S	960001–962178
	911S Targa	901/02	901/02	500001S–500718S	From S above
A-program					
1968	911 Coupe	901/06	902/01	11810001–11810720	3080001–3281606
	911 Coupe[5]	901/14	902/0 U.S.A.	11830001–11830473	3280001–3281606
	911 Coupe[6]	901/06	902/01	11835001–11835742	3080001 onward
	911 Targa	901/06	902/01	11880001–11880268	3080001 onward
	911 Targa[5]	901/14	902/0 U.S.A.	From Targa above	3280001 onward
	911 Coupe	901/07	Sportomatic	From Coupes above	3380001 onward
	911 L Coupe	901/03	902/01	11810001–11810720	3880001 onward
	911 L Coupe[5]	901/14	902/01 U.S.A.	11805001–11805549	3280001–3281606
	911 L Targa	901/03	902/01	11850001–11860307	3280001–3281606
	911 L Targa[5]	901/14	902/01 U.S.A.	11855001–11855134	3280001–3380464
	911 L[5]	901/17	Sporto U.S.A.	From 911L Coupe above	3380001–3380464
	911T	901/03	901/10	11820001–11820928	2080001 onward
	911T[6]	901/03	901/10	11825001–11825683	2080001 onward
	911T Targa	901/03	901/10	11870001–11870521	2080001 onward
	911T	901/13	Sportomatic	From 911T Coupe above	2180001 onward
	911S	901/02	901/02	11800001–11801267	4080001–4081549
	911S[6]	901/08	Sportomatic	From S Coupe above	4180001–4180227
	911S Targa	901/02	901/02	11850001–11850442	4080001–4081549
B-program					
1969	911T Coupe	901/03	901/06	119000001–119000343	6190001–6192455
	911T Coupe[6]	901/03	901/06	119120001–119123561	6190001–6192455
	911T Targa	901/03	901/06	119110001–119111282	6190001–6192455
	911T Coupe	901/13	Sportomatic	119110001–119111282	6193001–6193297
	911T	901/16	901/12 U.S.A.	119110001–119111282	6195001–6197292
	911T Coupe	901/19	Sporto U.S.A.	119110001–119111282	6198001–6198184
	911 E Coupe	901/09	901/07	119200001–119200954	6190001–6192455
	911E Coupe[6]	901/09	901/07	119220001–119221014	6190001–6192455
	911 E Targa	901/09	901/07	119210001–119210858	6190001–6192455
	911 E	901/11	Sportomatic	119210001–119210858	6298001–6298583
	911S Coupe	901/10	901/07	119300001–119301492	6390001–6392126
	911S Targa	901/10	901/07	119310001–119310614	6390001–6392126
	911S	901/10	901/13 U.S.A.	From 911S Coupe above	6390001–6392126

General notes

Chassis numbering The original six-digit numbering system used by Porsche since the 356 days lasted until 1967. The only distinction was between coupe (which started with 30-) and Targa (which started with 50-). The new S model was simply given an additional S to its chassis number. In 1968, the chassis numbers changed to an eight-digit system, which identified the model and build year, for instance, 11830001. The first two digits referred to the model type (i.e., 911). The third referred to the build year (e.g., 1968). The fourth digit was used for the bodyshell type (e.g., 5 = Targa S, 6 = Targa L, 7 = Targa T, and so on), but this description introduces conflict with some of the factory numbers given above, and the reader should take this into account. The fifth digit was used to denote a Karmann bodyshell (by using a 5). The last three digits were the build serial number. In 1969, the chassis numbers gained a ninth digit to allow the build serial number to go to four figures. Business was good!

Prototypes Chassis numbers are as follows: numbers 1–10, 13321–30; number 11, 13352; numbers 12–13, 300001–2 (November 1964). It is believed 235 cars were made after production began and before the end of 1964 (as 1965 models).

Gearboxes Generally, the 901 gearbox is five-speed; 902 is four-speed. These numbers derived from the original type designation for the 911 and four-cylinder 912, but to quote from Paul Frère's *911 Story*, it was quite normal to find 902 transmissions on 911 models, particularly export models, and 1968 U.S.A. 911L models had five-speed 902 gearboxes. Manual gearboxes were fitted with different gear sets for Europe and Rest of the World (RoW); hence, 901/01 and 901/06 are five-speed Europe; 901/0 and 901/12 are five-speed U.S.A.

Sportomatic Chassis numbers are to be found from the same series as equivalent manual models. Four-speed Sportomatic gearbox designation was 905/00 for 1968 U.S.A. models, 905/1 for European models on S and T, and 905/13 from start of 1969 model year.

Numbered notes

1. From March 1966, with Weber carburetors. 2. From November 1966. 3. From December 1966. 4. From October 1966. 5. With emissions control equipment (with air pump). 6. Body built by Karmann.

The chassis number on early models is found on the left-hand door pillar. Also shown on the plate is the paint code (Farbton) 6401, Slate Gray.

Production Changes

September 1963

The 901 is shown at Frankfurt Motor Show.

August 1964 (Start of 0-program)

Start of pilot production; short wheelbase (torsion bar cover next to rear wheel arch); 4.5-inch steel wheels; cone-shaped external mirror (early model Durant) with no flange; intake/exhaust valves are 39/35 millimeters, respectively; exposed pushbuttons on exterior door handles; chromed only bumper over-riders standard on U.S. models; opening front quarter windows; grab handle on passenger door; narrow vinyl-faced trim strip on sills under doors; single 12-volt battery; Eberspacher fuel heater for rapid interior heat/demist standard; single fuse panel at rear of luggage compartment; woven three-piece luggage compartment carpets; linked short (gold anodized) Porsche script on engine cover, angled 911 logo; engine grille with narrow wire horizontals. The five-speed gearbox ratios at the start of production were as follows: first, 12/34; second, 18/32; third, 23/28; fourth, 26/25; fifth, 28/23; and final drive, 7:31.

October 1964

Type number changed to 911.

February 1965

First models reach the United States (price $6,500).

May 1965

First RHD U.K. model (price £3,438).

Late 1965

From engine 903070, cam lubrication now by spray bar.

March 1966

Weber 40 IDAs replace original Solex overflow carburetors.

August 1966

911 script moved to below engine grille. Gearbox ratios changed to: first, 11/34; second, 18/34; third, 22/29; fourth 25/26; fifth, 28/24.

October 1966

The 911S (for Super) production started (announced July 1966); red engine cooling duct cover instead of black (with 5mm smaller diameter fan); Weber 40 IDS carburetors; intake/exhaust valves increased to 42mm/38mm; forged pistons and new three-into-one exhaust/heat exchangers; 4.5Jx15in five-spoke forged aluminum alloy wheels by Fuchs; thicker rubber strip on bumpers and side strips; ventilated disc brakes; front anti-roll bar increased from 13mm to 15mm; 16mm rear anti-roll bar introduced; Koni shock absorbers fitted; leather rim steering wheel; basketweave lower dash replaces wood trim. On all models, forged valve rockers replaced with cast-iron versions. Gear ratios were: first, 0.324; second, 0.529; third, 0.759; fourth, 0.962; fifth, 1.261.

December 1966

Start of Targa production (without vents in side of roll hoop and with zip-out soft rear window).

August 1967 (Start of A-program)

Black wipers; recessed pushbuttons on door handles; larger dual-circuit brake system; 5.5in wheel rims on 911S; all-plastic timing chain guides replace aluminum-backed early type; sealed unit chain tensioners replace open reservoir versions; engine weight of base model is approximately 182kg; brushed aluminum dash trim for 911; bright anodized aluminum replaces chromed brass for window frames; engine grille has thicker top and bottom horizontals; S gets bright trim on doors; three-piece felt (Perlon) carpet in front compartment; spaced-out (gold anodized) Porsche script on engine cover; front anti-roll bar reduced to 11mm 911L replaces basic 911 model. The 911T (for Touring) introduced, replacing four-cylinder 912: four-speed manual gearbox; bright anodized script on engine cover; no anti-roll bar; Weber 40 IDT carburetors; same valve sizes as S, but small ports and less overlap on cam timing. U.S. models, only 911 and 911L (for Lux) with Weber 40 IDAP carburetors and air pump; reflectors added to sides of body; five-speed gearbox; ventilated disc brakes; vinyl trimmed over-riders.

August 1968 (Start of B-program)

First major model upgrade for 911; extended wheelbase (torsion bar covers now set in from wheel arch); die-cast magnesium castings replace sand castings for crankcase, chain housings, and valve covers; 911S model uses Bosch mechanical fuel injection, intake/exhaust valves increased to 45mm/39mm, plus 6in wheels; S engine weight is approximately 196kg; 911 E (for Einspritzung or injected) replaces 911 with same injection as S, initially with

The earliest 911s had pencil-thin rubbing strips on the sills, and the circular cover that gives access to the rear torsion bar was completely exposed.

The sills of the 911S featured deeper aluminum trim extrusions and "wide" rubber trim. Peeping out from behind the trim is the circular torsion bar cover. The short-wheelbase 911s, built to the end of the 1968 model year, are visually identified by the closeness of the cover to the wheel arch.

Production Data

Model year	Model	Power (bhp DIN@rpm)	Torque (Nm@rpm)	Compression ratio	Weight (kg)	Number built
1964	901/911	130@6,200	162@4,600	9.0:1	1,000	13[1]
1965	911	130@6,100	174@4,200	9.0:1	1,080	235
1966	911	130@6,100	174@4,200	9,0:1	1,080	4,864
1967	911	130@6,100	174@4,200	9.0:1	1,030	3,421
	911 Targa	130@6,100	174@4,200	9.0:1	1,080	718
	911S	160@6,600	179@5,200	9.8:1	1,030	3,422
	911S Targa	160@6,600	179@5,200	9.8:1	1,080	718
1968	911	130@6,100	176@4,200	9.0:1	1,075	473
	911[2]	130@6,100	176@4,200	9.0:1	1,075	742
	911 Targa	130@6,100	176@4,200	9.0:1	1,125	268
	911L	130@6,100	176@4,200	9.0:1	1,075	720
	911L Targa	130@6,100	176@4,200	9.0:1	1,125	307
	911L U.S.	130@6,100	176@4,200	9.0:1	1,075	449
	911 Targa U.S.	130@6,100	176@4,200	9.0:1	1,125	134
	911T	110@5,800	156@4,200	8.6:1	1,075	928
	911T[2]	110@5,800	156@4,200	8.6:1	1,075	683
	911T Targa	110@5,800	156@4,200	8.6:1	1,125	521
	911S	160@6,600	180@5,200	9.8:1	1,075	1,267
	911STarga	160@6,600	180@5,200	9.8:1	1,125	442
1969	911T	110@5,800	156@4,200	8.6:1	1,020	343
	911T[2]	110@5,800	156@4,200	8.6:1	1,020	3,561
	911T Targa	110@5,800	156@4,200	8.6:1	1,070	1,282
	911E	140@6,500	175@4,500	9.1:1	1,020	954
	911E[2]	140@6,500	175@4,500	9.1:1	1,020	1,014
	911E Targa	140@6,500	175@4,500	9.1:1	1,070	858
	911S	170@6,800	183@5,500	9.9:1	995	1,492
	911S Targa	170@6,800	183@5,500	9.9:1	1,045	614

General notes

All cars have a capacity of 1,991cc, with a bore and stroke of 80x66mm. An assumption has been made here that Targas were approximately 50kg heavier than coupes.

Numbered notes

1. 1964 models include the two four-cylinder 901 prototypes built. 2. Body built by Karmann.

5.5Jx14in Fuchs wheels and Boge hydropneumatic gas/oil struts; E could be specified with conventional struts and 6in Fuchs wheels; E has green shroud on engine (generally!); E has same valve sizes as previous year's Sand T, timing as 911/911L; leather steering wheels for Sand E; T gets double valve springs of E and S and 5.5Jx15in wheels. Gear ratios for all models. Four-speed 902: first, 0.323; second, 0.613; third, 0.962; fourth, 1.261. Five-speed 901: first, 0.324; second, 0.529; third, 0.759; fourth, 0.962; fifth, 1.261. E and S use new Bosch CD ignition; S gets external radiator-type oil cooler in front right fender; now alternator on all models; in United States, T, E, and S replace 911 and 911L and air pump removed; slightly flared rear wheel arches; larger, flanged external door mirror (late model Durant); narrow horn grilles and wider indicator lenses; engine lid grille changes to thin chromed extrusions for horizontals, with three verticals; rear reflectors next to over-riders; two 12-volt batteries; reshaped spare wheel recess in fuel tank; vertical fuse panels on left front wall of luggage compartment; four-piece felt (Perlon) front compartment carpet; opening front quarter windows deleted on coupe and heater outlets moved from front of doorsills to a mixer unit under the dash; new internal ventilation system with three-speed fan, controls in left-center of dash (old position of ashtray, which moves below center dash); internal mirror now mounted to windshield; instrument lettering changed from green to white, basketweave dash trim standard on all models, with rubber knobs; hand throttle and heater control either side of handbrake lever; coat hooks change from beige 356 type to black; heated rear window on coupe; doors get separate storage compartments (not pockets) under armrest; gate pattern shown on top of gear lever; green tinted glass becomes standard; vents added to rear sides of Targa hoop.

Dimensions

Wheelbase

Prototypes, 2,204mm; O- and A-program, 2,211mm; B-program and subsequent models, 2,271mm.

Track (front/rear)

Prototypes, 1,332mm/1312mm; A-program, 1,337mm/1,317mm; A-program, 1,353mm/1,321mm; B-program, 1,360mm/1,342mm; B-program with 14in wheels, 1,362mm/1,344mm.

Length

Prototypes, 4135mm; subsequent production, 4,163mm.

Width

1,610mm.

Options

Factory list (1965)

9101 hubcap with colored emblem (901 361 031 00); 9107 Phoenix 165HR15 tires; 9108 Dunlop SP 165HR15 tires; 9118 chrome-plated wheels (901 361 013 22); 9127 external mirror, left (901731 11100); 9128 external mirror, right (901 731 111 00); 9131 external mirror, Talbot, left (644 731 111 00); 9132 external mirror, Talbot, right (644 731 111 00); 9189 sisal floor mats (901 551 102 15); 9198 Velouran floormats in carpet color (901 551 101 15); 9200/9201 lap belt, left and right (644 80390101); 9204/9205 lap and diagonal belt, left and right (644 803 90103 or 06); 9208 U.S.-approved lap belt; 9217 traveling kit; 9220/9221 bumper horns with rubber pads (front left, 901 505 031 21; front right, 901 505 032 21; rear, 901 505 033 21); 9224 four Koni shock absorbers (front, 901 341 067 05; rearm 901 333 051 12); 9229 gas heater (901 572 051 30); 9230

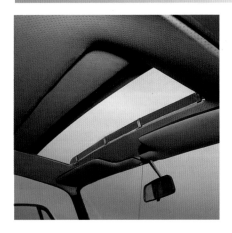

An electrically operated sunroof was an option from the start of production. The small wind deflector at the leading edge popped up as the roof was opened, inhibiting wind buffeting. The interior mirror was initially attached to the roof by three screws, but for 1968 the mounting became a "breakaway" design attached to the windshield.

A feature of O- and A-program model 5 with a sunroof fitted at the factory was drain slots in the roof adjacent to the rear window.

supplementary electric blower; 9237/9238/9248 black leather suitcases (small, medium, and large); 9248 canvas suitcase in red/black tartan; 9261 canvas bag in red/black tartan; 9264 suitcase SKAI-Dur in black; 9265 wooden (300 millimeters) steering wheel (901 347 082 01); 9266 horn button, black (901 347 802 00); 9267 raised steering wheel hub (901 347 082 11); 9290 rear wiper; 9293 foglights, pair (644 631 912 03); 9400 special paint, nonmetallic; 9403 special paint, metallic; 9425 leather interior; 9427 seats raised by 20 millimeters; 9428 leather seats only (left, 901 521 001 50; right, 901 521 002 50); 9442/9443 fittings for head rest (644 521 087 05); 9444/9445 fittings for leather head rest (644521 085 13); 9446/9447 fittings for leatherette head rest (644 521 085 07); 9474 Golde electric sunroof (901 564 003 65); 9481 Catacolor tinted glass (all); 9482 Catacolor tinted windshield; 9483 Catacolor tinted rear window (901 801 010 00); 9505 roof rack (901 801 010 00); 9506 leather straps for roof rack (901 801 953 00); 9507 roof ski rack with eight leather straps (901 801 015 20); the radio options were the contemporary Blaupunkt Bremen, Frankfurt, Frankfurt-U.S., Köln, and New Yorker, plus the Becker Monte Carlo, Europa, and Mexico.

Factory list (1969 additions)

9107 Phoenix 165VR15 tires; 9108 Dunlop SP 165VR15 tires; 9120 light alloy wheels, forged; 9121 chrome-plated wheels; 9168/9169 outside thermometer; 9186 chrome-plated flap light in engine compartment; 9189/9190 Velouran floor mats for Sportomatic; 9198/9199 Velouran floor mats for manual shift; 9216 traveling kit, 911S; 9218 traveling kit, 911T; 9219 traveling kit, 911 USA/911L/911L USA; 9222 bumper guards with rubber pads; 9232 air conditioner; 9239 two leather straps to fasten suitcases on rear seats; 9240 traveling bag, leatherette; 9241 traveling bag, leather; 9249 leather suitcase to fit on top of rear seats; 9250 leather shirt case to fit on top of rear seats; 9263 leather shirt case, rear seats; 9268 leather steering wheel; 9273 iodine headlamps; 9278 U.S. safety equipment; 9283 emergency flash light; 9291 iodine foglamps, yellow lenses; 9292 iodine foglamps, white lenses; 9294 foglamps, white lenses; 9297 electrically operated antenna; 9298 suppression of radio interference; 9303 antenna; 9305 suppression of radio interference; 9307 loudspeaker; 9320 Blaupunkt Bremen radio; 9322 Blaupunkt Frankfurt radio; 9323 Blaupunkt Frankfurt U.S.A. radio; 9325 Blaupunkt Köln radio; 9326 Blaupunkt New Yorker U.S.A. radio; 9327 Blaupunkt Boston U.S.A. radio; 9340 Becker Monte Carlo radio; 9341 Becker Europa radio; 9342 Becker Europa U.S.A. radio; 9349 Becker Grand Prix radio; 9350 Becker Grand Prix U.S.A. radio; 9356 tonneau for Targa; 9388/9389 Recaro sports seats; 9400 special paint, according to special color book; 9403 special paint, outside special color book and silver metallic; 9420 long-range iodine lamps above bumper; 9421 iodine foglamps, yellow lenses, above bumper; 9428 leather seats with dogtooth inlay; 9437 headrest, wrap dog-tooth fabric; 9438 headrest, wrap corduroy; 9439 headrest, leather; 9440 headrest, leatherette; 9480 tinted glass all round for Targa; 9481 tinted glass all round for coupe; 9482 tinted windshield; 9483 tinted rear window (coupe only); 9484 electrically heated rear window for coupe; 9485 electrically heated, tinted rear window for coupe; 9499 special fuel tank, 26 U.S. gallons; 9503 roof luggage rack with fittings for skis and straps; 9508 roof rack with eight leather straps for Targa; 9512 electrically heated fixed tinted rear window for Targa; 9520 stainless steel muffler skirt; 9521 towing hook, rear; 9574 limited slip differential; 9581 Sportomatic transmission; 9590 five-speed transmission.

Note: The four-digit option numbers were replaced by numbers prefixed by an M for 1970 onward. It is not possible to reproduce options for every year because some lists are very long and some information was unavailable from the factory at the time of publication.

Color Schemes

Color names in English-speaking markets could vary. In other markets, alternative names were sometimes used. For example, the British colors of Lemon Yellow and Bush Green were respectively called Canary Yellow and Leaf Green in the United States. The alternative names have been given where variations occur.

Early color codings had the year of manufacture as the first two digits. From 1968, the paint type and manufacturer was noted in a two-digit prefix number and a single suffix letter (e.g., 976802L, where 97 refers to the paint type and L refers to Lesonal, the manufacturer). Other paint suppliers were Glasurit (G), Herberts (H), and Herbol (HL). The prefix R indicates that a color could be obtained from all the manufacturers. The year indicator on the code appears to have been dropped after 1969.

1964–65
Standard body colors

Slate Gray (6401), Ruby Red (6402), Enamel Blue (6403), Light Ivory (6404), Champagne Yellow (6405), Irish Green (6406), Signal Red (6407).

Special order body colors

Dolphin Gray (6410), Togo Brown (6411), Bali Blue (6412), Black (6413).

Interior

Leatherette (vinyl) in red, black, brown, or beige (leather optional at extra cost). Seat inlays in basketweave leatherette or dog-tooth check (black with red or white, black with white, black with brown or white). The 912 interior was the same, except that seat inlays were in corduroy (red, black, cognac, or stone gray). For 911S, interior leatherette was ST grained in the same colors. Carpets were in black velour (square-weave) except on the 912, which used black boucle.

1966–67 (charts dated May 1965 and March 1967)
Standard body colors

Slate Gray (6601), Polo Red (6602), Gulf Blue (6603), Light Ivory (6604), Bahama Yellow (6605), Irish Green (6606), Sand Beige (6607), Aga Blue (6608), Black (6609).

Special order body colors

Burgundy Red (30868), Maroon (30736), Tangerine (P2002), Metallic Dark Red (30847), Champagne Yellow (16153), Signal Yellow (R1007), Lemon (Canary) Yellow (R1012), Medium Ivory (17657), Lido Gold (17656), Golden Green (62165), Signal Green (R6001), Bush (Leaf) Green (62163), Metallic Dark Green (62109), Turkey Green (R6016), Velvet Green (62162), Sea Green (62164), Crystal Blue (52254), Pastel Blue (R5012), Prussian Blue (R5009), Metallic Blue (52300), Ultra Blue (R5013), Olive (62166), Sepia Brown (R8007), Coffee Brown (80342), Stone Gray (75741), Light Gray (75742), Cloudy Gray (R7030), Beige Gray (70192), Black (95043), Silver Metallic (96024).

Interior

As for 1964–65.

1968 (chart dated May 1967)
Standard body colors

Slate Gray (6601), Polo Red (6602), Gulf Blue (6603), Light Ivory (6604), Bahama Yellow (6605), Irish Green (6606), Sand Beige (6607), Aga Blue (6608), Black (6609).

Special order colors

Burgundy Red (6808), Maroon (30736), Tangerine (6809/P2002), Metallic Dark Red (6854/30847), Champagne Yellow (6822116153), Signal Yellow (6823/R 1 007), Lemon (Canary) Yellow (6824/R 1 012), Medium Ivory (6821/17657), Lido Gold (17656), Golden Green (6828/62163), Signal Green (6829/R600I), Bush Green (6830/62163), Metallic Dark Green (6852/62109), Turkey (Turquoise) Green (6831/R6016), Velvet (Irish) Green (6806/62162), Sea Green (62164), Crystal Blue (6825/52254), Pastel Blue (6826/R5012), Prussian (Ossi) Blue (6803/R5009), Metallic Blue (6853/52300), Ultra Blue (68271R5013), Olive (6835/62166), Sepia Brown (6836/R8007), Coffee Brown (6837/80342), Stone Gray (75741), Light Gray (6832175742), Cloudy Gray (6833/R7030), Beige Gray (6834170192), Black (6838/95043), Silver Metallic (6851/96024).

Interior

For 911T and 912, basketweave leatherette in red, black, brown, or beige. Optional corduroy (in same colors) or dog-tooth check (in same colors as 1966–67). For 911L and 911S, ST grained leatherette in red, black, brown, or beige, with option of dog-tooth check and corduroy. Optional at cost was leather seating (with basketweave inlay on T, ST grain inlay on L and S) in the same four colors above. Carpet matched interior colors, with 911T in Perlon "special," 911S in velour.

1969 (chart dated October 1968)
Standard body colors

Slate Gray (6801), Polo Red (6802), Ossie Blue (6803), Light Ivory (6804), Bahama Yellow (6805), Irish Green (6806), Sand Beige (6807), Burgundy Red (6808), Tangerine (6809).

Special order colors

Medium Ivory (17657), Champagne Yellow (16153), Signal Yellow (R1007), Lemon (Canary) Yellow (R1012), Dark Red Metallic (30847), Crystal Blue (52254), Pastel Blue (R5012), Ultra Blue (R5013), Metallic Blue (52300), Lime Green (62165), Signal Green (R6001), Bush Green (62163) Dark Green Metallic (62109), Turkey Green (R6016), Gray White (75742), Fortuna Gray (R7030), Beige Gray (70192), Olive (62166), Sepia Brown (R8007), Coffee Brown (80342), Black (95043), Silver Metallic (96024).

Interior

As for 1968, but carpet on 911E in velour (and on T with "comfort" option).

Chapter 2

The 2.2-Liter 911 (1970–1971)

By the time we get to the 911s of the early 1970s we are into the stuff of romance. The previous decade had been a time of transition for Porsche on the international racing scene, the time when it made the move from being class winners to contending for outright wins. When the 917 was revealed to the public in March 1969, Porsche entered the big league. The following years were sports car racing's best: a period that was marked by ultra-competitive endurance racing between Porsche and Ferrari; the time of Siffert, Rodriguez, Ickx, and Andretti.

To have a Porsche 911 as a road car made a statement. You knew about the best things in life. Do you remember Steve McQueen, his steely eyes twitching as he viewed the repaired crash barrier at the start of that cult racing movie, *Le Mans*? He was leaning on a 911. It was silver, of course, and it was a 2.2S. How could we tell it was a 2.2S? By the glorious sound of its flat-six and virtually open fuel injection intakes.

The 2-liter engines of the early 911s were notable for lots of revs and power that tended to come in a rush toward the redline. In the mid-1960s, the chassis engineers had worked wonders on the handling and braking and made great progress with the refinement of the original design. The engine designers, meanwhile, had worked at reducing weight, reducing the effect of the engine overhang, and improving the road manners of the six-cylinder engine. Improved carburetion and, by 1969, the CD ignition system ensured that that year's 911s had had most of the bugs ironed out of the engine. The engineers then turned their attentions to improving the torque. In August 1969, the 911 received an engine with a capacity of 2,195cc. It gave the unit more flexibility, flattening the torque curve, and the change was most noticeable at lower revs on the T and E.

The S, however, was no less effort to drive. The maximum power had been edged up to 180-brake horsepower from 170-brake horsepower, but you had to keep the revs above 5,500 rpm to enjoy it. It meant the five-speed 'box earned its keep, and drivers got used to sweating as well as having silly grins on their faces. This inflexibility was expected on a racing car but could be a pain in normal town driving, especially in speed-restricted countries such as the United States. *Road & Track* magazine even advised that

A very clean 1971 2.2 Targa. Ventilation on the Targa had been improved for the 1969 model year by the addition of vertical cabin air outlets at the sides of the roll-over hoop. Although deleted from the coupe, the opening front quarter lights were retained on the Targa until 1977. Not often seen today is the "Weltmeister 1969/70" decal in the left lower area of the windshield, celebrating the factory's consecutive World Championship of Makes racing titles.

Evolution Outline

August 1969: The 911T, E, and S are now standardized as main production models, nominally with 2.2-liter engine; T (125-brake horsepower) has Zenith carburetors, E (155-brake horsepower) and S (180-brake horsepower) have mechanical fuel injection; T has CD ignition; Sportomatic deleted as an option on S.

August 1970: A selective hot zinc dip to exposed underbody sections is introduced.

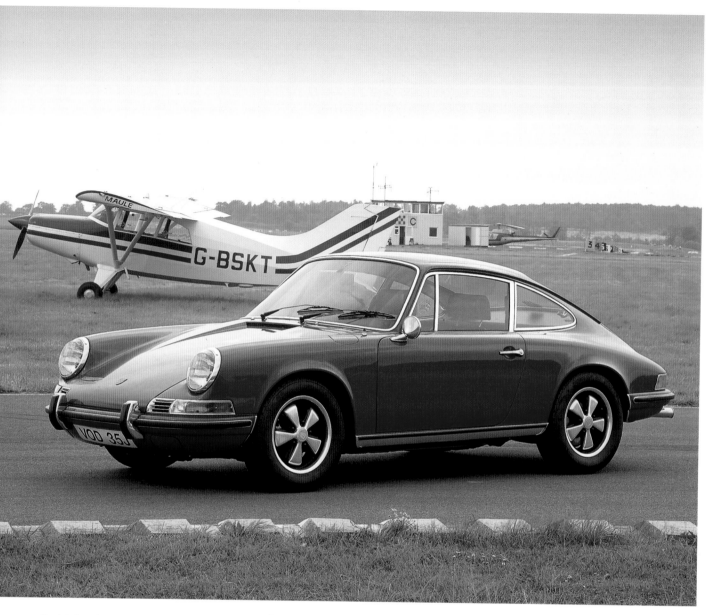

Patrick Amos' concours-winning 1971 911T at Silverstone. This car has a high specification, including 5.5-inch Fuchs wheels, tinted glass, and over-riders.

the T was a better car: "The 911T is a bit stronger this year. We recommend it for all-round use."

There was a secondary motive in increasing the engine capacity. It moved the 911 out of the up to 2,000cc class in international GT racing and into the 2,001cc to 2,500cc class. This offered scope for the racing department to explore further increases in capacity and power. In time, it would establish the 911 on the international racing scene as the competitive customer racing car.

Bodyshell

The 2.2-liter 911s are the C-and D-program cars. Weight reduction was still a major effort, especially at the extremities of the car.

For the C-program (August 1969) both the engine cover and the central part of the E and S bumpers were aluminum. All models received a flexible PVC underseal: This anti-corrosion treatment was a move toward extending the life of the 911, but it would prove to be a bane for restorers in later years. The undercoat has a habit of peeling away in highly stressed areas and forming a perfect rust trap. What might look like a small tear in the coating would, when picked back with a screwdriver, reveal an expanse of orange rust. The thought was there, and if the coating had not been applied, far fewer cars would be on the roads today.

For the D-program (August 1970), limited zinc coating of the exposed underbody parts was introduced. This in itself did not prevent the dreaded worm from gorging itself, but it was the start of a strategically beneficial move by the factory. The progressive improvement in anti-corrosion treatment Porsche was an industry leader in this and gives credibility to the claim that some 80 to 85 percent of Porsches ever made are still on the roads.

The Targa roof section was improved, recognizing that the open model was now becoming very popular. By 1970, the Targa was accounting for 31 percent of all 911s produced. The revisions affected the way the roof sealed to the windshield, side windows, and roll-over hoop. The method by which the roof section of the Targa collapsed down into a storable size was unaffected.

Racing was never far from the thoughts of Porsche engineers. An abortive effort had been made by racing manager Rico Steinemann to get the 911S accepted into the Touring Car category, but the 1970 production cars were affected by the paperwork tactic used to qualify a competitive car for the special GT class. The 1970 S was listed in the catalogue in very basic form, suitable for competition only, and weighed a remarkable 838 kilograms (1,848 pounds). This car was stripped of all luxury items, it used aluminum for the bumpers and

Here's a 2.2 911S owned by Mark Waring and finished in the unusual color of Olive. These cars make a quite glorious sound on hard acceleration, thanks to their largely unsilenced intake manifold and pre-emissions control exhaust.

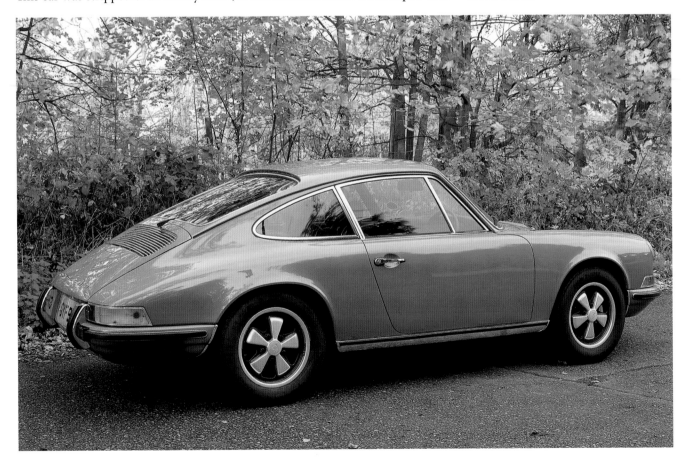

engine lid, lightweight seats were fitted, and pull straps replaced the door handles. A larger fuel tank of 110 liters (24.20 Imperial gallons, 29.06 U.S. gallons) and a space-saver tire were the standard fit. However, most Ss were built with the M470 option package that made the car suitable for road customers, bringing the car up to the full luxury specification of that year's E.

The interior of a 2.2 911 was now far removed from the early models. For the 1969 model year the lower dash had been revised to include more effective heating and ventilation controls. The ashtray was moved to the central area, the glovebox lid was further revised, and the speaker grille was now removable. From 1969, too, the seats could be tilted forward by operating a lever at the top of the seat back support, instead of down at the hinge point.

Recaro sports seats, as in this 1971 S, offered excellent sideways and thigh support. These seats have "crackle" finish back supports, which became standard across the range the following year.

Body Trim and Fittings

The most noticeable external change for the 1970 model year was new door handles with the opening trigger behind the handle. This offered a safer handle as well as being easier to use. Into 1971, this was the last year the pretty, round Durant external mirror was fitted as standard to cars for all markets. The following year legal requirements in the United States and Germany for a larger glass area forced the introduction of a rectangular type, but several markets (including the United Kingdom) retained the round Durant mirror for some years.

From August 1966, the 911 logo on the engine lid had been presented in block letters (rather than the original italic) and positioned centrally below the grille. By 1970, the three six-cylinder models were labeled accordingly, but it is worth pointing out that the 911T logo was normally in aluminum, with the other two in a gold anodized finish (although the gold finish was a T option). The 2.2 cars also had a unique decal—an outline drawing of the flat-six engine with large the number "2.2" on it—applied to the center of the rear window. What better way to let your neighbor know you had the latest model. The 1971 models also carried a small decal on the driver's side rear side window proclaiming victory in the 1969 and 1970 World Championship of Makes.

Interior Trim

The efforts being made to make the 911 more practical and more attractive to new buyers included improving the door trim and in particular the door pockets. The 1969 cars had featured a small locker in the door, and this was now replaced with a larger opening compartment below the door handle. On the safety side, the interior door handle was now a recessed pull-type lever rather than an exposed button. The forward part of the compartment was open, with the area below the armrest having an opening locker. The 1970 cars also offered electrically operated windows as an option.

Dashboard and Instruments

Ergonomics were improved with a revised stalk arrangement that improved accessory operation without the driver having to take his or her hands off the steering wheel. The left-hand stalk (a new four-way design) worked the indicators, headlight flash, and main/dipped control, and the right-hand stalk the windshield wipe/wash function.

From the 1970 model year, the main dials were each located by a neoprene ring around the circumference and inserted from the front, rather than being located by a rear bracket as previously. The instrument rims had lost their decorative 1960s chromed look from 1968 in favor of a more functional black look. The option of a steering lock had been introduced in 1969, and this went further on U.S. cars when a buzzer was introduced in 1970. This irritating device let you know when you had both the keys in the ignition and the door open. It was very useful. Incidentally, the 1970 cars were the first with a plastic handle to the ignition key.

The heavy basketweave finish to the dash was retained, and the radio controls could be integrated into this finish rather than being a more theft-prone separate unit. The 1970 model year was the last in which the model designation was shown on the glove compartment door.

Luggage Compartment

The higher specification 911s had been fitted with two luggage compartment lights, but 1971 was the last year this luxury was available. Subsequently, the E and S models copied the previous T in having a single light on the left-hand side (looking from the front). Fuel tank capacity remained at 62 liters (13.64 Imperial gallons, 16.38 U.S. gallons), but 110 liters (24.20 Imperial gallons, 29.06 U.S. gallons) was optional for the S.

Engine

Of all the changes, those to the engine were the most obvious. The capacity was now 2,195cc (133.90 cubic inches), found by increasing the bore from 80 millimeters (3.12 inches) to 84 millimeters (3.28 inches). In a pre–fuel crisis world, the increased fuel consumption was not regarded as a problem. While the E and the S needed 98 RON fuel, the T could use 96 RON.

Engine type numbers also changed, receiving a 911 prefix instead of the old 901 designation. Only the T had a special U.S. version. The engine team, under the

New door trims were introduced for the 2.2 models. Their features were rigid storage pockets (the rear one hinged outward) and a recessed door handle lever—much safer than the previous push-button release.

The instrument panel on a 1971 T, showing only detail changes: the hazard warning flasher button, introduced in 1970, is on the left-hand lower dash, and there are improved switches with large rubber surrounds. The labeling behind the steering wheel indicates headlamp flash and turn signal operation but is completely obscured from the driver!

This decal appeared in the rear window of all 2.2 models. The simple chromed engine lid grille has a black-painted mesh beneath to stop objects falling into the engine compartment.

The hinged panel behind the fuel tank covered the steering joints and the location for the optional petrol heater. The brake master cylinder was moved out of this compartment and up onto the left wing wall for the 1968 model year, when dual-circuit braking was introduced. The fuse box, larger than before, has been moved to just behind the left-hand battery.

guidance of Paul Hensler, evolved a common cylinder head for the 2.2 models with 46 millimeters (1.79 inches) inlet and 40 millimeters (1.56 inches) exhaust valves, although the port sizes were different. The Helicoil insert in the spark plug hole was also discarded. Bruce Anderson notes that the factory had felt the Helicoils caused "inconsistent effective spark plug heat ranges." A new cylinder head gasket, made up of a thin metal C-shaped ring trapping a continuous spring, replaced the earlier more conventional gasket. The barrels were designed to allow the racers to increase engine capacity still further, and the number of cooling fins was increased. Since the stronger con rods used longer big end bolts, the ends of the barrels were modified to clear the sweep of the longer bolts. A shell bearing was added to the internal end of the intermediate shaft as the new magnesium crankcases (introduced for the 1969 model year) had a tendency to wear faster than the original aluminum.

The T changed to the cheaper Zenith 40 TIN triple-choke carburetors, in place of Webers, and benefited from the CD ignition system. Some 1971 Ts used Webers, however, for reasons unknown. The T was becoming a very desirable and practical sports car. The E, meanwhile, was softened to improve its desirability to mainstream buyers, its engine receiving the cams (with less overlap) from the 1968 911 engine (the 901/06).

For 1970, all U.S. models received a new fuel evaporative control system to prevent the release of vapor into the atmosphere. The system passed vapor through an expansion tank and over an activated charcoal filter. Vapor was piped back into the air cleaner housing and drawn into the engine.

For the 1971 model year, the undersides of the pistons on all models were cooled by oil squirters. A feature that had been extensively tested in racing, this had the effect of dramatically reducing piston crown temperatures. On the 1971 models, the fuel pump was moved from the front suspension crossmember to a new position next to the left-hand rear suspension arm.

Transmission

With progressively increasing engine power, the clutch reached the point where it had to be improved. For 1970, the Fichtel and Sachs item was increased in diameter by 10 millimeters (0.39 inch) to 225 millimeters (8.86 inches) and included a redesigned diaphragm action to make pedal effort a little less tiring.

Like the engine, the gearbox was given a new prefix, being termed 911 rather than 901. The gearbox internals were largely unchanged and the five-speed 'box still offered a dog-leg first gear arrangement with first over to the left and back and reverse opposite, as on the 2-liter cars. The T retained the four-speed gearbox as standard with a five-speed as an option.

Recognizing that automatics, even semi-automatics, do not go well with the image of an out-and-out sports car, Porsche deleted the Sportomatic as an option for the S. Of interest to seriously sporty customers, however, was a new limited slip differential option. The ZF unit was offered with a locking factor of either 40 or 80 percent.

Electrical Equipment and Lighting
Another luxury feature introduced in mid-1969 was electrically operated side windows. These could be specified in place of the manual winders and had the added benefit that the driver could close the passenger window from the switches on the driver's door. All models retained a 770-watt alternator and two 36-amp/hour batteries. There were other detail improvements, too, like a small light for the ashtray mounted in the center of the knee-board under the dash. The ignition switch was now a four-position unit, with positions for accessory/off/run/start.

The Bosch H1 headlight continued for the majority of markets, with American 911s retaining Hella sealed-beam 50/40-watt units as standard.

Suspension and Steering
The anchorage points of the front suspension struts moved forward by 14 millimeters to reduce front wheel castor, making the steering lighter at lower speeds and reducing the amount of road vibration fed back to the steering wheel. A steering lock made its first appearance in 1970. On the T and S, the front torsion bars were made easier to adjust. The E kept the hydro-pneumatic struts.

Brakes
The 911T received the ventilated disc brakes that were standard fit on the E and S. The disc sizes were 282 millimeters (11.0 inches) front and 290 millimeters (11.3 inches) rear. The only other change was that the light alloy front calipers, previously only fitted to the S, were added to the E.

Wheels and Tires
The 6Jx15 Fuchs wheel became the usual fit across the range of models, not only because these wheels had become synonymous with Porsche and its success, but also because the other size that was available as an option—a 14-inch rim—was generally unpopular. The smaller wheel was produced to allow fitment of 85-series tires, which had more flexible sidewalls than the 70-series. The 14-inch rim was fitted to Sportomatics to start with, but many customers wanted to stay with the 15-inch wheels and the firmer ride that went with them. The 14-inch wheels were options on the T through 1970 and 1971 and were then deleted. On the T in many markets, the 5.5Jx15 steel wheel was still the standard offering, but few customers wanted these old-fashioned wheels.

The standard tire for the T was the 165HR15, but the 185/70VR15 option was much more popular. The 185HR14 was also available.

This 1971 S has the correct nonfrosted top edge to its Bosch H1 headlamp glass. From 1973, the top edge was frosted and many owners retrofitted the simpler single-bulb H4 unit.

The European 2.2T used two triple-choke Zenith TIN 40 carburetors. The oil filler neck is on the right-hand side with the oil filter just behind.

Production Changes

Engine cover and central part of the E and S bumpers made from aluminum; all models receive a flexible PVC undercoat; chromed engine lid grille has five verticals under the horizontal; sealing around Targa roof section improved; new door handles with the opening trigger behind the handle; door trim has larger opening compartment; steering column stalks revised; main dials located by neoprene ring; T gets two luggage compartment lights (like E and S); Bosch H1 headlight improved; engine capacity increased to 2,195cc; engine and gearboxes get 911 designations; Helicoil spark plug insert deleted; thin metal C-shaped head gasket replaces original type; more fins on barrels, longer big end bolts; shell bearing added to internal end of intermediate shaft; T uses Zenith 40 TIN triple-choke carburetors, plus CD ignition; E gets earlier softer cams; U.S.A. models have fuel tank vent kit; clutch size increased to 225 millimeters

diameter with redesigned diaphragm and action; gear ratios for four-speed gearbox: first is 0.324, second is 0.613, third is 0.962, fourth is 1.318. The five-speed gearbox (all markets) ratios are first, 0.324; second 0563; third, 0.821: fourth, 1.080; fifth, 1.318; reverse, 0.688; final drive, 0.226. Sportomatic (all markets) gearbox final drive is 0.259 with ratios 0.417, 0.645, 0.889, 1.167. Sportomatic was no longer available as an option for the S; anchorage points of front suspension struts moved forward by 14 millimeters to reduce front wheel castor; front torsion bar adjustment improved; T gets ventilated disc brakes; light alloy front calipers fitted to the E; 6Jx15 Fuchs wheel becomes standard fit on all models; intermittent wipe facility.

August 1970 (Start of D-program)

Selective hot dip zinc coating to exposed underbody sections; fuel pump moved from front suspension crossmember adjacent to the left-hand rear suspension arm; crankcase squirters introduced to improve piston cooling; new sealed-type chain tensioner universally introduced; fuel evaporative control system fitted to U.S. models; glove box top handle deleted, lock (at left of center) moved to middle of compartment lid, with integrated knob with twist and pull operation.

Dimensions

Wheelbase

2,268mm

Track (front/rear)

T, 1,362mm/1,343mm; E and S, 1,372mm/1,354mm

The European 2.2T used two triple-choke Zmith TIN 40 carburetors. The oil filler neck is on the right-hand side with the oil filter is just behind.

Options

1970 (popular new options)

Electric window lifters, ZF limited slip differential with either a 40 or 80 percent locking factor, 5.5Jx15 cast magnesium (Mahle) wheels for T (alongside the 5.5Jx14 Fuchs wheel or chromed 5.5Jx15 steel wheel).

1971 (popular new options)

Heated front windshield, H3 equipped foglights and spotlights in the United States, convex lens for Durant mirror.

For 1970, there was another revised exterior door handle with the introduction of the definitive hidden trigger-release. Door operation now had to be a deliberate activity with no possibility of accidental opening. The keyhole was given a hinged cover, which reduced the possibility of the lock freezing up.

Color Schemes

For 1970, the three-digit number given here is the code as it appears on the paint identification plate, attached to the left-hand front door pillar. For 1971, the four-digit number shown is the factory paint code as identified in the model color charts. On Targa models, the last two digits of the paint code are replaced by 10 (e.g., Olive is 3939 on a coupe, 3910 on a Targa). Beginning with the 1970 models, all metallic finishes were applied with a two-coat wet-on-wet process.

1970 (chart dated August 1969)
Standard body colors
Burgundy Red (017), Tangerine (018), Bahia Red (022), Signal Orange (116), Light Ivory (131), Medium Ivory (132), Irish Green (213), Turquoise Green (220), Conda Green (222), Pastel Blue (321), Albert Blue (325).

Optional body colors
Metallic Green (221), Metallic Blue (324), Metallic Red (021), Black (700), Silver Metallic (924, 925).

Special order body colors
Crystal Blue (320), Glacier Blue (326), Turquoise (340), Signal Yellow (114), Olive (414), Light Yellow (117), Light Red (023), Signal Green (217), Leaf Green (218), Sepia Brown (415), Gray White (620), Beige Gray (622).

Interior
Leatherette was standard in black, brown, or beige. Leather was an extra cost option in the same colors. Seat inlays were basketweave leatherette in black, brown, or beige, or leather with basketweave finish. Fabrics were corduroy in black, brown, or beige and dog-tooth check in black and white or black, brown, and white. Carpets were black or brown, in special Perlon on the T and in velour on the E and S.

1971 (chart dated August 1970)
Standard body colors
Light Ivory (1111), Bahia Red (1313), Signal Orange (1414), Irish Green (1515), Albert Blue (1818), Pastel Blue (2020), Tangerine (2323), Burgundy (2424), Conda Green (2626).

Optional body colors
Silver Metallic (8080), Green Metallic (8383), Blue Metallic (8484), Gemini Blue Metallic (8484), Gold Metallic (8888).

Special order body colors
Olive (3939), Ivory (4646), Light Yellow (6262), Turquoise (6464), Green Turquoise (6565), Glacier Blue (6666), Signal Yellow (7272), Crystal Blue (7373), Sepia Brown (7474), Beige Gray (7575), White Gray (7676), Leaf Green (7777), Signal Green (7878), Light Red (7979), Black (1010).

Interior
All unchanged from 1970.

Production Data

Model year	Model	Power (bhp DIN@rpm)	Torque (Nm@rpm)	Compression ratio	Weight (kg)	Number built
1970	911T	125@5,800	177@4,200	8.6:1	1,020	2,418
	911T[1]	125@5,800	177@4,200	8.6:1	1,020	4,126
	911T Targa	125@5,800	177@4,200	8.6:1	1,070	2,545
	911 E	155@6,200	191@4,500	9.1:1	1,020	1,304
	911 E[1]	155@6,200	191@4,500	9.1:1	1,020	667
	911 E Targa	155@6,200	191@4,500	9.1:1	1,070	933
	911S	180@6,500	199@5,200	9.8:1	1,020	1,744
	911S Targa	180@6,500	199@5,200	9.8:1	1,070	729
1971	911T	125@5,800	177@4,200	8.6:1	1,020	583
	911T[1]	125@5,800	177@4,200	8.6:1	1,020	1,934
	911T Targa	125@5,800	177@4,200	8.6:1	1,070	3,476
	911E	155@6,200	191@4,500	9.1:1	1,020	1,088
	911E Targa	155@6,200	191@4,500	9.1:1	1,070	935
	911S	180@6,500	199@5,200	9.8:1	1,020	1,430
	911S Targa	180@6,500	199@5,200	9.8:1	1,070	788

Numbered note
1. Body built by Karmann.

Identification

Model year	Model	Engine	Gearbox	Chassis numbers	Engine numbers
C-program 1970	911T	911/03	911/00	9110100001–9110102418	6100001 onward
	911T[1]	911/03	911/00	9110120001–9110124126	6100001 onward
	911T Targa	911/03	911/00	9110110001–9110112545	6100001 onward
	911T Sporto	911/06	905/20	9110110001–9110112545	6103001 onward
	911T U.S.	911/07	911/00	9110110001–9110112545	6103501 onward
	911T Targa U.S.	911/07	911/00	9110110001–9110112545	6103501 onward
	911T Sporto U.S.	911/08	905/20	9110110001–9110112545	6105001 onward
	911E	911/01	911/01	9110200001–9110201304	6200001 onward
	911 E[1]	911/01	911/01	9110220001–9110220667	6200001 onward
	911 E Targa	911/01	911/01	9110210001–9110210933	6200001 onward
	911 E Sporto	911/04	905/20	9110210001–9110210933	6208001 onward
	911S	911/02	911/01	9110300001–9110301744	6300001 onward
	911S Targa	911/02	911/01	9110310001–9110310729	6300001 onward
D-program 1971	911T	911/03	911/00	9111100001–9111110583	6110001 onward
	911T[1]	911/07	911/00	9111120001–9111121934	6110001 onward
	911T Targa	911/06	911/00	9111110001–9111113476	6110001 onward
	911T U.S.	911/07	911/00	9111110001–9111113476	6114001 onward
	911T Targa U.S.	911/07	911/00	9111110001–9111113476	6114001 onward
	911T Sporto	911/06	905/20	9111110001–9111113476	6119501 onward
	911T Sporto U.S.	911/08	905/20	9111110001–9111113476	6119501 onward
	911E	911/01	911/01	9111200001–9111201088	6210001 onward
	911E Targa	911/01	911/01	9111210001–9111210935	6210001 onward
	911E Sporto	911/04	905/20	9111210001–9111210935	6218001 onward
	911S	911/02	911/01	9111300001–9111301430	6310001 onward
	911S Targa	911/02	911/01	9111310001–9111310788	6310001 onward

General notes

Chassis numbering In 1970, the chassis numbering system changed to a 10-digit method, for instance 9110 12000 1. The first three digits referred to the model, the fourth to the model year (0 for 1970), the fifth to the engine type (I = RoW 2.2-liter T, etc.), the sixth to the body type (0 = coupe, I = Targa, 2 = Karmann-manufactured coupe), and the last four digits to the build serial number. This numbering method continued until 1979.

Engines E and S engines were the same for Europe and the RoW, including the United States.

Gearboxes 911/00 is four-speed gearbox for 911T, 911/01 is five-speed, 905/20 is Sportomatic.

Numbered note
1. Body built by Karmann.

Chapter 3

The 2.4-Liter 911 (1972–1973)

Amp/hour—the 2.4s! In these cars we see the fruits of all the development effort to produce an unmatched high-performance sports car. The classic mainstream production 911 is a 2.4, and depending on how far your pocket can stretch, the choice is between three outstanding examples of the automobile engineer's art: the T, E, or S. It has been said that the 911 is a triumph of development over design, and nowhere is it more apparent than on a 2.4. Even the T, supposedly the base model in the range, had so much appeal.

In mechanical terms, the 2.4s were a major upgrade. It was the factory's general intention to try to restrict major changes to every two years, but this policy became a little clouded through the 1960s as the engineers worked flat out to develop the 911. Things looked as though they were settling down after the announcement of the much-improved 1969 models, but the then-new 2-liter fuel-injected engine lasted only a year before being enlarged to 2.2 liters. Factory discipline more or less reigned after that and the next big changes arrived in August 1971. These included not only the extra cubic capacity, new camshafts, and improved breathing, but also the introduction of the 915 gearbox and improved high-speed handling.

There was more overall performance than previous models and, to the credit of the engineers, it was more manageable too. The new E was almost as quick as the 2.2S and would pull in fifth from as little as 2,500 rpm. But fuel

Evolution Outline

August 1971: The engine size increases to 2,341cc (2.4 liters), the oil filler flap becomes external in rear right wing, black anodized lettering replaces gold on the engine cover, cookie-cutter wheels are introduced on the E, and the S is fitted with a front lip spoiler.

August 1972: Horn grilles change to black, the front spoiler becomes standard on the E, and the Targa becomes available in right-hand drive for first time.

January 1973: Fuel-injected T models (U.S.) change to Bosch K-Jetronic.

Opposite above: By 1973, the performance of the production 911 had reached a peak. This German-registered 2.4T shows off the lip spoiler introduced with the previous year's S model and optional for the T and E. For 1973 models the finish for the horn grilles and the trim around the driving lights changed from bright plated to black.

Opposite below: Dave Gray's 1973 2.4E is a high-specification U.K. model. Note the Durant mirror, which in most other markets was superseded by a much plainer rectangular mirror, in order to give a larger glass area.

consumption was at an all-time low—14 miles per gallon would be typical for a hard-driven S, and it was just a year before the first major world fuel crisis.

We look back on the cars and tend to ignore the lifestyles of the time. This was the age of the beautiful people, long hair, and flared pants. But, as in any time, success was what every Porsche buyer craved and to be associated with Porsche was to be associated with winning. Sales of 911s continued to improve through the late 1960s and early 1970s, as the production volume data shows. This was in no small part due to the effectiveness of Porsche's main marketing tool: motor racing. In 1970 and 1971, the Wyer Engineering/Gulf 917s absolutely dominated endurance racing, driven by some of the world's top Grand Prix drivers. In 1972, the big sports car would be banned, and Porsche simply transferred the effort over to the American Can-Am Challenge and the European Interserie. It was a good time on the track and, if you cared what others thought about you, a good time to be seen driving a Porsche.

As well as producing some legendary prototype racing cars, the factory continued to develop the 911 for racing and rallying. The 1971 Le Mans 24 Hours saw a number of 911Ss with engines bored out to around 2.4 liters and one, driven by factory man Jurgen Barth, used an

A 1972 model 2.4 can be identified by the oil filler flap on the right-hand rear wing—where it remained for only one year. Placing the oil tank within the wheelbase helped the handling, but this arrangement proved to be impractical because filling station attendants sometimes put petrol in the oil tank.

experimental engine of 2,410cc with a longer-throw crank. This engine pointed the way to a reliable increase in capacity for the road cars, but in fact the Barth Le Mans 2.4 had little in common with the new production 2.4 introduced in August of the same year. The on-track variety was part of the learning experience and was typical of the meticulous way Porsche went about its development.

The main reason for achieving the capacity increase by lengthening the stroke was to comply with California's new air pollution laws; taking out the bores would not have met this requirement. With a move in the United States toward 91 RON lead-free fuel, compression ratios also had to be lower than before. In a speed-restricted United States, the T tended to be seen as the most practical 911: complete with an S option kit (spoiler, alloy wheels, and so on) it provided the looks of the higher-powered models without the temperament.

The 1972 models witnessed the first substantial increase in weight for the 911. Over the previous 10 years the engineers had managed to trim the weight of the basic car from the original 1,080 kilograms (2,381 pounds) to a best, in 1969, of just 995 kilograms (2,194 pounds). The objective had been to improve the handling, for instance by reducing the overhung weight of the engine and gearbox at the rear. But the progressive increase in power from 1970 meant components in the engine had to be strengthened, and the introduction of the higher torque 915 transmission in 1972 added some 9 kilograms (19.8 pounds) over the earlier 901 unit. The brakes and suspension had been improved, too, but with some weight penalty. Crash resistance, and with it chassis weight, was improved in response to changes in legislation across the world in the early 1970s. By 1972, the basic weight of the S was back up to around 1,075 kilograms (2,370 pounds), depending on fittings. A comparison of the power to weight ratios shows the overall improvement.

A 1964 2-liter car had 0.120-brake horsepower/ kilograms compared to the 1972 figure of 0.176-brake horsepower/ kilograms, but if we want an early "hot ship" then we need look no further than the 1969 S with its 0.171-brake horsepower/ kilograms. And the figures do not convey the 1969 car's almost kartlike lightweight feel. Of course, this is a discussion only to be found among classic Porsche enthusiasts. All the 1973 and earlier 911s feel wonderfully light and responsive compared with their later, more luxurious offspring.

The increases in capacity had originally been intended to improve the opportunity for success in GT racing. It worked. In 1972, bored-out 2.5-liter 911s with the new 915 gearboxes won the European GT Championship (John Fitzpatrick) and the U.S. IMSA GT Championship (Hurley Haywood). With some justification, some observers were saying the 911 was at its peak. They were asking how it could be improved further. There were rumors of a new 911 replacement in development at the brand new research facility at Weissach.

As a tailpiece to the general comments on the 2.4-liter 911, these models marked the peak of Ferdinand Piech's influence over the 911 as development chief. A big shake-out in the company's senior management came in 1972, when members of the Porsche and Piech families voluntarily stepped out of the day-to-day running of the business. Dr. Ferry Porsche was concerned that internal family politics were affecting the performance of the business. It meant that Piech, whose track record in the development engineering side of Porsche had been outstanding, joined Audi-NSU, where he would excel and later rise to head the giant VW-Audi empire. At the end of 1972, the Porsche company changed from being a limited partnership (Porsche KG) to a partly shareholder-owned

Porsche AG. It was a massive change in the way the company was run, allowing the management team to be selected on the basis of merit rather than background. That said, the implications of the loss of Piech, especially, were perhaps not fully realized at the time.

Piech's replacement was Ernst Fuhrmann, father of the four-cam racing engine of the 1950s and a firm believer that Porsche's racing cars should be developed from its road cars. That was good news for the 911. The first result of Fuhrmann's direction was the appearance of the Carrera RS at the October 1972 Paris Salon. It was Fuhrmann's decision to go for the RS in place of the proposed 2.7-liter 911S for 1973, a decision prompted by the change in international racing regulations in May 1972 that allowed stripped-out homologation specials to be built in series of at least 500. The concept of the racing department modifying the heavier production 2.7S was dropped, even though preparations for the 2.7S had gone as far as preparing all the marketing brochures, and photographs were taken of a number of prototypes. Instead we had the 2.4S for 1973, and the limited edition RS would act as a springboard to much greater things for Porsche in competition.

Bodyshell

The 1972 models were classified internally at Porsche as the E-program, and the 1973 models were classified as the F-program.

The no-expense-spared development effort to improve the handling of the 911 reached a peak with the E-program. The most obvious recognition feature of these models is the oil tank filler just behind the right-hand door with its flap opened from a button in the adjacent door pillar. The 2-gallon oil tank, larger and made of stainless steel, was moved from behind the right-hand rear wheel (where it had been filled from within the engine compartment) to a new position in front of the wheel. This, the engineers said, reduced the polar moment of inertia and improved the predictability of the handling. It was also claimed that oil surge was minimized in hard cornering (this had been proved in racing with the 911R), and on a purely practical level the new location took the oil tank out of the firing line of stones thrown up by the rear wheel. This detail was typical of the time, showing how much control the engineers had over the specification of the cars. The new oil system also included a remote oil filter housing so that the engine, complete with oil system, could be easily fitted to Porsche specials. Now, how many people would need that facility?

The trouble was that the new oil tank arrangement also had an unforeseen snag, and the following year the tank moved back to where it had been on the 2.2s. Too many filling station attendants put fuel in the oil tank.

The other main feature to change on the E-program was the adoption of a front air dam on the S as a result of intensive wind tunnel testing. The testing, on an earlier 2-liter car, had shown that aerodynamic lift was present over the front axle at high speed, but the lift was greater over the rear axle. In side winds, the lift appeared to increase. This confirmed the reports received from the racers that high-speed stability was not all it should have been. The engineers proposed a small spoiler at the front, and this was included on the S for 1972, as well as being optional on the E and T. It proved to be so popular that on the F-program it was standard across the range. By later standards, the air dam was merely a small lip on the bottom of the existing front valence, but it made a difference to stability (a

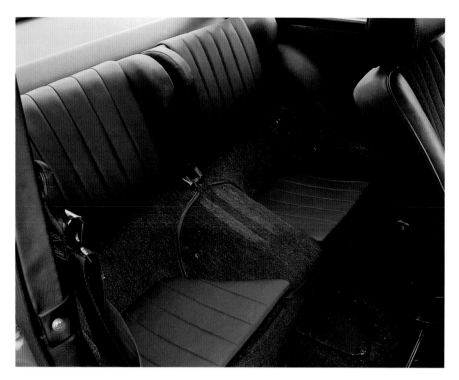

The interior of the 2.4E reflects a fashion in the 1970s for minimal chromework. An interesting point is the blank cover plate on the central tunnel. On early models (to 1967) a petrol heater was standard, but then became an option on left-hand-drive cars until 1973. Intake air for this device would have been drawn through an open grille mounted in this position.

claimed 40 percent reduction in front-end lift at high speed), and (probably more important for most customers) it looked great.

Tests also showed that the rear-end lift problem had not been addressed and subsequent testing led to a proposal for a rear spoiler mounted on the engine lid, the whole unit being made from glass-reinforced plastic. This was considered impractical for road use as well as likely to upset the authorities in several countries because of its hard, upturned edge. But the "ducktail" spoiler, as it became known, was very effective at curing high-speed over-steer and was adopted on the limited edition Carrera RS.

From 1972, U.S. models had the chassis number stamped onto a plate riveted to the windshield pillar, in accordance with new federal legislation.

Last, but by no means least, the London Motor Show in the autumn of 1972 saw the announcement of the Targa in right-hand-drive form. Deliveries of the T, E, or S in Targa form were promised in Britain from February 1973.

Body Trim and Fittings

The details that identify a 1972 model from earlier years are many. Look for the black engine lid grille with a "2.4" logo on the right-hand side. The "Porsche" and "911" lettering on the engine lid changed from the gold anodized finish to a dark gray (or gun metal) color. It is also quite easy to tell 1972 cars from 1973 cars. The most obvious trim differences are that the rims of the sidelight and taillight lenses changed from chrome to black, as did the horn grilles.

The European S, with its new front spoiler, now came without the standard over-riders of the earlier cars, although they were listed as an option and remained standard, in bright and dark chrome finish, on U.S. cars. In 1973, U.S. cars could be delivered with large foam rubber "bumper guards" that went some way to offering low-speed impact protection but looked awful. These would be replaced with a completely redesigned—and elegant—bumper the following year. The E became more frugal in that the standard external bumper and sill trim matched that of the T rather than the S, but the trim specification could be taken up to the S level at extra cost.

A change to the rules concerning rearward visibility meant American models had a larger, rectangular driver's door mirror. Getting into magnifying glass detail, the label on the engine fan housing and the chassis plate changed at the start of 1973 to acknowledge the fact that Porsche KG had become Porsche AG.

Interior Trim

The most noticeable difference in a period when interior changes were few was to the seats. These now had a black crackle finish to the back recliners and featured a new seat-locking mechanism for fore/aft adjustment. On the 1972 models the lock lever moved to the inside of the slider, and buzzers were fitted to the seat belt mechanisms on U.S. cars. The seat coverings could be in standard vinyl or optional leather.

Dashboard and Instruments

The center section of the dash was standardized in black, irrespective of the interior color, and covered in matching material. The basketweave vinyl that had covered the lower dash area of the earlier cars was replaced in 1972 by a leather-look finish that matched the door and upholstery trim. The 911 logo on the passenger side glove compartment lid was deleted. The familiar four-spoke design of the 400-millimeter (15.6-inch) steering wheel was largely unchanged, a leather-covered version being standard on the E and S, the T making do with an alternative hard rubber version.

Nancy MacLean's smart 1973 Sportomatic (above) has a two-pedal arrangement and a conventional-looking gear lever (top right). Porsche's automatic was quite different from any other manufacturer's. There was no clutch, but the driver still changed gears by moving the lever through a conventional gate. The Sportomatic's popularity waned through the 1970s.

For the 2.4 models the engine air intake ducting was revised to incorporate a cold-start flap, with the opening moved from the right-hand to the left-hand side of the engine compartment. When the engine was cold, the flap prevented ambient air entering the intake ducting, and warm air was drawn from around the left-hand heat exchanger.

Luggage Compartment

A new option was an 85-liter fuel tank (18.70 Imperial gallons, 22.46 U.S. gallons), a consequence of the thirstier engine now being used. This new tank was shaped to accept the new, more compact Goodrich Space-Saver spare tire, which came with a small compressor that could be powered from the cigarette lighter inside the car. The cross-ply construction of the Space-Saver made mixing this with the 911's standard radials illegal in the U.K. The T had a standard 62-liter tank (13.64 Imperial gallons, 16.38 U.S. gallons), with the S still being offered with the optional 110 liters (24.20 Imperial gallons, 29.06 U.S. gallons). With this latter tank, there was little room for anything else in the front compartment. The luggage compartment was now lit by just one lamp on the right-hand side of the car.

Engine

The obvious difference was that the engine was enlarged to 2,341cc (142.8 cubic inches). This was closer to 2.3 liters, but it suited Porsche's marketing people to label the car "2.4" because this seemed a more attractive increase in size. Whereas the previous capacity increase had been achieved by enlarging the bore, this time it was the stroke that was increased, going from 66 millimeters (2.57 inches) to 70.4 millimeters (2.75 inches). A lower compression ratio, achieved by lowering the height of the piston crowns, enabled low-octane (91 RON) fuel to be used.

The stroke increase was obtained by reducing the diameter of the big end journals, so the rod center could be moved farther from the crank center. The con rods were shortened by 2.2 millimeters (0.09 inch) and the big ends increased in width. The architecture and strength of these improved and lightened rods had been fully proven in the flat-12 engine of the 917 sports racing car.

These modifications were achieved while keeping within the envelope of the previous 2.2 crankcase (but with additional strengthening webs) and using the same crankshaft blank. The non-counterweighted cast crankshaft previously used on the T was deleted in favor of a common forged crankshaft across the range. On the 1973 models, airflow to the engine oil cooler was improved by modifying the air battles.

In the United States, all models used Bosch mechanical fuel injection, with closer tolerances on the injection pump and different setups for the fuel distributor for the T, E, and S models. Although the valve sizes stayed the same for all models, the size of the ports and the plastic intake trumpets increased with each more powerful model. For all other markets the T was fitted with Zenith 40 TIN triple-choke carburetors, which dropped power output to 130 brake horsepower compared with the 140 brake horsepower of the fuel-injected American T. Power outputs for the E and S were 165-brake horsepower and 190-brake horsepower.

From January 1973, the fuel injection system on the U.S. 911T changed to the new Bosch K-Jetronic Continuous Injection System (CIS). Although this sounds like an electronic system, it was another type of mechanical injection but using electrically operated sensors. The air sucked into the engine was measured by the displacement of a disc placed in an intake pipe shaped like a wine glass.

U.S. specification 911T models changed from carburetors to the Bosch K-Jetronic continuous fuel-injection system in January 1973. This gave American Ts a boost in performance and significantly changed the look of the engine compartment.

The new five-speed 915 gearbox for the 2.4 models had a conventional gear change pattern, with fifth to the right and forward. The larger gear lever boot seen here arrived for the 1973 model year.

The degree of displacement of the disc controlled the amount of fuel distributed to the cylinders. The U.S. 911T with this K-Jetronic injection also had new camshafts with reduced valve opening timing (overlap).

For 1972, the S came with a second oil cooler (a matrix-type) fitted in the right-hand front wing. Many cars were later converted to the labyrinth-type tubular system introduced in 1973.

Transmission

The gearbox was new for the 2.4s. Known as the 915, it was derived from the transaxle developed for the 1968–69 908 sports racing car and was designed for both four-speed and five-speed gear clusters. The gear cluster was contained in a magnesium casting separate from the aluminum differential housing. The fifth speed was housed with reverse in the end cover, while on the four-speed alternative the fifth gear wheel was simply deleted from the end of the gear set.

The principal benefit of the new gearbox was greater torque capacity, but the gears were also easier to use. The T and E came with the four-speed version as standard in most markets, including in the United States, but most customers chose the five-speed option, and the S was always five-speed. Gone was the race-bred "dog-leg" first gear that was rather inconvenient for town use: the new five-speed gearbox had a "street" pattern gate, with first to fourth in the conventional H with fifth over to the right and forward.

The popularity of the Sportomatic was dwindling, and it was now only available by special order.

Electrical Equipment and Lighting

The new Bosch H4 single-bulb headlight was standardized in all markets except the United States (which kept Hella sealed-beam units) and France (where the yellow H1 was still used). The H4 was rated at 60-watt (main) and 55-watt (dipped), compared with the 50/40-watt equivalent of the Hella sealed-beam unit. The H4's external glass looked slightly different from that of the H1 in that the ribbing inside the glass had a dipped-beam sector, and the face was slightly more vertical. Only two adjustment screws were used as opposed to four.

Another detail is that the frosted finish around the top of the rim of the H4 glass was a later addition. The glass was clear on the 2.4 models. That said, these H4 glasses have a reputation for cracking or chipping easily, and many cars received later glasses after stocks of the originals became exhausted. The later glasses also have a larger "H4" molded into the center of the lens.

This T has the more pronounced chromed headlamp flange that goes with the sealed-beam units fitted to U.S. cars. These headlamps were unpopular, as shown by this car having the more powerful Lucas H4 units retrofitted. Also visible is the large elastomer over-rider used only in 1973.

Suspension and Steering

The no-expense-spared development effort to improve the handling of the 911 reached a peak with the E-program, all the 2.4 cars having a detail change to the rear suspension geometry. The shock absorber strut had previously angled back from the mounting on the swingarm (when viewed from the side), resulting in a slight compound movement of the strut as the wheel moved up and down. The new arrangement changed the location of the top and bottom shock absorber strut mountings and eliminated that rearward tilt. In addition, a sharply inward angled mounting of the top of the strut (when viewed from the front) improved the response to wheel movement. It also improved the travel of the shock absorber, and thus gave a more comfortable ride over rough surfaces.

On the 911E, the Boge hydro-pneumatic front suspension struts were relegated to the option list, so this midrange model acquired the more popular torsion bar and MacPherson strut arrangement of the T and S. The T and E used Boge shock absorbers while the S continued with Konis.

Wheels and Tires

The standard factory fitting on the T for the 1972 and 1973 model years was the 5.5Jx15 nonchromed steel wheel with Dunlop CB57 165/70HR tires. The E used 6Jx15 steel wheels as standard in some markets with Dunlop CB57 185/70VR tires, while the S continued to use the (five times) more expensive 6Jx15 Fuchs forged-alloy wheels (an option for the other models) with Michelin XVR 185/70VR tires. In several markets, the forged-alloy wheels were fitted to the T and E as standard.

Earlier experiments with the Stuttgart-based Mahle company into magnesium casting had led directly to the development of a cast-aluminum alloy wheel. It was cheaper to make than the forged-alloy wheel, although it was not as strong. This new 6Jx15 wheel, made by the German company ATS and known as the "cookie-cutter" because of its appearance, was standard on the 1973 model year E and would remain in use until 1983.

Carrera RS

The RS was a unique limited-edition model that has become, perhaps, the most important of all 911 models. The term Carrera was first used by Porsche in 1955 to celebrate a class victory in the 1953 Carrera Panamericana road race. Carrera means "race" in Spanish and until 1974 was only given to Porsche's most sporting models. Much to the dismay of some enthusiasts, from this date Porsche began to use the title to adorn its regular production models, but that is another discussion.

Mark Waring's Carrera RS, painted Jade Green, is an M472 Touring model. Many RSs were delivered in the production colors available for the 1973 model year.

The evocative message on the tail of what is, for some, the most desirable 911 of all.

Just more than half of the 109 3-liter Carrera RS models built were roadgoing variants (below). This version used the heavier production bodyshell and featured a new whaletail rear spoiler. The M471 Sport model (above) is notable for its elementary equipment specification in the pursuit of performance.

The origins of the 1972–73 RS (RennSport) lay in the racing department's desire to widen the scope for the 911 in Group 4 Special GT racing. The RS was developed from the F-program and applied the lessons learned from earlier stripped-out rally and customer race cars. The RS could be specified by the customer in one of four forms.

The RSH (for homologation) was the basic model that was taken to the Stuttgart city scales for weight certification. It weighed just 960 kilograms (2,117 pounds). Only 17 cars were actually delivered to customers in this specification. From the RSH, two more practical models were offered for road use.

The RS Sport (the M471 option) was one stage up from the homologation cars and weighed around 975 kilograms (2,150 pounds). The M471 was still very basic, with minimal undercoating and soundproofing, elementary door trim with manual windows, and simple interior upholstery with felt carpets and rubber footwell mats. There were lightweight Recaro bucket seats for the driver and passenger, but the rear seats were deleted. There was no clock or passenger sun visor, but it did have black headlining.

The RS Touring (the M472 option) was trimmed like the contemporary S although a 380–millimeter (14.8-inch) steering wheel was fitted, and it weighed some 100 kilograms (220 pounds) more than the RS Sport. Nearly 200 RSH and RS Sport models were delivered; the remainder of the 1580 RS Carreras produced to the end of July 1973 were RS Touring versions.

The fourth model was the racing version, the 2.8-liter RSR (the M491 option). This model (55 were built) will not be discussed here.

The RS offered improved performance over the S, its 2.7-liter engine producing 210-brake horsepower at 6,300 rpm, with maximum torque of 255 Newton meters at 5,100 rpm. This was achieved principally through an increase in bore size to 90 millimeters (3.51 inches), using Nikasil-coated aluminum cylinders. Nikasil was a trade name for the nickel-silicon carbide coating deposited to a few hundredths of a millimeter on the bores. This technique was developed on the 917 racers and allowed the increased bore to be adopted without causing cylinder strength problems. The new coating also offered reduced sliding friction, leading to an increased power output over previous equivalent bores of the same

The interior of the M472 was equipped to the level of the production S model. Note the sports seats and the large gear lever boot—a new feature for 1973.

dimensions. The increased bore resulted in an engine capacity of 2,687cc (163.9 cubic inches). Apart from the bore sizing and the material, the 911/83 engine was the same as the 2.4S. A heavier clutch spring was required to cope with the additional torque, but the 915 gearbox had sufficient capacity for the 2.7 engine, although fourth (27/25) and fifth (29/21) gears were taller than on the S.

The suspension was improved by fitting gas-filled Bilsteins (lighter and stiffer than the Konis used on the S), 18-millimeter front and 19-millimeter rear anti-roll bars, and a light alloy front suspension support. The suspension mountings front and rear were strengthened, but the production brakes were unchanged from the S. The RS prototype's cross-drilled discs were not used for the series build cars.

In terms of running gear and bodywork, an early production RS differs considerably in detail from a 2.4S, and this is where the casual observer steps into a minefield of conflicting information. Because the model was planned as a homologation special, only 500 were initially scheduled for production, starting in November 1972. Lightness was a major goal for the engineers, so a uniquely lightened bodyshell with thinner gauge steel was used for its unstressed body panels, which included the roof, wings (with the rears flared by 50 millimeters each side for wider wheels), and hood. These bodyshell differences were common to all versions. On the M471, glass-reinforced plastic was used for both bumpers and the rear engine cover, which had an aluminum support frame. On the M472, the bumper trim, rear bumper, and center panel came from the 2.4S. On later Sport models the steel bumpers of the Touring models were used with plain chromed over-riders and an aluminum center panel. This was partly to do with restrictive regulations imposed by certain European countries. The windshield and rear side window glass were made from thinner safety glass (and was subsequently less robust), manufactured by the Belgian

Rear ends of an M472 RS Touring (above) and an early M471 RS Sport (below). The Touring has steel bumpers, a nudge bar, a chromed silencer skirt, and a molded badge under the ducktail. The Sport has a one-piece glass-fiber "bumper," the engine lid is secured with racing-style elastic toggles, and the badges are color-coded decals.

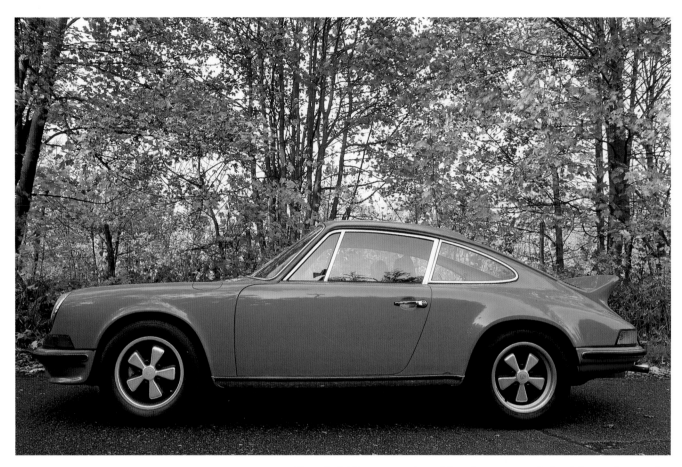

Pointing to the 911's aerodynamic future, the Carrera RS was the first model to sprout a rear spoiler, although the ducktail was actually an option.

Mechanical fuel injection manifolding on a European 1973 911E, with the correct green-finished cooling duct. The metal fuel-injection pipes enter the cylinder heads at the base of the intake trumpets.

company Glaverbel. The remainder of the glass was made by Sekurit, the regular suppliers of glass to Porsche. To the long-term detriment (from rust) of the early lightweight cars, the heavy PVC underseal was applied only around the wheel arch areas.

Interestingly, one story says that only factory competition and preferred customers received true lightweight RSs that had a complete complement of thin-gauge panels, but this has been disputed by the legendary Porsche development engineer Peter Falk, who has said that there was no conscious effort to make "lighter" lightweights. If some cars had a larger number of thinner panels or lighter plastic parts, it was simply due to the inconsistency of the manufacturing processes. There are those who would also argue that there is no conclusive evidence that the first 500 or 1,000 used up all the lightweight panels and that the remainder of the RS line used body parts from the heavier 2.4 production model, as has been generally thought to have been the case.

Externally, the RS can be identified by its ducktail spoiler (although it was an option and some cars may not have this fitted) and the larger rear wheel arch flares that accommodate the 7-inch Fuchs alloys used for the rear wheels. The RS was fitted with Pirelli CN36 tires of different sizes front and rear (185/70VR15 on 6J front wheels, 215/VR15 on 7J rear wheels), although Dunlops were used later in the production run. The most popular color was light yellow, while Grand Prix White was a special color for the RS. Many were delivered in the production colors available in the 1973 model year. Special side stripes were an option, derived from the Carrera logo first seen on the 356 four-cam model. These could be specified in blue, red, green, or black with matching color coding to the wheel centers. The RSH models were set apart by their black-only script. A "positive" decal was used for the two cars in the original sales brochure, but the series cars used a "negative" rendering.

The 915 five-speed gearbox (to the right) and the exhaust pipes leading forward into the heat exchanger boxes (to the left). Air is circulated around the exhaust pipes and taken forward to warm the cabin.

Once the RS was in the showrooms, demand exceeded the marketing department's dreams. The first 500 sold out immediately and production was extended to 1,000 in order to homologate the car in the Group 3 production GT racing class. These cars were still taken to the Stuttgart city scales and a certificate was produced that noted their lightweight specification compared to the mainstream production cars. But the demand still continued beyond 1,000, and subsequent RS bodyshells were manufactured on the main Zuffenhausen production line. Chassis numbers for the RS run from 11 to 1590.

Supplies of the lightweight components started to become short with the later models from late April 1973 (from around chassis 1230). Progressively, these later cars used more of the same heavier shell, panels, glass, and components of the regular production models (although they still retained the prestigious duck-tail engine lid), and by this time full underseal was being applied to the cars. Late model original RSs, therefore, are quite likely to have opening rear quarter windows and steel front support bars, among many other detail changes (and improvements) from the earlier RSs. These improvements make the later cars just as interesting, in that development was moving toward the 3-liter version. By the end of the series, the RS had the later Silumin alloy crankcase in place of the previous magnesium item and revised mounting points for the rear trailing arms.

To complete the RS road-going story, we will make a brief mention of the car that followed the 2.7RS in late 1973. Just 109 3-liter RS models were built. Because all the lightweight bodyshell parts of the original RS series had run out earlier in 1973, these cars used regular "heavy" bodyshells. The extra weight explains why the 3-liter RS is not much quicker than a 2.7 model. Just more than half (59) were road models, and only 6 right-hand-drive models were made (1 for Australia, 5 for the U.K.). The 3-liter RS was fitted with 8-inch front and 9-inch rear wheels wearing 215/60 and 235/60 Pirelli CN36 tires, respectively. Power was 230-brake horsepower at 6,200 rpm.

Production Changes

August 1971 (Start of E-program)

Oil filler flap now just behind right-hand door; S gets front spoiler lip, optional on E and T; black engine lid grille with 2.4 logo on right-hand side; lettering on engine lid changed from gold anodized to dark metalized gray; seat metalwork now black crinkle finish instead of chromed; H4 headlamp standard except in the United States; 911 logo on passenger-side dash deleted; leather-look finish on middle dash replaces previous basketweave; inertia reel seat belts and buzzers on U.S. models; larger rectangular external driver's mirror; doorsill kick plates standard on S, optional on E and T; E interior now based on T rather than S; front over-riders now optional; one lamp only for luggage compartment; rear suspension struts aligned vertically when viewed from side; rear swingarms revised to allow removal without removing the engine; Boge hydro-pneumatic front struts now only an option; ATS cookie-cutter wheels standard on E; chromed steel wheels deleted; door handles common on both sides; S has 15mm anti-roll bars front and rear; wheelbase extended by 3mm; engine enlarged to 2,341cc, stroke increased to 70.4mm by 2.2mm shorter steel rods, on S these were Tenifer-treated instead of soft-nitrided as on 2.2S; lower compression ratio (see production data table) from reduced-height piston crowns, which are cooled by individual oil jet sprays; larger big ends and full crankshaft counterbalancing; crankcase stiffened around main bearings; valves unchanged but porting improved; camshafts same for S but on E and T timing retarded by 1 degree (T) and 2 degrees (E); U.S. T gets six-plunger mechanical injection (and 140-brake horsepower) to meet emissions laws (this version also sold to Australia, Japan, and Canada); new remote oil filter housing, including thermostat and by-pass valve; new 915 gearbox with "street" pattern gate; 915 features torque capacity of 245Nm, three-piece transmission housing and fifth gear next to reverse at back of gear cluster; four-speed is standard in most markets, but for U.K. E and S have five-speed as standard; four-speed ratios are first, 11:35; second, 18:32; third, 24:27; fourth, 28:23; reverse, 12:21; final drive, 7:31; five-speed ratios are first, 11:35 (11:36 in U.S.); second, 18:35; third, 23:29; fourth, 26:25; fifth, 29:22; reverse, 12:21; final drive, 7:31; 925 Sportomatic introduced to cope with greater torque of E and S models (905 retained for T); torque capacity increased to 230Nm, using larger diameter torque converter and clutch, a larger crown wheel and pinion and a stronger differential; 925 transmission housing reinforced with extra ribbing; 925/00 (for E) and 925/01 (for S) are last of the four-speed Sportomatics.

August 1972 (Start of F-program)

Oil tank and filler moved back inside engine bay, now made from copper-coated steel; front lip spoiler and ATS cast wheels standard on E; rear wiper standard (except Carrera RS); rims of front driving light and rear taillight lens changed from chromed to black; front horn grilles changed to black; U.S. cars had large elastomer over-riders front and rear; interior upholstery more fire-resistant and seat anchorages strengthened; door beams for increased side-impact resistance; RHD offered for Targa for the first time; improved cast gear lever support mechanism and larger protective boot; S and Carrera RS models change to labyrinth (tube-type) secondary oil cooler in front of right front wheel.

January 1973

Fuel-injected T models change from mechanical to CIS (Bosch K-Jetronic).

Dimensions

Wheelbase

2,271mm.

Track (front/rear)

T, 1,360mm/1,342mm; E, Sand Sportomatic, 1,372mm/1,354mm; Carrera RS, 1,372mm/1,394mm.

Length

T, E, and S, 4,127mm; Carrera RS, 4,147mm.

Width

1,610mm.

Options

Factory list (dated September 1971)

M400 light metal wheels 6Jx15 with 185/70VR tires; M444 steel wheels 6Jx15 with 185/70VR tires; M485 pressure cast wheels 5.5Jx15 with 165HR tires; M976 chromed wheels with crest 5.5Jx15 with 165HR tires; M470 comfort kit; M429 foglight, white Halogen H3, under bumper; M430 foglight, yellow Halogen H3, under bumper; M433 foglight, white Halogen H3, above bumper; M434 foglight, yellow Halogen H3, above bumper; M432 spot light, white Halogen H3, above bumper; M571 foglight, rear; M425 rear window wiper; M650 electric

Production Data

Model year	Model	Power (bhp DIN@rpm)	Torque (Nm@rpm)	Compression ratio	Weight (kg)	Number built
1972	911T	130@5,600	196@4,000	7.5:1	1,050	1,963
	911T Targa	130@5,600	196@4,000	7.5:1	1,100	1,523
	911T U.S.	140@5,600	200@4,000	7.5:1	1,050	2,931
	911T U.S. Targa	140@5,600	200@4,000	7.5:1	1,100	1,821
	911E	165@6,200	206@4,500	8.0:1	1,050	1,124
	911 E Targa	165@6,200	206@4,500	8.0:1	1,100	861
	911S	190@6,500	216@5,200	8.5:1	1,050	1,750
	911S Targa	190@6,500	216@5,200	8.5:1	1,100	989
1973	911T	130@5,600	196@4,000	7.5:1	1,050	1,875
	911T Targa	130@5,600	196@4,000	7.5:1	1,100	1,541
	911T U.S.	140@5,600	200@4,000	7.5:1	1,050	1,252
	911T U.S. Targa	140@5,600	200@4,000	7.5:1	1,100	751
	911T U.S.[1]	140@5,700	201@4,000	8.0:1	1,050	1,944
	911T Targa U.S.[1]	140@5,700	201@4000	8.0:1	1,100	1,302
	911 E	165@6,200	206@4,500	8.0:1	1,050	1,366
	911 E Targa	165@6,200	206@4,500	8.0:1	1,100	1,055
	911S	190@6,500	216@5,200	8.5:1	1,050	1,430
	911S Targa	190@6,500	216@5,200	8.5:1	1,100	925
	911 RS Carrera	210@6,300	255@5,100	8.5:1	975	1,580

Numbered note
1. U.S. 911T with new fuel injection (Bosch K-Jetronic, Continuous Injection System) from January 1973.

Identification

Model year	Model	Engine	Gearbox	Chassis numbers	Engine numbers
E-program					
1972	911T	911/57	915/12	9112500001–9112501963	6520001–6523284
	911T Targa	911/57	915/12	9112510001–9112511523	6520001–6523284
	911T Sporto	911/67	905/21	9112510001–9112511523	6529001–6529224
	911T U.S.	911/51	915/12	9112100001–9112102931	6120001–6124478
	911T U.S. Targa	911/51	915/12	9112110001–9112111821	6120001–6124478
	911T U.S. Sporto	911/61	925/00	9112110001–9112111821	6129001–6129293
	911 E	911/52	915/12	9112200001–9112201124	6220001–6221765
	911 E Targa	911/52	915/12	9112210001–9112210861	6220001–6221765
	911 E Sporto	911/62	925/00	9112210001–9112210861	6229001–6229248
	911S	911/53	915/12	9112300001–9112301750	6320001–6322586
	911S Targa	911/53	915/12	9112310001–9112310989	6320001–6322586
	911S Sporto	911/63	925/01	9112310001–9112310989	6329001–6329147
F-program					
1973	911T	911/57	915/12	9113500001–9113501875	6530001–6533239
	911T Targa	911/57	915/12	9113510001–9113511541	6530001–6533239
	911T Sporto	911/67	905/21	9113510001–9113511541	6539001–6539197
	911T U.S.	911/51	915/12	9113100001–9113101252	6130001–6131926
	911T U.S. Targa	911/51	915/12	9113110001–9113110781	6130001–6131926
	911T U.S. Sporto	911/61	925/00	9113110001–9113110781	6139001–6139149
	911T U.S.[1]	911/91	915/12	9113101501–9113103444	6133001–6136092
	911T U.S. Targa[1]	911/91	915/12	9113110001–9113112302	6133001–6136092
	911T U.S. Sporto[1]	911/96	925/00	9113110001–9113112302	6139301–6139502
	911 E	911/52	915/12	9113200001–9113201366	6230001–6232125
	911 E Targa	911/52	915/12	9113210001–9113211055	6230001–6232125
	911 E Sporto	911/62	925/00	9113210001–9113211055	6239001–6239319
	911S	911/53	915/12	9113300001–9113301430	6330001–6332231
	911S Targa	911/53	915/12	9113310001–9113310925	6330001–6332231
	911S Sporto	911/63	925/01	9113310001–9113310925	6339001–6339136
	911 RS Carrera	911/83	915/08	9113600011–9113601590	6630001–6631549

General notes
Gearboxes The four-speed 915 was given the designation 915/12 and the five-speed version was 915/02. The four-speed Sportomatic was now designated 925/21 for Europe and 925/00 for the United States and the Rest of the World, but the 911S Sportomatic was 925/01.

Numbered note
1. U.S. 911T with new fuel injection (Bosch K-Jetronic, Continuous Injection System) from January 1973.

sunroof (coupe only, including RS); M258 seat head restraints, left and right; M409 sports seats, left and right; M410 sports seat, driver only; M419 automatic seat belts, left and right; M549 three-point seat belts, left and right. Other options not numbered: separately listed radios; special paints and fabrics; leather upholstery; leather seats; custom interiors; leather steering wheel on the T; five-speed gearbox; Sportomatic; limited slip differential; electric window lifters; air conditioning; 85-liter fuel tank with space-saver tire; S spoiler for T and E (1973 only, standard in some markets).

Color Schemes

1972 (chart dated July 1971)
Standard body colors

Tangerine (018), Bahia Red (022), Aubergine (025), Signal Yellow (114), Light Yellow (117), Light Ivory (131), Emerald Green (225), Albert Blue (325), Sepia Brown (415).

Special order body colors

Gulf Orange (019), Rose Red (024), Signal Orange (116), Ivory (132), Irish Green (213), Leaf Green (218), Lime Green (226), Jade Green (227), Glacier Blue (326), Gulf Blue (328), Oxford Blue (329), Royal Purple (341), Olive (414), Beige Gray (622), Black (700), Gold Metallic (133), Metallic Green (224), Metallic Blue (324), Gemini (blue/gray) Metallic (330), Silver Metallic (925).

Fabrics

Standard trim: leatherette (999.551.001.40) in brown (406), tan (502), red (003), blue (301), or black (708). Option at extra cost: leather (999.551.071.40) in brown (404), tan (503), or black (700). No-cost option on seats: corduroy fabric (999.551.032.40) in brown (400), tan (500), or black (700); dog-tooth check fabric (000.551.531.00) in brown, white, and black (430) or black and white (730); tartan Madras fabric (999.551.031.40) in reds (43), blues (41), or browns (42), optional with matching leather (or leatherette) and carpet. Seat fabric combinations: brown leatherette (406), tan leatherette (502), or black (708); leatherette or leather and cord in brown (487), tan (578), or black (779); leatherette and dogtooth check in brown (486), tan (577), or black (778); leatherette and Madras tartan in reds (079), blues (374), or browns (488).

Carpets

Pile carpet (000.551.570.00) in dark gray (401) or black (700); needle loom carpet (front compartment) in brown (401) or black (700); nylon velour carpet (999.551.052.40) in maroon (001), blue/green (301), or dark tan (402).

1973 (charts 1000.14 and 1001.14)
Standard body colors

Bahia Red (022), Emerald (Viper) Green (225), Sepia Brown (415), Light Ivory (131), Aubergine (025), Light Yellow (117), Tangerine (018), Signal Yellow (114).

Special order body colors

Gulf Orange (019), Rose Red (024), Signal Orange (116), Ivory (132), Irish Green (213), Leaf Green (218), Lime Green (226), Jade Green (227), Glacier Blue (326), Gulf Blue (328), Oxford Blue (329), Royal Purple (341), Olive (414), Beige Gray (622), Black (700), Gold Metallic (144), Metallic Green (230), Metallic Blue (334), Gemini (blue/gray) Metallic (335), Silver Metallic (936). Note: RS Carrera body colors included alternative special order colors (e.g., Grand Prix White).

Fabrics

Generally same as 1972. Leatherette (standard) in black, brown, or beige; leather optional at extra cost; seats were leatherette in black, brown, or beige with inlays in corduroy or dog-tooth check (black/white or black/brown/white).

Carpets

The T had special nylon; the E and S had velour pile in black or brown.

Note

Custom external colors and interiors were available to special order.

Chapter 4

The 2.7-Liter 911 (1974–1977)

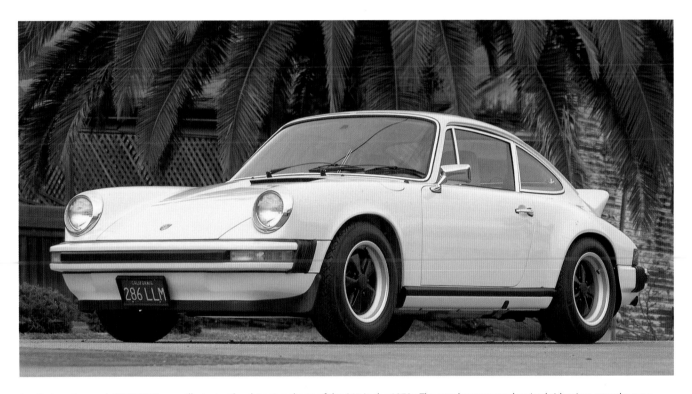

Joe Hartman's superb 1974 2.8 Carrera illustrates the changing shape of the 911 in the 1970s. The new bumpers and revised side trims gave the car a lower look.

The first major fuel crisis hit the world in 1973. The effect on Porsche sales was dramatic, with volumes falling some 25 percent. Fuel was no longer cheap, and customers were looking for more efficient use of this now-valuable commodity. It was not acceptable that a hard-driven 911S would only cover 12 or 15 miles to the imperial gallon. What was suddenly a difficult time for Porsche was compounded by two other external influences, both initiated in the United States, that would also force changes to the 911.

In a series of new laws that aimed to institutionalize the motor car into a more environmentally friendly armored

Evolution Outline

August 1973: The 911 (150-brake horsepower), 911S (175-brake horsepower), and 911 Carrera (210-brake horsepower) replace previous T, E, S, and RS models; new cars all have 2.7-liter engines and impact-absorbing bumpers; side window demist vents on dash; start of models with significant emissions control devices for American and certain other markets (with even tighter specifications for California).

August 1974: New whaletail spoiler is introduced for the U.S. Carreras.

August 1975: The Carrera 3.0 is introduced in non-U.S. markets; all models receive hot-dip zinc galvanizing over whole bodyshell; Sportomatic goes from four speeds to three; electric external door mirror is introduced, along with the Silver Anniversary model.

August 1976: Central face level vents in the dash are introduced.

August 1977: Dilavar cylinder head studs are used, and the Targas get a black roll-over hoop.

The ducktail rear spoiler was offered as an option in most markets for 1974. It was banned in Germany, however, because the authorities judged that there was too great a risk of pedestrian injury from its hard edges.

vehicle, the U.S. federal government, and in particular the state of California, gave notice of a significant tightening-up of exhaust emissions and crash resistance. It seemed to outsiders that American legislators wanted to wipe out the sports car completely.

The two-year cycle of 911 upgrades was now well-known in the industry, and many observers suggested that in fact the 911, now 10 years old, would be replaced by a new model in 1974. There were rumors of a new four-seater project (the 928), so the observers had some credibility. But there was never really any doubt within Porsche about the continuation of the 911. Certainly it would have to grow up and become a bit more serious and maybe more concerned with the world around it, but there was life in the old dog yet. The new Research and Development Center at Weissach, west of Stuttgart, had recently opened, and in this new environment the engineers and stylists would have to innovate their way out of the problems.

Exciting new 911 types appeared in racing in 1974, like the 3.0-liter RSR for customers and the 2.8-liter Turbo Carrera—a 911 like no other. These were cars that would point the way to new chapters in the history of Porsche in racing and of the 911. The production 911 was on the verge of a new lease of life and would find a new maturity in the changed economic climate of the 1970s.

The 1973 model 911T for the United States had been the first Porsche to use the cleaner-running Bosch K-Jetronic injection, and this ingenious and effective system appeared on the new 2.7-liter 911 and 911S lines in 1974. Extra engine capacity combined with more fuel-efficient injection to give the 911 more flexibility, with better power delivery at low revs. This allowed the 911 to meet the new American legislation for exhaust emissions.

The other change that had to be made for the 1974 models was the introduction of energy-absorbing bumpers to improve low-speed crash resistance. Other manufacturers, such as MG, had made beautiful cars look awful with the addition of ugly black deformable bumpers, but the Porsche stylists (notably Wolfgang Mobius) introduced impact bumpers, and by a clever mix of design and function, actually managed to lift the image of the 911. The transformation was complete. Sales steadied and then started to rise through the mid-1970s. The new 911 had defied its critics.

In 1974, the model line changed from the familiar T/E/S format to a more marketable 911, 911S, and 911 Carrera. It was, frankly, a cheapening of the Carrera name to use it on the top-of-the-range production model. The models sold to the United States became a little more complex, and this is explained further in the Engine section (page 69).

The regular 911 was a better car than the previous T, its 150-brake horsepower up 10-brake horsepower on the old fuel-injected version and 20-brake horsepower on the carburetor type. The 1974 S gained 10-brake horsepower (to 175-brake horsepower) over the previous year's E model, against which it must be compared. Because it was fitted with the new fuel injection, the S engine had a more flexible torque curve, peaking at 235 Nm at 4,000 rpm (compared with 206 Nm at 4,500 rpm for the old 2.4E). You did not have to stir the gearbox so much, and on the world's progressively more congested roads this made for a more manageable car. Fuel consumption did indeed reduce, and on the regular 911 more than 20 miles per gallon (8 kilometers per liter) was now possible. Refinement was further enhanced by 12,000-mile (or 20,000-kilometer) service intervals, quite something for a high-performance sports car in the mid-1970s, as it is today.

The 1974 European Carrera shared the 210-brake horsepower of the previous year's RS, but there the comparison blurs. It should not be confused with the 1973 RS and probably aligns more with the 1973 911S model. The 1974 Carrera retained the mechanical fuel injection, and the ducktail was an option for those who had missed out on the RS. The engine was identical to the RS's unit, and this endowed the 1974 Carrera with excellent performance, certainly better than the previous year's S. The Carrera was only available with full equipment, to a similar specification to the end-of-line RSs. The ducktail, however, had run into controversy in its home market concerning its safety and had been outlawed there.

The late Tony Knapp's 911 is a superb example of a European-specification 1975 2.7 Carrera. Note that this British car still has the round Durant external mirror, an item deleted in many other markets in 1973 because the glass area did not meet local regulations.

The Targa took on a new maturity with the elimination of chrome from its exterior. This 1975 German model is typical of many 911s in not having an external passenger door mirror. Oddly this feature was an extra-cost option until the late 1980s.

Porsche 911

The Carrera 3.0 revitalized the image of the 911 in Europe for the 1976 model year. There were many improvements that year, but surely the most far-reaching was the introduction of hot-dipped zinc coating for the entire bodyshell, a process applied across the 911 range. This U.K.-specification Sport version is owned by Peter Hafield.

This 1976 U.K.-specification 2.7 911 shows off the ATS cookie-cutter wheels that had first appeared on the 1973 911E. The electrically operated driver's door mirror was new for the 1976 model year.

By a superbly clever mix of design and function, Porsche's stylists turned a potentially disfiguring legal requirement for energy-absorbing bumpers into an image-enhancing feature. Just visible here is the flexible lip extension to the new front spoiler, an important detail that improved the aerodynamic balance of the car when the rear ducktail was fitted.

In the United States, however, the 1974 picture was not so good for those with a thirst for power. The regular 911 delivered 150-brake horsepower, but the bad news was that the Carrera shared the S's 175-brake horsepower engine. In 1975, the standard 911 was dropped altogether, and two versions of the S engine were now required with different levels of emissions equipment. The first was termed a "49-state" engine with 165-brake horsepower, while California's ever-stricter legislation resulted in its own 160-brake horsepower variant, complete with air pump, thermal reactors, and exhaust gas recirculation. Both these engines were detuned versions of the 175-brake horsepower engine in the 2.7 911S sold to the rest of the world. The Californian engine did find another 5-brake horsepower to reach 165-brake horsepower in 1976, but the 2.7 Carrera model, unsurprisingly, was deleted after 1975.

In 1974, the factory celebrated 25 years of the Porsche sports car. This was marked with a special run of Silver Anniversary 911s, using the new 1975 model year 911 as a base. Each was painted in what was termed Diamond Silver Metallic. The cars featured a special silver-and-black tweed interior and had a numbered plaque attached to the passenger side of the dash. Another special was sold in 1976 called the Signature 911S. This version was fitted with the Carrera's three-spoke steering wheel with an embossed Ferry Porsche signature. It had the "black-look" and beige tweed upholstery and was painted in metallic platinum with color-coded wheels. Porsche was getting the hang of profitable special edition models.

American enthusiasts, offered only the 911S alongside the new Turbo in 1976, had to look in envy at the new 911 model that was not available to them but was on sale to the rest of the world. The Carrera 3.0, as it was known, replaced the 2.7 Carrera and received what was effectively a 930 engine without the turbocharger, with an output of 200-brake horsepower. Given that the 2.7 engine was recognized as being at the end of a long development cycle, the adoption of the large redesigned turbo engine was a smart move.

The 911 was moving toward a new type of buyer, one who did not look for the last fraction of performance but who demanded comfort, smoothness, and easier driving. By 1977, the transition of the 911 into a thoroughly refined automobile was nearly complete.

Bodyshell

The 1974 model year cars were termed the G-program models and were instantly recognizable by their new bumpers.

The bumpers were designed to absorb impacts up to 5 miles per hour and then recover their original position. Unlike other manufacturers' efforts, the Porsche bumpers absorbed impacts by moving backward in their entirety (rather than deforming) up to a maximum of 50 millimeters, either against collapsible steel tubes (Europe) or hydraulic shock absorbers (United States). The hydraulic rams resulted in the American cars having bumpers that projected farther than their European counterparts, although hydraulic rams could be fitted as an option to a car destined for any market.

The new bumpers required changes to the front and rear wings and the front bonnet (hood) to accommodate the higher bumper line. The potential movement meant that between bumper and body was a gap, which was filled by flexible concertina-type bellows that were integrated into the body shape with an additional side panel at the front and a shaped lower panel at the rear. At the back of the car, the central panel over the silencer disappeared (it did anyway after a few years, thanks to rust!) and was replaced with a one-piece wraparound bumper formed from a complex aluminum extrusion. Two large flexible over-riders carried the number plate lights, and the gap between engine lid and bumper line was filled by a reflective band, a much-copied Porsche styling innovation. As a footnote to the introduction of the new bumpers, the overall dry weight only increased by 25 kilograms, demonstrating some careful design work.

The side sills were extended so that the jacking points came through the panel rather than being sited below them. Some road testers felt that the slightly increased length of the 911, with its new bumpers, improved the response to side winds. On Targas, the fold-away roof was replaced by a fixed panel, which could be stowed in the front luggage compartment. The folding roof now became an option for cars with air conditioning. The 1973 RS could not be ordered in Targa form, but the 1974 Carrera could—and came in the black-look. Standard Targas would not be delivered in standard form in the black-look until the 1977 model year, although it was an option from 1976.

The H-program cars (1975 model year) had extra sound insulation as an added refinement, but otherwise there were no changes.

The I-program cars (1976 model year) brought one of the most far-reaching improvements to the 911 line with the introduction of Thyssen zinc-coated steel. A hot dip process was applied to both sides of the steel and was used for all chassis and bodywork parts. This was a significant improvement on the previous level of zinc-coating, applied to the underside only of cars after August 1970, and new cars were immediately offered in most markets with a six-year anti-corrosion warranty. It was the final effort in the continuing battle against rust, which unfortunately could affect the earlier models quite badly, sometimes after only two or three years in a poor winter climate. It also ensured that in later years those enthusiasts who could not afford the new cars would be able to buy near showroom condition models, even when five or more years old. It was an astute business move by the factory because it underwrote a good resale price for their customers and contributed much to the "hewn from stone" image of quality that the 911 was gaining.

The new bumpers were neat one-piece aluminum extrusions front and rear. The rear aspect of the 911 was further changed by the addition of a full-width reflector strip between the light clusters. Possibly too flashy on some cars, it worked well on the 911. The Carrera logo had always been reserved for limited-edition high-performance models.

Keeping the 911 stable at speed had become a priority in the early 1970s. Following the introduction of the ducktail, this whaletail arrived in 1975 to satisfy German legal requirements. This was a production version of the rear spoiler first seen on the 3-liter Carrera RS.

The wipers on the 911 had changed for 1968 so that they always parked in front of the driver, whether the car was left-hand or right-hand drive. Since then, the 911 designers have not been able to change the wiper arrangement significantly through the entire life of the model because of the cost of retooling.

The design of the impact bumpers allowed them to move backward in a low-speed collision. Movement was resisted either by two shock absorber units or collapsible tubes fitted between the bumper and the front part of the wing inner walls. The external bellows at the sides of the bumpers were a tidy method of accommodating this potential for movement.

The fuel filler flap has hardly changed throughout the life of the 911. The canvas flap shields the paintwork from drips, while the washer bottle filler is to the left.

Large exterior mirrors were introduced in 1976. The body of the mirror was color-coded, while the mirror itself was electrically adjustable and heated.

The 1974 model year saw the introduction of high-pressure headlamp washers as an option in most markets (and standard in some). The new Carrera 3.0 had them as standard, as well as color-coded headlamp surrounds.

Body Trim and Fittings

A neoprene rubbing strip on the impact bumpers allowed touch parking without risk of damage to paintwork. At the front, the sidelights and indicators were integrated into the bumper. Fitted to the top of the front bumper were optional (but standard in some markets) high-pressure headlamp washers. These were fed from an 8.5-liter reservoir mounted in the wing behind the left-hand headlight. This was to meet a new Swedish law, but Porsche adopted the washers across the product range. The front spoiler was not so pronounced as on earlier models. It was the elegant integration of all these features that made the change to the impact bumpers so visually successful on the 911.

Black trim had been used earlier for details like wipers (from the 1968 models), badging (from the first 2.4 models), and the horn grilles (from the 1973 models); but on the 1974 Carrera the fashion could be extended to all brightwork, including the window trim and door handles. When a car was finished in this way, no chrome was visible on the exterior.

The ducktail rear spoiler was only available as an option outside Germany (where it was criticized by the authorities for being dangerous to pedestrians in the event of an accident), but 1975 saw a so-called safer rear spoiler emerge in the form of the whaletail that could be specified for the Carrera. To balance the increased aerodynamic forces of the larger rear spoilers, a mandatory elastomer "chin" extension was now specified for the front spoiler. The whaletail was formed mainly from flexible elastomer and addressed the earlier arguments against the ducktail in Germany. The whaletail was derived from the spoiler first seen in 1973 on the 3-liter RSR and then on the new production 930 Turbo model. Unlike the ducktail, the whaletail could be specified in conjunction with a rear wiper. Other details to distinguish these 1975 Carreras from the 1974 models were color-coded headlamp surrounds, new wheel arch protection moldings, and anti-stone chip steel under-doorsill covers.

The badges on the engine lid changed to a simple "911" for the base model, with a chromed "2.7" on the right-hand side of the grille. There was no "Porsche" script at the lower edge of the lid, this being embossed in red on the full-width reflector strip that bridged the gap between the lid and the rear bumper.

The 1976 model year saw the debut of another Porsche feature that would become an old friend to enthusiasts: the "elephant's ear" door mirror. This unit was electrically adjusted and heated and was sprayed in the body color. The way it protruded brought a new thrill to driving past oncoming traffic in narrow country lanes.

In 1976, the new European Carrera 3.0 could be distinguished from the other models by the black look introduced for the 1974 Carreras and wider flares for the rear wheels.

There were new seats for 1974, featuring more thigh support and integral head restraints. Although rear passengers found it more difficult to see ahead, getting in the back was easier because the releases on the seat backs were more accessible. When air conditioning was fitted, as here, the outlets ran across the lower dash area, integrating well with the existing design but reducing knee room.

Interior Trim

A glance at this chapter's Color Schemes section (page 76) shows the incredible selection of interiors available to 911 buyers. Exclusivity has always been a major selling feature of Porsche, and customers could choose from a wide range of materials and colors, within the bounds of the model. Alternatively, they could decide to use their own fabrics and colors and create a completely customized interior. This area of special orders would grow for Porsche as more customers sought to make unique statements about their lifestyles.

New seats with better lateral and thigh support, achieved by lengthening the front of the seats, were found on the 2.7s. These had integral head restraints in the seat backs. Repa inertia reel seat belts were now standard in all markets. Opening rear quarter windows were standard on the Carrera but optional on the 911 and S. Carpets were now all velour pile, with the earlier—and cheaper—"special" nylons of the 911T being discontinued. The door trim was redesigned to provide a more accessible storage bin, with a lid that opened from the top and doubled as an armrest.

The heater had always been an area for criticism on the 911 because deriving warmth from the exhaust heat was not easy. The design of the heating system had basically changed little since the car's launch 10 years before. Heat exchangers wrapped around the exhaust manifolds on each side of the engine, fresh air was warmed by passing it over the hot exhaust pipes contained within these heat exchangers, and the amount of warmed air admitted to the cabin was controlled by a single lever next to the handbrake. This lever opened or closed butterfly valves mounted just downstream of each heat exchanger. If no heat was required in the cabin, then the butterfly valves exhausted the warmed air to the atmosphere. If the valves were closed, then all the warmed air was ducted through

The door trim on the 1974 models received another revision. The rear compartment was now deeper and had a conventionally hinged top lid to replace the elastic bungee sprung "clamshell" of the previous design.

The door trim changed again in 1976, in response to the growing problem of car theft. Instead of the mushroom-shaped lock pull (which a thief could easily "hook" open) at the top of the door trim, this knob had to be turned to lock or unlock the car from the inside.

The 1974 Carrera retained the 380-millimeter steering wheel of the RS. The new side vent in the lower dash greatly improved side window demisting. The redline on the rev counter starts at 6,300 rpm and shows that this model was no RS. The latter was redlined at 7,200 rpm.

A new option for 1976, and standard on the 3-liter Carrera, was automatic regulation of cabin temperature. A controller was fitted between the seats and monitored inputs from sensors. The controller drove a servo motor that opened or closed butterfly valves on the heat exchangers.

the sills and into the cabin. In theory, heat control was performed by mixing this warm air with fresh cool air from the inlet ahead of the windshield, but the reality was that the supply of warmed air was fairly unpredictable. If the engine ran fast you had a lot of heat, but around town with a slow-running engine, heat tended to come in bursts. It would be a while before 911s had heating and ventilation that was effective, but the engineers were working on it.

For 1974, side window demisting vents were fitted into each end of the dash—at last the side windows could be demisted on wet days! Then, in 1975, an additional electrical fan boosted the heater output (but not on European Carreras because of their mechanical fuel injection) at low engine speeds, and there were left and right side heat controls. The interior sound insulation was improved, too, but a new option (standard on the new 3-liter Carrera and Turbo) offered in 1976 went a long way toward providing regulated hands-off control of the interior heat. A thermostat was fitted into the heat exchanger and another into the cabin between the sun visors, and there was a third manual selector switch. Between the seats a control unit monitored the inputs from these three sensors and drove a servo motor remotely attached to the butterfly mechanism on the exchangers. It was a complex system and over the years it proved to be fragile, but it was a significant improvement for new car buyers. In some markets this automatic system was termed "dial-a-heat."

Not until the 1977 model year did the occupants finally have the luxury of face-level ventilation, with the introduction of two adjustable vents in the middle of the dash. These also doubled as air conditioning outlets when this was fitted.

Improved door locks for 1976 reflected growing concern about theft. This was followed in 1977 by an arrangement that allowed the interior pushbuttons to disappear into the top of the doors when they were locked. A recessed knob in the door trim was turned to raise the button and unlock the door. At the same time the opening quarter windows on the Targa were deleted altogether. They were largely redundant now that there was adequate face-level ventilation inside the cabin.

The 1977 models were more lavishly trimmed than ever, with improved carpeting and rear bulkhead sound insulation, together with a new pinstripe fabric for the Carrera 3.0. The doors now had their lower edge carpeted and sported a smart slanted pleat pattern.

Dashboard and Instruments

A new 400-millimeter (15.6-inch) steering wheel was to be found on the 911 and 911S. Derived from the horizontal X pattern of previous models, the new wheel obscured the lower dash in front of the driver completely because most of the X was filled with padding. It was said the new wheel would be the basis for a future air-bag system. The Carrera, however, used a 380-millimeter (14.8-inch) three-spoke design with a thick leather-trimmed rim.

The main instruments were changed slightly, using new colors and regrouped warning lights. The most obvious change was the elimination of the central chromed disc on each of the instruments. A new electronic rev counter and a quartz clock were fitted. Chrome was eliminated from the dash and the doors generally, while new soft knobs had clear symbols indicating their function.

The 1976 model year saw the introduction of the first cruise control for a Porsche, termed "Tempostat" in Europe and Automatic Speed Control in the United States. In 1977, the heater controls on the dash were revised so that there were individual controls for fan and heater delivery.

Luggage Compartment

G-program cars used a new steel 80-liter (17.60 Imperial gallons, 21.14 U.S. gallons) fuel tank, complete with a recess for the Goodrich Space-Saver tire. On European cars this was pumped up from a storage bottle; whereas, a small electric compressor did the job more effectively in the United States.

The new fixed-panel Targa top would not fit into the front luggage area on 1974 cars when air conditioning was specified, so in this case the old folding top had to be used. The 8.5-liter (1.87 Imperial gallons, 2.25 U.S. gallons) water reservoir for the headlamp and windshield washer system was sited ahead of the left front wheel inside the luggage compartment. The system was replenished from a supplementary filler neck next to the fuel filler.

Engine

By now there were significant differences between U.S. engines and those available to the rest of the world. Before we get into this, the engine type numbers given here refer only to manual transmission versions: Sportomatics would have a different number (see page 75).

For 1974, the standard Rest-of-the-World range was the 2.7-liter 911 (engine type 911/92), 911S (engine type 911/93), and Carrera (engine type 911/83, still with mechanical injection). In the United States the model offering shared the same titles, but the 911/93 engine was found in 175-brake horsepower form (with retarded cams) in both the S and the Carrera. The 1974 2.7-liter engines entered production with the Nikasil barrels that had been used on the Carrera RS, but these were soon changed to a new material called Alusil. This new alloy of aluminum and silicon was formed as a die-casting and used no cylinder liner. The piston skirts were plated with cast iron to prevent pick-up between the piston and the bore. The use of aluminum improved heat transfer away from the cylinders as well as enabling the larger 90-millimeter (3.5-inch) bore, without a liner, required for the 2,687cc (163.9-cubic inch) engine.

The 1974 cars had a new 80-liter fuel tank (top) with a spare wheel recess reshaped for a Goodrich Space-Saver tire. With the introduction or impact bumpers, the chassis plate moved to the right-hand wall or the luggage compartment, adjacent to the spare wheel. The two batteries of the previous models (above) were replaced by a single unit for 1974. The 66Ah battery was now charged by a 770-watt alternator. In front of the Space-Saver spare wheel can be seen the air compressor, used for inflating the tire.

While European 1974 Carreras used the engine from the previous year's RS, U.S. models adopted that market's S engine and Bosch K-Jetronic injection. With just 175-brake horsepower, the U.S. Carreras were at a significant power disadvantage against the 210-brake horsepower Carreras offered in most other markets.

During 1974, work progressed on improving the exhaust system in response to the higher temperatures that were now being generated, partly as a result of the lower exhaust emissions. It is worth mentioning, too, that noise was becoming an issue, especially in Switzerland. Until then, European 911s had used an efficient three-into-one manifold system sheathed by the heat-exchanger jacket. A new system was developed that used an aluminum coating on the heat exchangers and a double stainless steel skin design for the silencer. The new system, which was further developed in 1975, was quieter, but some power was again lost in the process of making the 911 a more refined sports car. The oil tank was now also made from stainless-steel and was enlarged, permitting an increase from the previous 6,000-mile (10,000-kilometer) service intervals to 12,000 miles (20,000 kilometers).

The 1975 model offering in the United States was driven by ever stricter exhaust emissions policy. Only the 2.7-liter S engine (911/43) was used, with K-Jetronic injection and an air pump (injecting clean air downstream of the exhaust valves) for what were termed the "49-state" cars. For California, where the exhaust laws were even more difficult to meet, separate models were offered with engine type 911/44. These had the unloved thermal reactors and exhaust gas recirculation. The California 911S managed just 160-brake horsepower at a time when the 911S in Europe delivered 175-brake horsepower, which itself was nothing to write home about. The 1975 models used 6-millimeter-thick sound absorbing material on the lower (exhaust) valve covers in an effort to reduce exterior noise levels. That year also saw an updated, but not fundamentally changed, chain tensioner—a small step forward in improving the reliability of this suspect item—that was accompanied by new harder wearing but noisier chain guide ramps in brown plastic.

In Europe, things started to happen in autumn 1975 with the introduction of the new 3-liter Carrera, which replaced the 2.7 Carrera. The S was also dropped for the 1976 model year. The new 3-liter engine, type 930/02, was derived from the Turbo unit. It used the same 95-millimeter (3.70-inch) bore and 70.4-millimeter (2.75-inch) stroke as the Turbo, but the compression ratio was increased to 8.5:1 by using higher domed pistons. Valve size was unchanged at 49 millimeters (1.91 inches) for the inlets and 41.5 millimeters (1.62 inches) for the exhausts. These sizes would remain the same for all later 930-based engines (SC, Turbo, and the later 3.2 Carreras to 1989). The Carrera 3.0 used the aluminum die-cast crankcase, Nikasil cylinders, and Bosch K-Jetronic injection from the 930. The output for the 930/02 was 200-brake horsepower at 6,000 rpm on 91 RON fuel.

In markets where it was available, the 911 Lux adopted the old S engine (911/81) and went from 150-brake horsepower to 165-brake horsepower for the 1976 model year. It used the four journal camshaft housings from the 930 engine. Most noticeable on the 1976 cars was the five-blade cooling fan, which had the same 245-millimeter (9.6-inch) diameter as the earlier 11-blade unit but ran at a higher speed (1.8:1 instead of 1.3:1) to improve alternator output. Inside the engine, the oil pump was revised to improve oil circulation in the hotter-running engines.

In the United States, the range for the 1976 model year was simpler, but the engines were not. There were still separate engines for "49-state" cars and for California, but things were simplified for the factory in 1977 when all cars destined for the United States could at least use the same emissions equipment air pump, twin thermal reactors, and exhaust gas recirculation. These 2.7-liter 911s were also sold to Canada and Japan. That year also, the K-Jetronic was improved with more stainless-steel components and finer fuel filters, and a return circuit was provided around the fuel accumulator to cope with higher fuel delivery pressure.

The 1974–75 European Carreras still used the 911/83 engine from the RS. Combined with the same overall weight, these cars were almost as desirable as the preceding limited edition. This car is fitted with air conditioning. The compressor is on the right, driven from the crankshaft pulley, and the condenser is mounted on the engine lid.

The 3-liter Carrera's engine was derived from the Turbo's, its designation changing from 911 to 930. The faster-running five-blade cooling fan is the most obvious distinguishing feature of these cars.

Transmission

The fact that the 2.7-liter engines were more flexible and produced their torque at lower revolutions allowed longer ratios to be used in both the 1974 and 1975 models, as the improvements were introduced. In America, four speeds were the standard offering on the 915 gearbox across the range, with the fifth speed being an option. On manual cars, except the European Carrera, the clutch pedal was 30 percent lighter to operate owing to a new center plate, cable, and throw-out mechanism. The S had new ratios in the gearbox and the crown wheel and pinion to maximize the benefits of its greater engine torque.

In 1977, the 915 gearbox was improved by machining first gear to prevent accidental engagement at speed, an alarming possibility. The first and second gear arm of the H pattern was fitted with detents for the same reason.

As torque levels rose, the Sportomatic transmission reached the limit of its torque capacity for a second time, so it had to be uprated in 1976. This time it was reduced to three speeds and became the 925/09 unit. It was said at the time that three speeds were sufficient for the broader torque curve of the new 2.7 engines, but the Sportomatic's popularity declined even further, despite it now being a no-cost option.

The 1976 Carrera 3.0 used the same 915 gearbox as specified for that year's 2.7 911 and American S.

Electrical Equipment and Lighting

Because of the location of the new bumpers, a single 66-amp/hour battery replaced the twin batteries of previous models. This was located in the front left-hand side of the luggage compartment, ahead of the front wheel. The alternator changed to a 55A/770-watt unit. The new impact bumpers also meant revisions to the sidelights, indicators, rear taillights, and number plate lights. Electric windows were listed as a factory option, but several markets (including the U.K.) specified them as standard.

In 1975, the alternator was upgraded to 70A/980 watts to handle the increasing amount of electrical equipment, especially the new constant-running heater system fan.

Suspension and Steering

On the 911 and 911S, a 16-millimeter front anti-roll bar was standard and made to a simpler design than before; the Carrera front anti-roll bar was stiffer at 20 millimeters. When the Carrera's 18-millimeter rear anti-roll bar was fitted as an option to the 911 or 911S instead of the standard 16-millimeter item, the front bar was also uprated to 20 millimeters on these more basic models to maintain an understeering tendency. The Carrera was fitted with Bilstein gas-filled shock absorbers all round.

The main change at the rear was the move to forged aluminum alloy semi-trailing arms. These new "bananas" were 3.5 kilograms (7.7 pounds) lighter than the original fabricated steel items and were also considerably stiffer. At the same time a stronger rear wheel bearing was incorporated into the arm design.

In 1976, the standard 911 front struts were angled inward slightly to improve camber adjustment. In 1977, the sheet steel rear spring plates were made in two pieces, clamped together by eccentric bolts to allow easier—but not easy!—adjustment of the rear ride height. The new Carrera 3.0 suspension used the same anti-roll bar sizes as the outgoing 2.7 Carrera, but the torsion bar diameter increased to 19 millimeters at the front and 23 millimeters at the rear. Among the options available for the 3-liter Carrera (but standard in the U.K.'s Sport package) were Bilstein shock absorbers to give a firmer ride.

This underside view shows the forged semi-trailing arms (with embossed build date) that replaced the more flexible fabricated steel units in 1974. Other points of interest are the glimpse of the green Bilstein gas shock absorber, the fuel pump tucked away behind and above it, and the delicate mounting for the anti-roll bar.

Brakes

There were no significant changes to the brakes for the 1974 or 1975 model years, except that the pedal was made slightly longer to reduce effort. The standard 911 and 911S used the M-type caliper front and rear (of a 52.5-square centimeter swept area); whereas, the Carrera used S-type aluminum calipers on the front (of a 78-square centimeter swept area). In 1976, the standard 911 received cast-iron A-type calipers (also of a 78-square centimeter swept area). The A-type caliper, derived from the earlier S-type, was stronger and narrower in section than the previous M-type and earned its designation because it had been developed under contract for Alfa Romeo.

The 1977 model year saw the introduction of a brake servo on the Sportomatic 911. This was a major improvement in drivability and made the car more attractive to those who were not endowed like Tarzan, but much of the feel provided by the original heavy pedal was lost.

By 1975, the Fuchs forged-alloy wheel had become the required fitting. From the early narrow examples, changes had centered on increasing the wheel width and improving the finish of the rim. The RS had introduced different front/rear wheel sizes, and this practice was carried over to the later 2.7 Carreras. This is a rear 7Jx15 wheel with a nonstandard 225/50 tire.

Wheels and Tires

For 1974 in the United States, the standard wheels for the 911 were still in steel, size 5.5Jx15 with 165/70HR tires. For most other markets the cast-alloy ATS cookie-cutter wheels were specified. The S used the 6Jx15 ATS wheels with 185/70VR tires while the Carrera sported the now-classic Fuchs five-spoke alloy wheels of 6Jx15 at the front (with 185/70VR tires) and 7Jx15 (with 215/60VR tires) at the rear. The spare for all models (except the U.K.) was the Goodrich Space-Saver. This was naturally much narrower than the tires on the car. Its use was limited to low-speed "get-you-home-only" mode, and if the car was full of luggage there was nowhere to put a dirty flat tire.

New bumper height rules in the United States prevented the use of 50-series tires on the new 911s, although these were an option on the 1976 Carrera 3.0 in Europe. A 1977 option list defined a comfort pack for that year's 911s. This included softer Bilstein shock absorbers (Boges were standard) and 14-inch Fuchs forged-alloy wheels with Uniroyal 185HR Rallye tires. Curiously, these tires were not rated for speeds above 130 miles per hour, so the engine was governed to that maximum. In the United States the comfort pack came with cruise control and electric windows.

Silver Anniversary Model

A total of 1,063 Silver Anniversary 911s were made in coupe and Targa form during the 1975 model year to celebrate 25 years of Porsche sports car manufacture. Production was split as follows: 154 Rest-of-the-World coupes, 150 Rest-of-the-World Targas, 510 U.S. coupes, and 249 U.S. Targas. The anniversary models were customized 911 and 911S models.

Grouped as the option M426, the following options enhanced the standard car's specification: two-stage heated rear window (M102), headlamp washers (M288), Blaupunkt Bamberg radio (M422), electric antenna (M461), pressure-cast 6-inch wheels (M458), 18mm rear anti-roll bar (M404), black-look trim (M496), 380mm-diameter sports steering wheel (M565), and a five-speed gearbox (M481). The cars were finished in a special diamond silver metallic paint finish. Each car carried a "*25 Jahre Fahren in seiner schonsten Form*" plaque on the dash.

Comparison views of a 1975 2.7 Carrera with body trim in the normal chrome (above) and a 1977 Carrera 3.0 Sport with the black-look and side decals (below).

Production Changes

August 1973 (Start of G-program)

Impact bumpers front and rear with integrated sidelights and indicators, new fenders, new reflective strip under engine lid; "Porsche" logo moved from rear lid to reflector strip; side sills extended; black-look trim for Carrera (with ducktail and lettering in the United States); Carrera available in coupe or Targa form; wide rubbing strips face bumpers front and rear with two large elastomer over-riders at rear (including number plate lamps); new seats with integral head restraints, side window demist vents on dash, and inertia reel seat belts standard in all markets; top entry storage bins in doors; new 400mm four-spoke steering wheel; chrome disc removed from center of restyled instruments; restyled indicator stalk; electronic rev counter and quartz clock fitted; soft knobs on center dash; 80-liter steel fuel tank (although some markets used the plastic version) and Goodrich Space-Saver tire; new hard Targa top (for cars without air conditioning) with third locating peg on windshield; single 55Ah battery replaces previous twin arrangement; batteries now charged by a 55A/770W alternator; engine size increased to 2,587cc with Bosch K-Jetronic injection

for standard 911 and 911S, and cast (not forged) pistons (see text for U.S. model differences); transition to Alusil barrels (from Nikasil); new heat exchanger design; 13-liter engine oil capacity (Sporto is 15-liter); valve overlap retarded relative to 1973 2.7 engine and port size on both models reduced; new silencer to fit new bumper design, new heat exchanger design; larger (stainless-steel) oil tank allows 12,000-mile service intervals to be introduced; longer ratios (fourth, 0.926; fifth, 0.724) in top two gears for 915 gearbox; new over-center mechanism for clutch pedal; brake pedal lengthened from 232mm to 250mm to enable lighter action; one-piece front anti-roll bar; towing eye welded to right-hand side wishbone mount; standard 911 and 911S use cast-iron M-type front calipers; 15mm front/rear anti-roll bar on 911 and 911S, 20mm front and 18mm rear on Carrera; forged-alloy semi-trailing arms at rear (with larger wheel bearing); standard 911 and 911S use ATS cookie cutter wheels.

August 1974 (Start of H-program)

Extra sound insulation; color-coded headlamp surrounds for Carreras; new whaletail rear spoiler and front chin spoiler for U.S. Carreras; additional electric fan for heating system with left- and right-side heater control; noise insulation on engine cam covers; alternator increased to 70A/980W; U.S. 49-state models receive exhaust air pump, California cars have this plus thermal reactors and exhaust gas recirculation (EGR); in U.S. Carrera uses S engine, but S gets tinted glass, five-speed gearbox, intermittent front wipe and heated rear window as standard; steel wheels deleted; high-pressure headlamp washers with 8.5-liter water reservoir introduced for specific markets as an option.

August 1975 (Start of I-program)

In Europe, all models receive hot dipped zinc-coated steel for all bodyshell parts; Carrera 3.0 introduced with 2,994cc Turbo-based 930 engine (weight is 184kg); standard 911 uses previous year's S engine (155bhp) with larger capacity oil pump (weight is 175kg, with magnesium crankcase); five-blade, faster turning (1.8:1) cooling fan; K-Jetronic has automatic cold start enrichment; lower valve covers changed to die-cast aluminum (not magnesium), for better sealing; fuel pump moved to front of car; Sportomatic gearbox drops from four speeds to three; clutch cable strengthened and mounting improved; standard 911 (911 Lux in U.K.) gets larger (A-type) cast-iron calipers; inward angle of front struts increased; cast front suspension crossmember introduced (first seen on RS Carrera and Turbo in 1975); improved door locks; one-piece interior carpet; new door trims; Targa has improved front three-quarter window locking; driver's door mirror now color-coded, electrically adjustable and heated; more sound insulation; 80-liter fuel tank lead-lined.

August 1976 (Start of J-program)

Reduced section middle air deflectors fitted below cylinders for improved cooling; Dilavar cylinder head studs introduced for lower line on late model Carreras and 2.7 engines; higher flow rate fuel pump and fine mesh fuel filters; upgraded K-Jetronic components; supplementary air slide (controlled by a bi-metallic spiral) on intake pipes for numbers 5 and 6 cylinders improves hot starting; first/second gear arm of selector gate baulked on 915 gearbox; booster spring to make clutch operation lighter; two-piece steel spring plates with ride height adjustment; Targas get black-look roll-over hoop; central face-level fresh air/heater vents in top of dash; improved heater controls; carpet on door storage boxes; Targa loses opening three-quarter windows; door buttons disappeared into door as locked, opened with knurled knob; 7-inch brake servo, auto heat control and pressure headlamp wash standard on Carrera 3.0; new option is Comfort kit, which includes 185HR14 tires on Fuchs wheels, automatic speed governor (to 130mph) and softer gas dampers (in United States this included Automatic Speed Control and electric windows); brake servo on Sportomatic models; center console ahead of gear lever (M590).

Dimensions

Wheelbase
2,271mm.

Track (front/rear)
911 and 911S, 1,360mm/1,342mm; Carrera, 1,372mm/1,354mm.

Length
4,291mm.

Width
911 and 911S, 1,610mm; Carrera and Carrera 3, 1,652mm.

Options

Factory list dated August 1973

Metallic paint and custom colors to order; Sportomatic gearbox; leather upholstery; M058 impact-absorbing dampers for bumpers; M060 additional heater; M197 88Ah battery; M093 external manual passenger door mirror; M102 two-stage rear window heater; M220 limited slip differential (80 percent); M261 external electric passenger door mirror; M288 high-pressure headlamp washers with 8.5-liter water reservoir; M402 Koni dampers; M404 rear anti-roll bar, 18mm; M405 protective lacquer finish, orange; M406 protective lacquer finish, green; M407/8 front seats raised 26mm left/right; M409 Sports Recaro seats, both; M410 Sports Recaro seat, driver only; M412 front oil cooler; M414 oil pressure and oil level gauges (basic 911 only); M416 leather steering wheel with raised hub; M417 Porsche script on doors, orange; M419 Porsche script on doors, green; M422 Blaupunkt Bamberg stereo; M425 rear window wiper; M427 Carrera script on the doors, gold; M428 protective lacquer finish, gold; M429 foglight, H3 white, rectangular under bumper; M430 foglight, H3 yellow, rectangular under bumper; M432 protective lacquer finish, black; M436 Targa folding roof; M438 Porsche script on doors, gold; M439 Porsche script on doors, black; M440 mechanical antenna (left) with speakers and wiring; M441 electric antenna (right) with speakers and wiring; M443 tinted side front glass, heated windshield and rear window; M446 chrome trim (Carrera only); M449 Blaupunkt Lubeck stereo; M450 light alloy wheels, black, 6Jx15 with 185/70VR15 front tires and 7Jx15 with 215/60VR15 rear tires (Carrera only); M451 as M450 but in comet diamant metallic; M452 Blaupunkt Frankfurt radio; M454 Blaupunkt Coburg radio; M458 6Jx15 light alloy wheels in silver green diamant finish with 185/70VR 15 tires; M459 as M458 but comet diamant metallic; M460 as M458 but gray-blue metallic; M461 electric antenna (right) with wiring; M462 Carrera script on doors, black; M468 air compressor for spare wheel; M469 black headlining; M474 Bilstein dampers; M477 6Jx15 light alloy wheels with 185/70VR 15 tires (standard on S); M477 6Jx15 front, 7Jx15 rear light alloy wheels with 185/70VR15 front, 215/60VR15 rear tires (Carrera only); M481 five-speed gearbox; M482 engine compartment light; M485 5.5Jx15 light alloy wheels with 165HR/15 tires; M490 mechanical antenna (left) with wiring; M497 self-starter; M498 engine lid without model designation; M559 air conditioning; M567 graduated tint windshield; M568 tinted side and windshield glass for Targa or coupe; M571 rear foglight; M650 electric sliding sunroof; M651 electric window lifters; M652 intermittent windshield wipe; M659 as M429 with rear protection light; M565 sports steering wheel, 380mm.

Factory list dated September 1975 (where different from above)

M009 three-speed Sportomatic transmission; M220 limited slip differential (80 or 40 percent); M392 interior in Scottish tweed; M393/4 turbo decal in black (or white) for rear fender (Turbo only); M395 Pirelli P7 205/50VR 15 (front) and 225/50VR 15 (rear) tires; M399 air conditioning; M400 forged-alloy wheels, 6Jx15 (front and rear) with 185/70VR 15 tires; M401 forged-alloy wheels, 7 Jx15 (front) and 8Jx15 (rear) with 185/70VR15 and 215/60VR15 tires (Carrera only); M403 aluminum trim strip under door; M418 aluminum trim strip around wheel

Identification

Model year	Model	Engine	Gearbox	Chassis numbers	Engine numbers
G-program					
1974	911	911/92	915/16	9114100001–9114104014	6140001–6146625
	911 Targa	911/92	915/16	9114110001–9114113110	6140001–6146625
	911 Sporto	911/97	925/02	9114110001–9114113110	6149001–6149517
	911S	911/93	915/16	9114300001–9114301359	6340001–6342804
	911S Targa	911/93	915/16	9114310001–9114310898	6340001–6342804
	911S Sporto	911/98	925/02	9114310001–9114310898	6349001–6349236
	Carrera	911/83	915/16	9114600001–9114601036	6640001–6641456
	Carrera Targa	911/83	915/16	9114610001–9114610433	6640001–6641456
	Carrera U.S.	911/93	915/16	9114400001–9114400528	6340001–6342804
	Carrera U.S. Targa	911/93	915/16	9114410001–9114410246	6340001–6342804
	Carrera RS 3.0	911/77	915/08	9114609001–9114609109	6640001–6640200
H-program					
1975	911	911/41	915/48	9115100001–9115101238	6150001–6152007
	911 Targa	911/41	915/48	9115110001–9115110998	6150001–6152007
	911 Sporto	911/46	925/04	9115110001–9115110998	6159001–6159252
	911S	911/42	915/45	9115300001–9115300385	6350001–6350567
	911S Targa	911/42	915/45	9115310001–9115310266	6350001–6350567
	911S Sporto	911/47	925/04	9115310001–9115310266	6359001–6359105
	911S U.S. 49	911/43	915/45	9115200001–9115202310	6450001–6452440
	911S U.S. 49 Targa	911/43	915/45	9115210001–9115211517	6450001–6452440
	911S U.S. 49 Sporto	911/48	925/04	9115210001–9115211517	6459001–6459135
	911S Cal	911/44	915/45	9115210001–9115211517	6459001–6459135
	911S Cal Targa	911/44	915/45	9115210001–9115211517	6459001–6459135
	911S Cal Sporto	911/49	925/04	9115210001–9115211517	6459001–6459135
	Carrera	911/83	915/16	9115600001–9115600518	6650021–6650712
	Carrera Targa	911/83	915/16	9115610001–9115610197	6650021–6650712
	Carrera U.S.	911/43	915/16	9115400001–9115400395	6450001–6452440
	Carrera U.S. Sporto	911/48	925/04	9115400001–9115400395	6459001–6459135
	Carrera Cal	911/44	915/16	9115400001–9115400395	6450001–6452440
	Carrera Cal Sporto	911/49	925/04	9115400001–9115400395	6459001–6459135
I-program					
1976	911	911/81	915/49	9116300001–9116301868	6360001–6363029
	911 Targa	911/81	915/49	9116310001–9116311576	6360001–6363029
	911 Sporto	911/86	925/09	9116310001–9116311576	6369001–6369435
	911S U.S. 49	911/82	915/44	9116200001–9116202079	6460001–6462305
	911S U.S. 49 Targa	911/82	915/44	9116210001–9116212175	6560001–6561837
	911S Cal	911/84	915/44	9116210001–9116212175	6560001–6561837
	911S Cal Sporto	911/89	925/12	9116210001–9116212175	6569001–6569160
	Carrera 3.0	930/02	915/44	9116600001–9116601093	6660001–6661385
	Carrera 3.0 Targa	930/02	915/44	9116610001–9116610479	6660001–6661385
	Carrera 3.0 Sporto	930/12	925/13	9116610001–9116610479	6669001–6669212
J-program					
1977	911	911/81	915/60	9117300001–9117302449	6370001–6373531
	911 Targa	911/81	915/60	9117310001–9117311724	6370001–6373531
	911S U.S.	911/85	915/61	9117200001–9117203388	6270001–6276041
	911S U.S. Targa	911/85	915/61	9117210001–9117212747	6270001–6276041
	911S U.S. Sporto	911/90	925/17	9117210001–9117212747	6279001–6279113
	Carrera 3.0	930/02	915/61	9117600001–9117601473	6670001–6671932
	Carrera 3.0 Targa	930/02	915/61	9117610001–9117600646	6670001–6671932
	Carrera 3.0 Sporto	930/12	925/16	9117610001–9117600646	6679001–6679215

General notes

U.S. specification For 1975–1976, American specification models are divided into "49-state" cars (*US 49* above) and California cars (*Cal* above). For 1977, U.S. cars were all to the same specification. The above listing excludes models specific to the Japanese market, which were delivered with California specification emissions equipment on the 911/41 or 911/42 engines.

Gearboxes For 1974, the five-speed 915 gearbox was known as the 915/06 (with the four-speed being the 915/16). For 1975, the gearbox was variously defined as the 915/48 (four-speed for 911 RoW), 915/43 (five-speed for 911 RoW), 915/45 (five-speed for 911 RoW and U.S.), 915/40 (five-speed for 911S RoW and U.S., and Carrera U.S.), 915/16 (four-speed for Carrera RoW), or 915/06 (five-speed for Carrera RoW). For 1976, it was 915/44 (five-speed for 911 and 911S U.S.) or 915/49 (four-speed 911 RoW). For 1977, it was 915/60 (five-speed for 911 RoW), 915/65 (four-speed for 911 RoW), 915/61 (four-speed 911S U.S.), or 915/66 (911S for Japan).

arches; M424 automatic heating control; M454 Tempostat speed control; M494 two stereo loudspeakers on the rear shelf; M496 black-look trim with color-coded headlamp surrounds (standard on Carrera).

Color Schemes

1974

Standard body colors

Guards Red (Indischrot, 027), Peru Red (042), Signal Orange (116), Light Yellow (117), Lime Green (GelbgrÜn, 137) Orange (156), Mexico Blue (336), Bitter Chocolate (Cockney, 408), Sahara Beige (516), Grand Prix White (908),

Special order body colors

Magenta (Karminrot, 009), Rose Red (Fraise, 024), Aubergine (025), Irish Green (213), Jade Green (Hellgrün, 227), Birch Green (Lichtgrün, 253), Gulf Blue (328), Royal Purple (Flieder, 341), Bahama Blue (Acid, 354), Olive (414), Black (700), Salmon Metallic (036), Emerald Green Metallic (Vipergrün, 249), Ice Green Metallic (Silbergrün Diamant, 250), Metallic Blue (334), Gemini Metallic (335), Gazelle Metallic (Comet Diamant, 406), Copper Brown Metallic (Braunkupferdiamant, 432), Steel Blue Metallic (Graublaudiamant, 631), Silver Metallic (936)

Fabrics

Leatherette light grain (000 551.615.11) in dark red (002), tan (503) or black (709); leatherette light basketweave (999.551.002.41) in dark red (002), tan (503) or black (709); leatherette Roy Flex heavy grain (999.551.001.40) in red (003), blue (301) or black (406); leather (999.551.07141) in red (002), tan (504) or black (701). Madras check fabrics (999.551.031.40) in reds (000), blues (300), or browns (400). Available as no-cost options were Shetland seat center panels (999.551.032.41) in dark red (000), tan (500), or black (700); Tweed seat center panels (999.551.034.40) in red/white (000), black/white/ turquoise (300), or tan (500); and Twill seat side panels (999.551.035.40) in dark red (000), tan (500), or black (700).

Carpets

Nylon velour 430 (999.551.052.40) in red (001), blue/green (301), or tan (402); nylon velour 626 (999.551.051.41) in red (001), tan (501), or black (701); special velour (999.551.061.41) in red (001), tan (501), or black (701).

1975 (chart 1050, 51.14)

Standard body colors

Guards Red (Indischrot, 027), Peru Red (042), Light Yellow (117), Lime Green (Gelbgrün, 137), Orange (156), Mexico Blue (336), Bitter Chocolate (Cockney, 408), Sahara Beige (516), Grand Prix White (908).

Special order body colors

Magenta (Karminrot, 009), Rose Red (Fraise, 024), Aubergine (025), Signal Orange (116), Irish Green (213), Jade Green (Hellgrün, 227), Birch Green (Lichtgrün, 253), Gulf Blue (328), Royal Purple (Flieder, 341), Bahama Blue (Acid, 354), Olive (414), Black (700), Salmon Metallic (036), Emerald Green Metallic (249), Ice Green Metallic (250), Metallic Blue (334), Gemini Metallic (335), Gazelle Metallic (406), Copper Brown Metallic (432), Steel Blue Metallic (631, wheels for 25-year model), Silver Metallic (936)

Fabrics

No-grain leatherette (000.551.615.03) in black (713), tan (413), or ivory (513); basketweave (pierced hole stitched appearance) leatherette (000 551.615.12) in black (713), tan (413), or ivory (513); light-grain leatherette (999.551.001.41) in dark red (002), tan (503), or black (709); leatherette light basketweave as 1974; leatherette Roy Flex light-grain (999.551.021.41) in red (003), blue (301), or brown (406). Leather, Madras check, twill, Shetland, and Tweed as 1974.

Carpets

Perlon 999.551.051.41 (Needle velour 626) in red (001), tan (501), or black (701); nylon velour and special velour as 1974. Velour pile (Carrera only) 999.551.075.41 in yellow (1 AG), dark

green (2AG), burgundy (4AG), tan (5AG), dark blue/gray (7 AG), jubilee car, dark red (8AG), or orange (8AP)

1976 (chart 1080,81.14)

Standard body colors

Guards Red (027), Talbot Yellow (106), Continental Orange (107), Light Yellow (117), Ascot Green (Speedway, 258), Arrow Blue (305), Bitter Chocolate (408), Black (700), Grand Prix White (908).

Special order body colors

Magenta (009), Peru Red (042), Lime Green (137), Irish Green (213), Apple Green (Daphne, 260), Ice Blue (Coppaflorio, 360), Sahara Beige (516), Emerald Green Metallic (264), Oak Green Metallic (265), Ice Green Metallic (Silver Green, 266), Minerva Blue (304), Copper Brown Metallic (443), Silver Metallic (936), Platinum Metallic (944), Sienna Metallic (436). Note: some colors have new codes because of finer bronze powder (e.g., Ice Green Metallic changes from 250 to 266); an A suffix to the paint code would indicate an acrylic paint.

Fabrics

Light grain and light basketweave leatherettes as 1975; leather (999.551.073.40) in orange (1AG), brown (2AG), green (2AP), blue (3AG), dark brown (4AG), tan (5AG), black (7AG), midbrown (8AG), red (8AT), or white (9AG); Twill, Tweed, and Shetland as 1974. Tartan Dress tweeds (new no-cost option, 999.551.083.40) in red (8AB), green (2AC), or brown/beige (4AD).

Carpets

Velour pile as 1975 Carrera; special velour as 1974.

1977

Standard body colors

Guards Red (027), Talbot Yellow (1 06), Continental Orange (107), Light Yellow (117), Ascot Green (Speedway, 258), Arrow Blue (305), Bitter Chocolate (408), Black (700), Grand Prix White (908).

Special order body colors

Magenta (009), Peru Red (042), Lime Green (137), Irish Green (213), Apple Green (Daphne, 260), Ice Blue (Coppaflorio, 360), Sahara Beige (516), Emerald Green Metallic (264), Oak Green Metallic (265), Ice Green Metallic (Silver Green, 266), Minerva Blue (304), Copper Brown Metallic (443), Silver Metallic (936), Platinum Metallic (944), Sienna Metallic (436).

Fabrics

Heavy-grain leatherette standard (999.551.012.40) in black (7AU), red (8AU) or tan (5AU); leatherette new light basketweave (999.551.009.40) in black (7AT), lobster (8AT), or cork (5AT); leather (999.551.073.40) in gold/yellow (IAG), dark green (2AG), light green (2AP), blue (3AG), dark brown (4AG), cork (5AH), black (7 AG), lobster (8AH), light red (8AT), or white (9AG); pin-stripe velour (999.551.039.40), no-cost option in black with white stripes (7AK), lobster with black stripes (8AK) or cork with black stripes (5AK); Tartan Dress tweeds as 1976.

Carpets

Velour pile (999.551.092.40) in yellow (1AY), green (2AY), dark brown (4AV), cork (5AZ), black (7AZ), lobster (8AB), or light red (8AZ).

Production Data

Model year	Model	Power (bhp DIN@rpm)	Torque (Nm@rpm)	Compression ratio	Weight (kg)	Number built
1974	911	150@5,700	235@3,800	8.0:1	1,075	4,014
	911 Targa	150@5,700	235@3,800	8.0:1	1,125	3,110
	911S	175@5,800	235@4,000	8.5:1	1,075	1,359
	911S Targa	175@5,800	235@4,000	8.5:1	1,125	898
	Carrera	210@6,300	255@5,100	8.5:1	1,075	1,036
	Carrera Targa	210@6,300	255@5,100	8.5:1	1,125	433
	Carrera US	175@5,800	235@4,000	8.5:1	1,075	528
	Carrera RS3.0	230@6,200	275@5,000	9.8:1	900	59
1975	911	150@5,700	235@3,800	8.0:1	1,075	1,238
	911 Targa	150@5,700	235@3,800	8.0:1	1,125	998
	911S	175@5,800	235@4,000	8.5:1	1,075	385
	911S Targa	175@5,800	235@4,000	8.5:1	1,125	266
	911S U.S. 49	165@5,800	225@4,000	8.5:1	1,100	2,310
	911S U.S. Targa	165@5,800	225@4,000	8.5:1	1,150	1,517
	Carrera	210@6,300	255@5,100	8.5:1	1,120	518
	Carrera Targa	210@6,300	255@5,100	8.5:1	1,170	197
	Carrera U.S.	165@5,800	225@4,000	8.5:1	1,100	395
1976	911	165@5,800	235@4,000	8.5:1	1,120	1,868
	911 Targa	165@5,800	235@4,000	8.5:1	1,170	1,576
	911S U.S.	165@5,800	235@4,000	8.5:1	1,145	2,079
	911S U.S. Targa	165@5,800	235@4,000	8.5:1	1,195	2,175
	911 Japan	165@5,800	235@4,000	8.5:1	1,195	130
	Carrera 3.0	200@6,000	255@4,200	8.5:1	1,120	1,093
	Carrera 3.0 Targa	200@6,000	255@4,200	8.5:1	1,170	479
1977	911	165@5,800	235@4,000	8.5:1	1,075	2,449
	911 Targa	165@5,800	235@4,000	8.5:1	1,170	1,724
	911S U.S.	165@5,800	235@4,000	8.5:1	1,145	3,388
	911S U.S. Targa	165@5,800	235@4,000	8.5:1	1,195	2,747
	911S Japan	165@5,800	235@4,000	8.5:1	1,195	383
	Carrera 3.0	200@6,000	255@4,200	8.5:1	1,120	1,473
	Carrera 3.0 Targa	200@6,000	255@4,200	8.5:1	1,170	646

The 911SC (1978–1983)

Sue Baker's black 1979 911SC Targa. The "tea-tray" spoiler, first seen on the Turbo the previous year, was introduced on Targas before coupes, which at this time retained the whaletail spoiler.

Thirteen years in production would be a significant achievement for any modern car, and by 1977, this was the point the 911 had reached. This was despite the hurdles imposed by the fuel crisis and new U.S. legislation concerning emissions and impact resistance. Yet here was the 911 going from strength to strength. The change to impact bumpers had been a triumph for the stylists at Weissach and, combined with a deliberate move to make the 911 more attractive to the non-enthusiast, a transformation had occurred. The 911 was now a more subtle, refined grand tourer on which you could depend completely.

Evolution Outline

August 1977: The 911SC (180-brake horsepower) replaces the 911, 911S, and Carrera (3.0) models, a brake servo is added, and Martini stripes become available for the SC.

August 1979: The 50-state car introduced in United States with a three-way catalytic converter and Lambda sensor, power on Rest-of-World models is raised to 188 brake horsepower, the Sportomatic is discontinued, and the special "Weissach" model is introduced in the United States.

August 1980: Power on Rest-of-World models is raised to 204-brake horsepower; small side repeaters are added on the front wings.

August 1981: Options are now listed on the vehicle identification plate.

March 1982: The Cabriolet is launched at the Geneva Motor Show.

October 1982: Cabriolet production starts (left-hand drive, Germany).

This 1980 911SC is the special edition Weissach model sold only in the United States and has been owned from new by Brian Carleton.

As the 1970s had progressed, Porsche had deliberately sought not just the enthusiast-drivers who until then had made up the core of its customers, but the company also went looking for a new type of owner. Market research had shown that the profile of the new owner might typically be a small business person, perhaps with a young family, who could justify the 911 as a business tool while enjoying its performance abilities. This new type of driver wanted easier drivability, better reliability, and good value for money. The first two factors were achieved, but poor value for money was a recurring comment in contemporary road tests from around the world. The factory argued—and still does—that you had to pay for exclusivity.

As ever, the racing association was a vital selling ingredient. At the end of 1971, the mighty 917 sports racing cars that had dueled with Ferrari were banned. This had seemed a body blow to the racing department, but it soon picked itself up, dusted down the 917, turbocharged it for the Can-Am, and set about turning the 911 racer into a world beater in Europe. By 1976, the prototype 936 had won Le Mans with an engine derived from the 911 and Porsche was back at the top of sports car racing. Once again, to buy a Porsche was to be associated with that success.

After the impact bumpers of 1974, there had been two more stepping stones to what might be termed the ubiquitous production 911: the 1978 911SC. The first had been the adoption of a fully galvanized bodyshell, an industry-leading development that at last offered longevity over years of exposure to salt-covered winter roads.

The second had been to seek complete reliability. The 2.7 unit had been good, with a broader torque curve than the peaky 2.4, but it had stretched the original design to its limits. Some parts had tended to wear at a higher rate than was expected in a Porsche, and the engine ran hot in warmer climates. Although this engine was reliable compared with most others, it did not offer the bullet-proof reliability the engineers were seeking. The new Turbo's 3-liter engine, unblown, offered that potential.

While the Carrera 3.0 had combined power and reliability with improving refinement, the launch of the 911SC in August 1977 extended the refinement still further. The SC was now the only normally aspirated 911 available, replacing the 911S in the United States and the Carrera and the 2.7 in Rest-of-the-World markets. For Americans, the SC offered a useful extra 15 brake horsepower over the 911S, but for all other buyers, power fell from the Carrera's healthy 200-brake horsepower to 180-brake horsepower. However, the engineers had worked to achieve a flatter torque curve, thus increasing the appeal of the car to that much-sought new type of customer. The new buyer probably would not have noticed new details like the brake servo (fitted for the first time across the range), which greatly improved drivability around town and reduced pedal effort when the brakes were cold.

The SC was Porsche's first attempt at a "world" car, for an exhaust emission air pump was fitted even to European models. Hardened 911 enthusiasts, who also grumbled about the new "soft" brakes having lost their feel, soon had these air pumps decorating their garage walls.

The SC used the same mechanical components as the Carrera 3.0 and kept the attractive flared rear wheel arches. Outright performance was not much changed by the loss of 20-brake horsepower, but the effect of advancing the timing of the same camshafts by just six degrees allowed the SC to pull confidently from surprisingly low revs, a feature of the 911 that has remained ever since. The problem for enthusiasts was that as the 911's appeal was broadened to a

Peter Foskett's 1982 911SC is a U.K. Sport model, recognizable by its front and rear spoilers and black-finished wheels. The flush-mounted headlamp washers were introduced for 1980, while the side repeaters are the mark of a post-1981 model.

The black-finished Targa hoop was attractively accented by gold "Targa" script. Even the beading in the window trim was darkened.

U.S. models with impact bumpers had an extra indicator lens in each side of the front bumper molding. This Weissach model also shows off its additional driving lights below the bumper.

Unleaded fuel only for U.S. 911s. Californian cars had their previous two-way catalytic converters replaced with more effective three-way systems in 1980.

wider market, it was losing power (in Europe at least) and putting on weight. The SC's increase in curb weight to 1,160 kilograms (2,558 pounds) ensured that it was not the best performer among 911s. With the addition of items like electric windows, an electric sunroof, and, from 1980 especially, air conditioning in the United States, weight continued to rise.

The 911 was due for replacement in the early 1980s, but demand continued strongly with the SC outselling its declared successor, the 928, by nearly 50 percent. Power improvements hurriedly introduced in 1980 (not for the United States) and 1981 (this time including the United States) were intended to give the car new life in its twilight years by addressing criticisms that it was becoming middle aged and, with all the weight, slower. To be fair, these power rises were accompanied by useful improvements in fuel consumption, even if the 1981 204-brake horsepower world model reverted to using premium 97 RON fuel. By 1981, however, the factory had changed its mind over the future of the 911, and with this new direction the SC began to rediscover some of the aggressiveness that had been lost with the Carrera 3.0.

The British weekly newspaper *Motoring News* tried one of the new 204-brake horsepower SCs in December 1980. Its comments are interesting and showed where the 911 was at the start of the decade: "The 924 and 928 should have marked the death of this 15-year-old model. However, this 1960s design remains in production. . . . I'm sure the 911 is still *the* Porsche . . . as yet the 924 and 928 lack the charisma."

Bodyshell

The 1978 models were known as the K-program, and the bodies were largely unchanged from the previous year, except for color variations. The SC kept the flared rear wheel arches from the Carrera, while the SC Targa lost the opening front quarter-lights that had been unique to this model.

The internal factory "program" designation changed for the 1980 model year. Since the original A-program cars of 1964 would be followed by another potential A-program of the same car 16 years later, a change was necessary to prevent duplication and possible confusion. It coincided with the adoption of a new chassis numbering system, which came about as a result of new European Community and U.S. legislation requiring that the chassis should be identifiable worldwide for a period of 30 years by a 17-digit number. Starting in 1980, a preliminary 10-digit system was used across all Porsche models, not just the 911. The following year the full international 17-digit vehicle identification number (VIN) was used. For an explanation of the new numbers, see the Identification table (page 88).

A concept car called the "Studie" was revealed on the Porsche stand at the Frankfurt Motor Show in 1981. This was a four-wheel-drive 911 with a Cabriolet body. So strong was the reaction that by the following March's Geneva Motor Show, a prototype 911SC Cabriolet was shown, with the press being allowed rides in preproduction cars through the summer of 1982. Production models started to be delivered in Germany in October 1982, with most other markets (including right-hand-drive markets) receiving theirs from February 1983.

Surprisingly, the Cabrio required few structural stiffening changes to the basic building block, the Targa bodyshell. Stripped of the Targa's roll-over hoop, production Cabrios were claimed to equal the coupe's weight by being about

14 kilograms (31 pounds) lighter than the Targa, but the reality was that both open models weighed about the same. Mounted on a light alloy hood frame, the hood material was a three-layer sandwich with a tough polyester/polyacrylic surface, a middle insulating layer, and waterproof soft cotton lining. The hood had a detachable rear screen to allow covered but ventilated motoring, but an optional heated panel could replace the plastic screen. The hood was manually operated as standard (electric operation was a later option) and folded back into a space behind the rear seats; a roll-over bar was also an option.

The Cabrio's windshield was left at the existing model's rake angle in preference to the lower roofline of the Speedster model that the engineers also proposed at the time. The Cabrio's launch turned out to be the beginning of the end for the Targa model: In the early 1980s, sales of Targas had virtually matched those of the coupe, especially in the United States, but as Cabrio production increased, Targa production decreased. The Targa took a long time to die, however, finally being deleted in 1993.

Body Trim and Fittings
The SC came with chrome trim as standard, but the black-look option (M496) first seen on the 2.7 Carrera, was growing in popularity.

The usual comprehensive range of other factory options was offered for the SC in all markets. In the larger markets, importers would often group together a collection of options to make life easier for their customers. Typical of these was the Sport package offered to U.K. customers. These models were identified by an all-elastomer whaletail, front spoiler chin extension, Bilstein gas dampers, and forged-alloy 16-inch wheels with Pirelli's new low-profile P7 tires. Inside, the driver and passenger were held firmly in place by sports seats and what the press handout called "a high-quality stereo cassette/radio player with electric aerial."

The 1980 models had the black-look as standard on the coupe and the Targa (including the roll-over hoop). This also meant the headlamp surrounds were color-coded to the body. The protruding headlamp washers were replaced with units that were flush-fitting to the top of the bumper surface. In 1981, side repeaters were fitted to the front wings, a good way of spotting the later 204-brake horsepower models.

In September 1981, a revised and more elegant form of rear spoiler structure was fitted to the SC, with a large, flat central cooling grille as on the Turbo but cut back on the underside.

On the new Cabrio, both driver and passenger door mirrors were standard. From the 1982 model year the options fitted to a particular model could now be found (by M code) on the vehicle identification plate.

First used in series production on the 1975 Carrera, the whaletail spoiler changed in detail on the 911SC. At first the most noticeable difference was a deeper black flexible part of the assembly (above), but further revisions for 1982 meant that the center section was built up on its top surface, like the Turbo version, and the underside was cut back (below).

Interior Trim
The smart interior choice of pinstripe, as well as the popular tartan schemes, were carried over from the Carrera 3.0, but into the 1980s Porsche became much more adventurous with its interior fabrics. In 1980, a wavy check upholstery style called Pascha was introduced. It was probably one of the more controversial Porsche fabrics that had been first seen on the 928. You either loved it or hated it. The following year the more conservative Berber fabric was introduced.

Until the 1980 model year the steering wheel diameter had been 400 millimeters (15.6 inches) except for the 380-millimeter (14.8-inch) wheel used on

The seating of this Weissach model is full leather in Doric Gray with Burgundy piping. The Burgundy theme extends to the door pockets and carpeting. Note the modest speedometer calibration—a new dial for U.S. cars arrived for the 1980 model year and read to only 85 miles per hour!

Smart Berber upholstery was introduced for 1981. The plaque on the glove compartment lid indicates that this car has been a Porsche Club GB concours competitor.

the 2.7 Carrera and the Turbo, but from August 1979 the 380-millimeter three-spoke wheel was transferred to the SC. This attracted some criticism from road testers as it was now more difficult to read the speedometer—quite important in a 911!

For 1980, the folding rear seats were upholstered in the same cloth material as the front seats. A center console, first seen on the Turbo, now kept cassettes and oddments tidy. For the 1982 models the heater control was revised to improve warmth at low engine speeds, and on 1983 models the over-ride lever for the heater (positioned between the seats) was deleted.

On the new 1983 Cabrio model the automatic heater control, standard on most 911s, was replaced by a manual system because the automatic system could become confused during open-air motoring. The rear seat backs were reduced in height by 125 millimeters (4.9 inches), and the Cabrio was unique in having leather seats as standard.

Dashboard and Instruments

The introduction of an oxygen sensor in 1980 for U.S. models resulted in an "OXS" warning lamp appearing on the upper dash between the rev counter and the speedometer. This would light when sensor replacement was due at 30,000 miles. As with the Carrera 3.0 and the 2.7s, the SC was equipped with a 7,000-rpm rev counter.

Luggage Compartment

The new brake servo and fluid reservoir fitted from 1978 reduced the space in the rear area of the front compartment. In 1981, the engine compartment received a light.

Engine

The SC used the Turbo-based 930 2,994cc (182.63-cubic inch) engine that had been developed for the European Carrera 3.0. The extra capacity was achieved by increasing the bore size from 90 millimeters (3.5 inches) to 95 millimeters (3.71inches). Stroke remained at 70.4 millimeters (2.75 inches) although a new crankshaft with larger main and con rod bearings was used. The crankcase was made from die-cast aluminum; whereas, between 1968 and 1977 it had been magnesium. The SC continued the use of Nikasil for the cylinder barrels. Milder camshafts pushed up the maximum torque and improved the engine's flexibility.

The instrument panel of the SC was little changed from the European Carrera 3.0. Points to note are the 380-millimeter steering wheel (which obscured important sections of the speedometer) and the rocker switch for the headlamp washers sited between the speedometer and the clock.

The cooling fan reverted to an 11-blade item that was smaller at 226 millimeters (8.8 inches) than the previous five-blade fan, although it ran at the same 1.8:1 speed. A new capacitor discharge and contactless system was introduced for the ignition. This system can be recognized because the distributor rotor turns anticlockwise. A dual vacuum advance and retard was standard on U.S. cars from 1980.

Camshaft chain noise was reduced by fitting new, taller, black chain guides in five of the six positions. The previous brown guide was still being used in the lower right-hand position. The reliability of the earn drive was improved again in 1980, when a new timing chain tensioner idler arm was introduced to ease the workload

A busy engine compartment on this Californian-specification 1980 911SC, with the air conditioning compressor (and revised condenser coil) on the right. This was the first year the SC was not fitted with an air-injection pump: This was replaced by a sensor that measured the oxygen in the exhaust and was linked to the fuel-injection system.

Rest-of-the-World models retained the air-injection pump, seen here on the left of this 1982 engine compartment. The air filter for the pump can be seen behind it, with a red wing nut on top. After a brief period when a five-blade cooling fan had been used, the SC returned to an 11-blade version. This fan and many of the fittings around the engine have been highly polished, to good effect.

of the tensioner. Porsche studies had found that a proportion of the unexpected tensioner failures had been due to idler arms seizing on their shafts, so the arm was modified to include a wider double bush. The modified arm needed more space to operate in, so the tensioner body itself was slimmed down (but the internal mechanics remained the same). This improved timing chain tensioner reliability, but the engineers still had not eliminated this notorious problem. A once-and-for-all solution was still a few years away.

The front wing oil cooler was revised for most markets in 1980 with the use of a finned brass tube unit that improved heat dissipation. U.S. models retained the older coiled pipe type of cooler until the 1983 models.

The first SCs were fitted with an air-injection pump, which did nothing for access to the left-hand spark plugs. The pump was driven from the crankshaft pulley and was fitted for all markets. Its output was controlled by a diverter valve that vented the pump to the atmosphere in conditions of low-intake vacuum. The continued efforts of the Environmental Protection Agency in the United States also led to the introduction for that market of a new two-way catalytic converter in place of the transverse silencer or muffler. Californian cars continued to require exhaust gas recirculation (EGR). The two-way converter was replaced in 1980 by a three-way unit and, combined with a new oxygen sensor linked to the fuel injection system, eliminated the need for the air-injection pump. The pump was soon dropped on European models as well. A Lambda sensor accurately measured the oxygen content of the exhaust and then adjusted the injection to provide the correct fuel/air mixture to suit the load conditions.

U.S. models also used a simplified fuel evaporative control system, without a line from the charcoal filter to the fan housing. From 1977, engine fumes were piped back from the crankcase directly to the oil tank instead of into the air cleaner as on earlier models. Another pipe connected the oil tank breather to the ribbed throttle housing upstream of the airflow sensor.

The 1980 engines were "optimized," to use the factory's description. The improvements that led to an extra 8-brake horsepower in Rest-of-the-World markets were revised ignition and camshaft timing, a tightening of design tolerances in certain areas of the engine, and an increase in compression ratio to 8.6:1. As well as more power, there was a claimed 10 percent improvement in fuel consumption.

In the United States, power was held at 180-brake horsepower in 1980, but the compression ratio was increased to 9.3:1 and, combined with the ignition timing improvements, the effect was to make the new model American SCs more flexible and lively.

In January 1981, the power deficiency of emissions-equipped SCs widened when Rest-of-the-World cars received yet another output rise. The engine was uprated to 204-brake horsepower, but fuel consumption improved still further. The engine changes were minor on 1982 and 1983 models: The camshaft sprockets were attached to the cams by bolts rather than nuts, and the oxygen sensor was upgraded for U.S. models.

Transmission

The 915 five-speed gearbox became standard for all markets on the introduction of the SC. It differed from the transmission in the Carrera by having even taller ratios, to take advantage of the flatter torque curve, and to benefit emissions by reducing engine speed. A new clutch hub design with a rubber center overcame low-speed gear chatter. This would, in time, prove to be more trouble than it was worth, as the rubber center tended to part with the rest of the clutch. Clutch adjustment was simplified on the SC, and a new transmission mounting for the linkage overcame some reliability problems found with the earlier design.

Sportomatic was now offered only as a special order, but its popularity was waning, and the stick shift semi-automatic was deleted altogether after the 1979 model year.

Electrical Equipment and Lighting

On 1978 U.S. models, a 770-watt alternator charged a single 66-amp/hour battery, but for the 1979 model year the alternator became the 980-watt unit that was already in use on Rest-of-the-World cars. In 1982, the alternator received an integrated voltage regulator, and output went up to 1,050 watts for all markets.

Suspension and Steering

A performance option for the 1978 SC Targa was Bilstein gas shock absorbers, but when these were fitted they tended to accentuate the fact that the Targa had a fairly flexible bodyshell. The following year, in markets where the Bilsteins had been offered as part of a performance package on the Targa, they were replaced by the Boge struts that had been fitted to earlier models.

The 1981 model SCs had slightly stiffened rear suspension with torsion bar size increasing from 23 to 24 millimeters.

Brakes

The big braking change on the SC was the introduction of a Hydrovac servo, lightening the pedal significantly and making the 911 less attractive to those who wore gold medallions around their necks. The attraction of the servo was that it did not make the brakes ultra-light but just assisted them. The improvement was most noticeable around town, especially when the big ventilated disc brakes were cold. The disc diameters were now 287 millimeters (11.2 inches) front and 295 millimeters (11.5 inches) rear, and the cast-iron calipers were the A-type front and the M-type rear.

Wheels and Tires

The standard specification for the SC were the ATS cookie-cutter wheels with Dunlop SP Super tires, sizes being 6Jx15 wheels with 185/70VR tires at the front and 7Jx15 wheels with 215/60VR tires at the rear. The U.K. Sport came with

By 1979, when this car was built, the two-pedal Sportomatic transmission was available only on special order. This novel but halfway house automatic shift was deleted the following year.

The addition of a brake servo was a significant improvement for the 911 SC. Its effect was most noticeable around town when the discs were cold. The bulk of the assembly seriously reduced the usefulness of the luggage compartment.

Weissach models were available in Black Metallic or, as here, Platinum Metallic. The centers of the Fuchs alloy wheels were color-coded to the body.

The paint code plate on the left-hand front door pillar notes the special Platinum Metallic finish of the Weissach model.

16-inch diameter forged-alloy Fuchs wheels with Pirelli P7 tires, sizes being 6J wheels with 205/55VR tires at the front and 7J wheels with 225/50VR tires at the rear. These sizes were an option in other markets. The Fuchs wheels of the 1982 models had highly polished rims with black gloss centers.

Special Editions

The "Martini" model was never actually a mainstream variant of the SC because any 911SC from 1978 could be specified with option number M42, which gave the owner a set of side stripes similar to those first seen on the 1976 British Motor Show 911 Turbo. That car had been a "special," to celebrate the combined victories in the World Manufacturers' Championship (with the 935) and the World Sports Car Championship (with the 936). It was also the fourth season that the factory racing team had been supported by the Italian drinks company Martini and Rossi. The stripes proved so popular on the Motor Show Turbo that they were quickly made available as a factory-fit or retro-fit option, usually on cars in Grand Prix White. The numbers shown in the Production Data table (page 89) refer to cars that had M42 applied at the factory.

A total of 408 Weissach limited-edition models were produced solely for the American market in the 1980 model year. With the option number M439, the standard SC was embellished with special paint. Half were in Black Metallic, and half were in Platinum Metallic. The interior was full leather in Doric Gray with burgundy piping. Otherwise, the specification was similar to a U.K. market Sport model, with a flexible lip added to the front air dam and a whaletail rear spoiler added to the rear.

Bilstein dampers gave a firmer ride, and special Fuchs wheels with Platinum Metallic centers were used irrespective of body color. These wheels were fitted with Pirelli CN36 tires of sizes 185/70VR15 front and 215/60VR15 rear, on 6-inch and 7-inch rims, respectively. Other decorations included a passenger door mirror, electric sunroof, foglights below the front bumper, and an electric aerial with speakers fitted in the doors and on the rear shelf.

The 911SC Ferry Porsche, a special model to celebrate 50 years of the Porsche company, was finished in Meteor (gray with a tint of purple) metallic paint and had a full burgundy leather interior. Other trim was in burgundy/gray striped material with cut-pile velour carpet in burgundy. These models carried a "Ferry Porsche" autograph on the head restraint area of the seat backs and were to a high general specification. The equipment included a rear wiper, an electric aerial, and color-coded 7J and 8J Fuchs wheels using 185/70VR15 and 215/60VR15 tires. A total of 200 were built from the start of the 1982 model year.

Production Changes

August 1977 (Start of K-program)
The 911SC is introduced with a 3-liter 930 engine of 2,994cc (bore 95mm, stroke 70.4mm); valves 49mm inlet, 41.5mm exhaust; ports are 39mm and 35mm, respectively, for all markets; softer cams, new crankshaft with larger main and con rod bearings; die-cast aluminum crankcase; Nikasil barrels; new camshafts; 11-blade 226mm-diameter cooling fan, running at 1.8:1 speed; new capacitor discharge and contactless ignition; runs on 91 RON fuel and all models have air-injection pump; Hydrovac 7in brake servo introduced; front anti-roll bar 20mm, rear 18mm; rear torsion bar now 24mm instead of 23mm; clutch pedal spring assistance improved again; rubber torsion damper in center of clutch reduces transmission noise at low speed; 7,000rpm rev counter fitted; front opening window vents deleted from Targa; in U.K., SC Sport model given following extra front and rear spoilers, 6J front and 7J rear Fuchs wheels with 205/55VR 16 and 225/50VR 16 tires, sports seats, uprated shock absorbers, Porsche stereo with electric aerial; M42 option specified Martini stripes.

August 1978 (Start of L-program)
No major changes from K-program except for colors, fabrics, and carpets. Gear ratios (915/44): first 0.314, second 0.546, third 0793, fourth 1.000, fifth 1.217, reverse 0.301, and final drive 0.571. Sportomatic ratios (925/09 or 12 or 13) first 0A07, second 0.700, third 1.080, reverse 0.553, and final drive 0.296.

August 1979 (Start of new A-series)
Center console becomes standard; new checkerboard Pascha upholstery available; U.K. models have Panasonic stereo and electric aerial as standard; in the United States, many previous options made standard and include air conditioning, power windows, black-look window trim, leather-covered 380mm three-spoke steering wheel; 911SC becomes a 50-state car in U.S. with three-way catalytic converter and Lambda sensor, meaning EGR is shelved; U.S. models go to 9.3:1 compression ratio, vacuum advance, and retard distributors and have a new suction venturi attachment to the oil pump (with mesh filter) to assist oil scavenging in the crankcase; U.S. models have an 85mph speedo; flush-fitting headlamp washers introduced; Sportomatic discontinued; new design of brass tube oil cooler in front wing for RoW, but U.S. models keep serpentine-type cooler; automatic light for engine compartment; clutch pedal pressure reduced (improved mechanism); new timing chain idler arm and slimmer body to sealed tensioner unit, and all models receive stiffer lower valve covers with horizontal double ribs; longer fifth gear (from 1.217 to 1.273) in gearbox (becomes 915/62) for RoW models; cylinder head inlet port size drops to 34mm, exhaust to 35mm (all models); special model finished in

U.K. Sport specification, seen on Peter Foskett's 1982 911SC, included front spoiler chin extension, whaletail rear spoiler, Bilstein gas dampers, 16-inch alloy wheels, Pirelli P7 low-profile tires, and sports seats.

The introduction of the SC was marked by a new flat-profile script for the model designation. For the first time since the 911's launch, the script adopted the European style of writing the number 1, with a peak.

This factory label shows that the 911SC was comfortably within Californian emissions limits for hydrocarbons, carbon monoxide, and oxides of nitrogen.

Identification

Model year	Model	Engine	Gearbox	Chassis numbers	Engine numbers
K-program					
1978	911SC	930/03	915/44	9118300001–9118302438	6380001 onward
	911SC Targa	930/03	915/44	9118310001–9118311729	6380001 onward
	911SC U.S. 49	930/04	915/61	9118200001–9118202436	6280001 onward
	911SC Cal	930/06	915/61	9118200001–9118202436	6580001 onward
	911SC U.S. 49 Targa	930/04	915/61	9118210001–9118212579	6280001 onward
	911SC Cal Targa	930/06	915/61	9118200001–9118212579	6580001 onward
	911SC Japan	930/05	915/15	9118309501–9118309804	6180001 onward
L-program					
1979	911SC	930/03	915/62	9119300001–91J9303318	6390001 onward
	911SC Targa	930/03	915/62	9119310001–9119311874	6390001 onward
	911SC U.S. 49	930/03	915/63	9119200001–9119202013	6290001 onward
	911SC Cal	930/06	915/63	9119200001–9119202013	6590001 onward
	911SC U.S. 49 Targa	930/04	915/63	9119210001–9119211965	6290001 onward
	911SC Cal Targa	930/06	915/63	9119210001–9119211965	6590001 onward
	911SC Japan	930/05	915/63	9119309501–9119309873	6190001 onward
A-series					
1980	911SC	930/09	915/62	91A0130001–91A0134831	6300001 onward
	911SC U.S.	930/07	915/63	91A0140001–91A0144272	6300001 onward
	911SC Japan	930/08	915/63	91A0130001–91 A0134831	6308001 onward
B-series					
1981	911SC	930/10	915/62	WPOZZZ91 ZBS 100001–3181	6310001 onward
	911SC Targa	930/10	915/62	WPOZZZ91ZBS140001–1703	6310001 onward
	911SC U.S.	930/16	915/63	WPOAA091 BS 12000 1–1573	6410001 onward
	911SC U.S. Targa	930/16	915/63	WPOEA091 BS 16000 1–1407	6410001 onward
	911SC Japan	930/17	930/63	WPOZZZ91ZBS129500–9622	6318001 onward
	911SC Japan Targa	930/17	930/63	WPOZZZ91ZBS169500–9510	6318001 onward
C-series					
1982	911SC	930/10	915/62	WPOZZZ91ZCS 1 00001–3307	63C0001 onward
	911SC Targa	930/10	915/62	WPOZZZ91ZCS140001–1737	63C0001 onward
	911SC U.S.	930/16	915/63	WPOAA091 CS 120001–2457	64C0001 onward
	911SC U.S. Targa	930/16	915/63	WPOEA091CS160001–2426	64C0001 onward
	911SC Japan	930/17	915/63	WPOZZZ91 ZCS1 09501–9628	63C8001 onward
	911SC Japan Targa	930/17	915/63	WPOZZZ91 ZCS149501–9562	63C8001 onward
D-series					
1983	911SC	930/10	915/62	WPOZZZ91Z0S100001–2995	6300001 onward
	911SC Targa	930/10	915/62	WPOZZZ91Z0S140001–1258	6300001 onward
	911SC Cabriolet	930/10	915/62	WPOZZZ91Z0S 150001–2406	6300001 onward
	911SC U.S.	930/16	915/63	WPOAA091 0S 120001–2559	6400001 onward
	911SC U.S. Targa	930/16	915/63	WPOEA0910S160001–1430	6400001 onward
	911SC Cabriolet	930/16	915/63	WPOEA0910S170001–1718	6400001 onward
	911SC Japan	930/17	915/63	WPOZZZ91 ZDS 109501–9645	6308001 onward
	911SC Japan Targa	930/17	915/63	WPOZZZ91 Z0S 149501–9562	6308001 onward

General notes

Chassis numbering The 1980 chassis numbers had a new 10-digit formula: The first two digits were the model type, the third is the model year (A is 1980, B is 1981, and so on), the fourth is the plant code (0 is nondescriptive on 1980-only models), the fifth is the last digit of the model type (1 for 911, 0 for 930), the sixth is the engine code number (e.g., 3 for RoW 3-liter, 4 for U.S. 4-liter, 7 for 930 RoW 3.3-liter, and so on), and the last four digits were the build number. For the 1981 model year, the 17-digit VIN system was started. For instance, consider WPOZZZ91ZBS100001: WPO is the world make code. ZZZ is the U.S. VSD code, 91 are the first two digits of the model number (911), Z is a test number, B refers to the model year (B = 1981), S refers to the plant code (for Stuttgart), the next digit is the third of the model type (911) followed by the body code number, the last four digits are the build number. Model years are identified as follows: A 1980, B 1981, C 1982, D 1983, E 1984, F 1985, G 1986, H 1987, J 1988, K 1989, L 1990, M 1991, N 1992, P 1993 (note no O), R 1994, and so on.

1980 models For this model year, coupes and Targas shared the same chassis number series but defined between RoW (including Japan) and the United States.

U.S. specification For 1978–1979, U.S. specification models are divided into 49-state cars (U.S. 49 above) and California cars (Cal above). For 1980, there was just a single U.S. specification. For 1981–1983, cars for Canada also shared U.S. specification.

Japanese specification Japan had its own engine type with specific exhaust emissions equipment: 1978–1979, 930/05; 1980, 930/08; 1981–1983, 930/17.

Sportomatic Engine codes for this transmission were as follows: for 1978–1979, RoW 930/13, U.S. 930/14, Japan 930/15; for 1980, engine was always 930/19; a 9 as the fourth digit of the engine number denotes special mountings for the Sportomatic. Gearbox type was 925/16. Not listed after 1980.

pewter metallic paint with Doric Gray leather interior and russet cut pile carpets, known in U.S. as the Weissach special edition, and receives whaletail and extension spoiler at front, sport dampers, etc.; alarm is offered for first time as a special option.

August 1980 (Start of B-series)

New Berber tweed upholstery, rear seats cloth-fronted; double-peak domed pistons raise compression ratio to 9.8:1 on RoW models, power rises to 204bhp, torque unchanged; Bosch K-Jetronic fuel injection improved (capsule valve for better snap throttle opening and new cold start injector spray added to airbox); nonadjustable fuel distributor on U.S. models, with improved cold running mixture control; now uses 97 RON fuel (not 91 RON) and braided fuel lines replaced by seamless steel tubes; gearing raised slightly in fifth (0796 from 0.821); improved diaphragm springs fitted to clutch; side repeater flashers on front wings; improved sports seats optional; anti-corrosion warranty increased to seven years; 915 transmission casing now pressure die-cast in aluminum; U.S. models' anti-roll bars now 20mm front, 18mm rear.

August 1981 (Start of C-series)

Special Ferry Porsche model finished in Meteor Metallic (gray with a tint of purple) with burgundy leather, burgundy/gray striped material, and cut pile velour carpet in burgundy; camshaft sprockets fastened with a hex bolt instead of a hex nut; alternator has integrated voltage regulation and rises to 1,050W output; options include the front and rear (tea-tray) spoilers of the 911 Turbo.

August 1982 (Start of D-series)

The 911 Cabriolet introduced (experimental Studie 4WD Cabrio shown at Frankfurt in September 1981, European launch in March 1982 Geneva Salon), stiffened bodyshell allowing first true open 911; new range of colors and cloths; from April 1983, a new stiffer crankcase was used with deleted sump plate and screen and quieter silencer (muffler); heater's manual control deleted; 160mph speedometer standard in all models: lap and diagonal seat belts could be fitted to rear seats; four speakers standard; U.S., Canadian, and Japanese models had revised acceleration enrichment controls, an improved Lambda sensor, and the brass tube oil cooler first fitted to RoW models from September 1979; interesting new options include an electrically heated windshield with graduated tint, Blaupunkt Monterey stereo, 16in wheels with 6in front and 7in rear rims (to take 205 and 225 tires, respectively).

Dimensions

Wheelbase
2,271mm

Track (front/rear)
1,369mm/1,379mm (with standard tires)

Length
4,291mm

Width
1,626mm

Options

Refer to the list of options presented at the end of the chapter on the Carrera 3.2 (see page 100). From 1982 the M numbers were shown on the vehicle identification label (VIL).

Color Schemes

1978

Standard body colors

Guards Red (027), Talbot Yellow (1 06), Continental Orange (107), Apple Green (260), Oak Green Metallic (265), Fern Green (273), Olive Green (274), Light Green Metallic (275), Minerva Blue Metallic (304), Arrow Blue (305), Petrol Blue Metallic (376), Bitter Chocolate (408), Copper Brown Metallic (443),

Production Data

Model year	Model	Power (bhp DIN@rpm)	Torque (Nm@rpm)	Compression ratio	Weight (kg)	Number built
1978	911SC	180@5,500	265@4200	8.5: 1	1,160	2,438
	911SC Targa	180@5,500	265@4,200	8.5:1	1,210	1,729
	911SC U.S.	180@5,500	237@4,200	8.5:1	1,190	2,436
	911SC U.S. Targa	180@5,500	237@4,200	8.5:1	1,240	2,579
	911SC Japan	180@5,500	237@4,200	8.5:1	1,190	304
1979	911SC	180@5,500	265@4,200	8.5:1	1,160	3,319
	911SC Targa	180@5,500	265@4,200	8.5:1	1,210	3,319
	911SC U.S.	180@5,500	237@4,200	8.5:1	1,190	2,013
	911SC U.S. Targa	180@5,500	237@4,200	8.5:1	1,240	1,965
	911SC Japan	180@5,500	237@4,200	8.5:1	1,190	373
1980	911SC	188@5,500	265@4,200	8.6:1	1,160	4,831
	911SC U.S.	180@5,500	244@4,200	9.3:1	1,190	4,272
	911SC Weissach U.S.	180@5500	244@4,200	9.3:1	1,250	408
1981	911SC	204@5,900	267@4,300	9.8:1	1,160	3,181
	911SC Targa	204@5,900	267@4,300	9.8:1	1,210	1,703
	911SC U.S.	180@5,500	244@4,200	9.3:1	1,190	1,573
	911SC U.S. Targa	180@5,500	244@4,200	9.3:1	1,240	1,407
	911SC Japan	180@5,500	244@4,200	9.3:1	1,190	132
1982	911SC	204@5,900	267@4,300	9.8:1	1,160	3,307
	911SC Targa	204@5,900	267@4,300	9.8:1	1,210	1,737
	911SC U.S.	180@5,500	244@4,200	9.3:1	1,190	2,457
	911SC U.S. Targa	180@5,500	244@4,200	9.3:1	1,240	2,426
	911SC Japan	180@5,500	244@4,200	9.3:1	1,190	190
	Slant-Nose	180@5,500	244@4,200	9.3:1	1,250	4
1983	911SC	204@5,900	267@4,300	9.8:1	1,160	2,995
	911SC Targa	204@5,900	267@4,300	9.8:1	1,210	1,258
	911SC Cabriolet	204@5,900	267@4,300	9.8:1	1,210	2,406
	911SC U.S.	180@5,500	244@4,200	9.3:1	1,190	2,559
	911SC U.S. Targa	180@5,500	244@4,200	9.3:1	1,240	1,430
	911SC U.S. Cabriolet	180@5,500	244@4,200	9.3:1	1,240	1,781
	911SC Japan	180@5,500	244@4,200	9.3:1	1,190	207
	Slant-Nose	180@5,500	244@4200	9.3: 1	1,250	1

General note
Weights are DIN curb weights, but use as a guide only because some are ex-factory (no options) and some are fully equipped.

Numbered notes
The Weissach was option number M439 (see page 86). Slant-Nose models refer to stock 911SCs customized in the *Sonderwunsch* (Restoration) Department and later to become part of the Porsche Exclusive program. The 1982–1983 Slant-Nose cars had headlights housed in front spoiler; pop-up lights started to appear in 1983.

Mocha Brown (451), Cashmire Beige (502), Black (700), Grand Prix White (908), Silver Metallic (936).

Fabrics
Leatherette (999.551.012.40) in Lobster (8AU), Cork (5AU), or Black (7 AU); light basketweave leatherette (999.551009.40) in Lobster (8AT), Cork (SAT), or Black (7 AT); leather (999.551.073.40) in Lobster (8AH), Cork (5AH), Black (7AG), Blue (3AG), Yellow (IAG), Light Green (2AP), Light Red (8AT), or White (9AG); pinstripe velour (999551.039.40) in Lobster with black stripe (8AK), Cork with black stripe (5AK), or Black with white stripe (7 AK); tartan dress (999.551.08340) in Beige (4AD), Green (2AC), or Red (8AB).

Carpets
Velour pile (999.551.092.40) in Lobster (8AB), Cork (5AZ), Black (7AZ), Yellow (1AY), or Light Red (8AZ).

1979
Standard body colors
Guards Red (027), Talbot Yellow (106), Oak Green Metallic (265), Olive Green (274), Light Green Metallic (275), Light Blue Metallic (30T), Minerva Blue Metallic (304), Arrow Blue (305), Petrol Blue Metallic (376), Bitter Chocolate (408), Copper Brown Metallic (443), Moccha Brown (451), Casablanca Beige Metallic (Opal, 463), Tobacco Metallic (464), Cashmire Beige (502), Lilac (Flieder, 601), Black (700), Black Metallic (708), Grand Prix White (908), Silver Metallic (936).

Fabrics
Leatherette (BSP) in Brown (40A), Cork (5AU), or Black (7 AU); light basketweave leatherette (999551009.40) in Brown (4AT), Cork (SAT), or Black (7AT); leather in Blue (3AG), Brown (40A), Dark Green (20B), Yellow (1AG), Light Red (8AT), Cork (5AH), Black (7AG), or White (9AG); pinstripe velour colors as in 1978.

Carpets
Cut-pile velour (999.551.098.40) in Brown (4AC), Dark Green (2AC) Yellow (IAC), Light Red (8AC), Cork (5AC), or Black (7 AC).

1980
Standard body colors as in 1979 models.
Fabrics
Leatherette in Beige (50 B), Brown (40A), or Blue (30B); leather (EHS) in Beige (50B), Brown (40A), Dark Blue (30B), Blue (30A), Dark Green (20B), Yellow (10A), Cork (40D), Light Red (80B), Black (70A), or White (99A); checkerboard velour (TPB) in Beige/Brown (54A), Blue/Black (37A), Brown/Black (47A), or Gray/Black (67A); tartan dress fabrics as 1978.

Carpets
Cut-pile velour (TFK) in Beige (50B), Brown (40E), Dark Blue (30B), Dark Green (20E), Yellow (10A), Cork (41D), Red (80B), or Black (70E).

1981
Standard body colors
Guards Red (027), Chiffon White (182), Mint Green (20A), Moss Green Metallic (20C), Light Blue Metallic (30T), Pacific Blue Metallic (31G), Minerva Blue Metallic (304), Arrow Blue (305), Mocha Brown (451), Rosewood Metallic (474), Bamboo (523), Caramel (524), Platinum Metallic (for special, 055), Black (700), Black Metallic (708), Wine Red Metallic (895), Grand Prix White (908), Zinc Metallic (956).

Fabrics
Leatherette (BPE) in Beige (50B), Brown (40A), Blue (30B), or Black (70A); leather (EHS) in Beige (50 B), Brown (40A), Dark Blue (30B), Red (80S), Hannibal Gray (60S), Papyrus White (95S), Mint Green (20S), Black (70A), or Doric Gray (for special, 6AD); checkerboard velour (TPB) in Beige/Brown (54A), Blue/Black (37A), or Gray/Black (67A); textured cloth (TPU) in Beige (50C), Blue (30C), or Black (70F); Berber tweed (TPB 000 000 00 plus code) in Beige (54B), Blue/Black (37B), or Gray/Black (67B).

Carpets
Cut pile velour (TFK) in Beige (50B), Brown (40E), Dark Blue (30B), Mint Green (20S), Black (70E), or Russet (for special, 8AY).

1982
Standard body colors
As in 1981 models but Platinum Metallic (655) now available for all models, plus special model in Meteor Metallic (961).
Fabrics
Leatherette (BPE) in Beige (50B), Brown (87S), Blue (30B), or Black (43S); leather (EHS) in Beige (50B), Brown (3NG), Dark Blue (30B), Red (80S), Hannibal Gray (60S), Papyrus White (95S), Mint Green (20S), Black (1AJ), or Burgundy (for special, 2LB); checkerboard velour, textured cloth, and Berber tweeds as in 1981 models; special model burgundy/gray stripe design (TPC).

Carpets
As in 1981 models, plus cut-pile velour Burgundy (TKF) for special model.

1983
Standard body colors
Guards Red (027), Moss Green Metallic (20C), Glacier Blue (32Z), Pewter Metallic (655), Slate Blue Metallic (661), Quartz Gray Metallic (662), Black (700), Ruby Red Metallic (810), Kiln Red Metallic (811), Grand Prix White (908), Zinc Metallic (956), Light Bronze Metallic (966), Chiffon White (182).

Fabrics
Leatherette (BSP) in Burgundy (3MK), Brown (87S), Blue (30B), or Black (43S); leather (EHS) in Burgundy (7LD), Gray Beige (6FL), Brown (3NG), Black (IAJ), Blue (30B), Red (80S), Pearl White (8YD), Dark Green (6JD), or Champagne (1VD); cloths with wavy stitch pattern (TPU) in Brown (7NU), Blue (30C), Black (70F), Gray Beige (8FU), or Burgundy (5MU); Berber tweeds (TPE) in Beige/Brown (54B), Blue/Black (37B), Gray/Black (67B), Burgundy/Gray (6LB), or Gray-Beige/ Gray (1FB); checkerboard velour (TPB) in Light Gray/Black (4FH), Brown/Gray (5RH), Blue/Gray (7GH), or Burgundy/ Gray (9LH)

Carpets
Cut-pile velour (TFK) in Light Gray (60A), Brown (40E), Dark Blue (30B), Dark Green (6JD), Black (70E), Gray/Beige (2FL), Red (80S), Burgundy (80E), or Champagne (1VD).

Chapter 6

The Carrera 3.2 (1984–1989)

Andy Frost's 1985 model year 3.2 Carrera in Guards Red, probably the most popular Porsche color of the 1980s, shows off the controversial "telephone dial" wheels that were the standard fitting until the 1988 model year.

The late 1970s had seen Porsche shrug off doubts that such a small firm could profitably run three separate and very different product lines for the 911, the 924, and the 928. The company was coming back strongly from yet another world oil crisis and, once again, the racing team was winning, this time with the 911-derived 935. By 1983, the new 956 Group C endurance racing car, also using an engine derived from the 911's flat-six, had won Le Mans at its first attempt. Through the 1980s and into the 1990s the 956 and its derivative, the 962, would become the most successful racing car family ever, still winning 12 years later.

Evolution Outline

August 1983: The Carrera 3.2 (207-brake horsepower U.S., 231-brake horsepower Rest-of-the-World) replaces 911SC, and the engine is increased in size to 3.2-liters with Motronic engine management.

August 1985: A new dashboard with larger side window and central vents is introduced and the Turbo-Look model launched.

August 1986: A G50 five-speed gearbox with hydraulic clutch operation is introduced, U.S. engines are remapped for 217-brake horsepower, and the unique Australian Carrera (207-brake horsepower) is introduced.

August 1987: Telephone dial wheels are replaced by Fuchs forged alloys.

September 1987: The Speedster Club Sport is displayed at the Frankfurt Show.

August 1988: The Celebration 911 limited edition is introduced.

January 1989: The Speedster limited edition is introduced.

Success on the track combined with the ever broadening appeal of the 911—there were now three body styles with the Coupe, the Targa, and the new Cabriolet—would lead to Porsche's best ever trading years in the mid-1980s. But it was a time when the company's followers realized that development was slowing. In order to increase production volumes ever higher, engineering staff worked on factory problems as a top priority, and there was relatively little forward thinking about what new models would be required by the end of the decade. Was it a question of make money now and tomorrow would look after itself?

If life at Porsche to the outsider still seemed good early in the decade, inside all was not well. CEO Dr. Ernst Fuhrmann was apparently happy to accept a waiting list that stretched to more than a year on the basis that exclusivity was still important. It was his view that the 911 was finished and that the future lay with the new 924 and 928 models. Production of 911s had eased from some 45 911SCs per day at Zuffenhausen through 1981, but Fuhrmann's strategy to phase out the 911 and replace it with the 928 was stalling because the 18-year-old 911 was outselling the V-8-engined car two to one. It was clear that stopping development of the 911 was out of the question.

Fuhrmann's reluctance to accept that the 911 was still needed in part led to his early retirement at the end of 1981. He would make way for new blood, something that was seen by the Porsche and Piech families as the only way to revive falling 924 and 928 sales and save the 911. Only the 911 was selling steadily, and that was not enough. A successor had to be found.

Outsiders would have gone for Ferdinand Piech, the brilliant manager who had led the development of the 911 up to the 2.4-liter versions and had been controversially responsible for developing the prototype racers of the late 1960s and early 1970s. By 1980, he was head of engineering at VW-Audi, where he had led Quattro development. With hindsight he would have been absolutely the right choice for Porsche's new boss, but internal politics got in the way. Piech was part of the family, and the family had stepped out of the day-to-day running in 1972. They blocked his election and chose Peter Schutz, a German-American headhunter from a German subsidiary of Caterpillar, the truck maker.

Schutz brought a pure market-led management style to Porsche, in contrast to the technology-driven style of his predecessors. For the 911 and for Porsche, this

The 1987 Carrera Club Sport was about 50 kilograms lighter than the standard Carrera. Combined with a new engine management chip, this lightness gave slightly better performance. This is photographer John Colley's own car.

Martini stripes (option M42) on a Grand Prix White 911 made a bold statement about the owner's enthusiasm for the company's racing successes. It was possible to specify the "Turbo-Look" for the Cabriolet version as a special order from 1984.

The Turbo-Look (top) became a standard Carrera model from 1985. This is Terry Davison's 1987 example. Note the Turbo tea-tray rear spoiler, with its deep underside. The 1989 Speedster (above)—this one is owned by Mike Flannery—offered open-air 911 motoring in a leaner form. The most obvious difference from the standard Cabriolet is the lower line of the hood, resulting in changes to the windshield and side windows. The absence of a model designation was a no-cost option.

would have excellent short-term business results as volumes started to climb steadily through the first half of the 1980s. Schutz threw all the profits into upgrading the production facilities, and volumes hit all-time highs. The improvement in production efficiency was desperately needed, but more of the profit should have been spent on development and some of it was wasted on, for instance, over-lavish improvements of staff facilities. Moreover, one of the company's cornerstones of success, exclusivity, was being undermined in a dash for increased volume.

Enthusiast customers, who still made up the core of Porsche business, noted that Porsche's attitude seemed to be to get away with the minimal amount of development needed to justify ever-rising prices. Improvements to the 911 slowed because the engineers were occupied with the limited-edition 959 project or were being seconded to production to keep the lines running. But those production lines were producing 911s at a rate never seen before. In 1985, the peak year, some 21,000 of the new 3.2 Carreras were made.

The 911 was now selling to a new type of customer who wanted a Porsche just for its image and who could not care less about anti-roll bar stiffness or maximum torque figures. What the factory could not—or would not—see was that the new breed of customer was fickle. In time, the "yuppie" tag was virtually to destroy that all-important image of sporting purity and exclusivity.

But back in 1982, in his first year as chairman of Porsche, Schutz immediately set about giving the 911 a boost. He approved the Cabriolet's development, but a four-wheel-drive proposal was made a low priority in deference to an agreement between Porsche and VW-Audi (which was developing the Quattro at the same time). Most important, Schutz set in motion the engineering work that would lead to the replacement for the 911SC—the 3.2 Carrera—in late 1983. He also realized that the 911 would need a facelift to improve its aerodynamics, but that work was not approved until much later.

The first public sign of the new development effort was a special 3.3-liter SC that the factory press department used in 1982. But as far back as 1976, 3.5-liter engines had been tested by the engineers at Weissach and subsequently used by development head Helmut Bott as personal transport. The experience was broadened in racing from 1979 when the twin turbo 935 had a capacity of 3,164cc, the same as the subsequent production Carrera of 1984.

The revised model was targeted for launch in September 1983 and brought back the hard-worked Carrera name, surrendering again the exclusivity of that title for marketing expediency. The marketing men had come to appreciate the cachet of the name with the 2.7-liter and 3-liter models of the 1970s. The new 1984 model Carrera came out with 3.2 liters, and its engine was the most impressive development on the new 911.

Bodyshell

There were no major changes in the bodyshell for the 3.2 Carrera, save for detail revisions to improve manufacturing efficiency. This enabled an easy transition of the three bodyshell types—Coupe, Targa, and Cabriolet—to the new Carrera specification. The optional Turbo-Look Coupe and Targa followed for 1985.

The guarantee against rust perforation was extended to 10 years for 1986. The Cabrio received the long-awaited power hood in September 1986, for the 1987 model year. The operation of this hood was fully automatic, with two small electric motors in the windshield frame locking the front of the hood into place.

The introduction of a larger clutch in 1987 meant that the pick-up points for the rear semi-trailing arms had to be repositioned. This was achieved using a new torsion bar tube, with a profiled cast-iron center section to clear the clutch housing.

Three major new developments of the 911 theme became available during the life of the 3.2 Carrera. These were the Turbo Look, Club Sport, and the Speedster models, all of which are described later in this chapter (see pages 97–99).

Body Trim and Fittings

The new model received a new front spoiler with integrated foglamps and was identified by the word "Carrera" in script on the engine cover. The new Carrera Targa was given the better-fitting weather seals (with rain channels) for 1987 that had been developed for the Cabrio, to reduce high-speed wind noise. Heater output on all models was improved not only by a new heat exchanger design and a larger main fan, but also by booster fans at each side of the dashboard where the air was drawn from the sills. The air conditioning pump, driven from the end of the crankshaft, was uprated and ran faster.

For the 1985 model year, the radio aerial, previously electrically operated and fitted to the front wing, became integrated into the windshield and central locking became an option. But if you preferred a conventional aerial, you could separately specify a graduated tint to the top of the windshield or a Securiflex laminated type. The windshield washers were more powerful and were heated. For 1986, central locking became standard, while for 1987 the single rear foglamp was joined by another. Both were integrated into the reflective strip between the taillights. The reversing lights were also integrated into the strip. From September 1987, the passenger door mirror (already standard on the Cabrio) and headlight washers became standard.

Incidentally, in 1987 the Sport package was renamed in the U.K., and cars became known as the 911 with Sport Equipment (to complement the Turbo

Telephone dial wheels were one feature of Porsche's attempt to update the Carrera 3.2's appearance without excessive cost. Another external difference was that the front driving lights became more integrated into the shape of the front spoiler.

An enduring feature of the 911 has been that customers could always buy a car that was not covered in aerodynamic hardware. The Carrera script on the engine lid returned to its original style.

The Cabriolet hood stowed neatly under a tonneau. On the Cabriolet the folding rear seats were smaller in order to make room for the hood.

By 1987, the original black fabric of the Cabriolet hood was supported by Mahogany, Blue, Burgundy, or Gray-Green, depending on body color.

The pinstripe style is one of Porsche's best interiors, being both practical and smart. New features for the 1985 model year, one year after the Carrera 3.2's introduction, included a four-spoke steering wheel, taller seat backrests, and seat release catches on both sides of the backrests.

The ventilation system was improved again for the 1986 model year, with larger face level and side window vents. The headlamp level adjustment was introduced for 1987. The nonstandard slot next to the sunroof rocker switch is the keyhole for an aftermarket engine immobilizer.

The seats on the Carrera 3.2 have electric adjustment for height, cushion angle, and recline, with this control panel set on the side of the cushion.

Look or SE). As well as the ubiquitous rear spoiler and front spoiler extension, there were Bilstein shock absorbers and 16-inch forged-alloy wheels with black centers with 205/55 front tires on 6J wheels and 225/55 rear tires on 7J wheels. By this stage sports seats were no longer part of the package.

From September 1988, an alarm system was linked to the operation of the central locking circuit and the tempostat heating control system was improved.

Interior Trim

Leather was a standard fit on the well-equipped U.S. models from 1984. Sport option cars still had special seats with height adjustment, this feature being a no-cost option on the standard cars.

For 1985, there was a new leather steering wheel with four horizontal spokes. The first electrically operated seats were offered with new switches for height/squab angle and recline. The seat belt buckles were now on the seats themselves and the backrest release catches were fitted on both sides of the seats for the first time. Seat heating was an option. The new seats are identified by the headrests being 40 millimeters (1.6 inches) taller than those on the earlier seats. For 1985 and 1986, there were successive reductions in gear lever travel of 10 percent, to make the 911's gear change more contemporary in feel. Electric height adjustment was an option on sports seats from the 1986 model year, this feature becoming standard for 1988 (with lumbar adjustment as well). Electric operation became standard on the passenger seat for 1988.

A wider selection of materials was presented for the 1984 model year and extended in 1985. These are listed in the Color Schemes section at the end of this chapter (page 101).

The interior was changed in detail for the 1986 model year, particularly the seats. The front seats were lowered by 20 millimeters (0.8 inch) and given extra front-to-back travel. Heating control was improved, and a new temperature sensor was mounted on top of the dash instead of between the sun visors. The switchgear was revised, and the sun visors were given covered vanity mirrors.

The 25th Anniversary Carreras had special Recaro seats with Dr. Porsche's signature monogrammed into the head restraints.

Dashboard and Instruments

There were only detail changes from the 911SC to the Carrera in 1984, one being the addition of a brake pad wear indicator. In 1986, a new dash panel had larger and restyled fresh-air vents, and there were new switches and better heat regulation. For 1987, headlamp beam height could be adjusted from the dashboard.

Luggage Compartment

The luggage capacity of a Cabrio could be improved by replacing the rear seats with optional lockers, which also added to security when the hood was down. The fuel tank increased in size from 80 liters (17.60 Imperial gallons, 21.14 U.S. gallons) to 85 liters (18.70 Imperial gallons, 22.46 U.S. gallons) for 1985, and for 1986 the luggage area carpets were color-coded to match the interior carpets.

Engine

The 3.2-liter production engine was claimed to be 80 percent new, although its basis was still the proven 3-liter assembly, coded 930/20 for Rest-of-the-World models or 930/21 for the United States, Canada, and Japan. It used the 95-millimeter (3.71-inch) Nikasil barrels from the SC and the 74.4-millimeter (2.90-inch) stroke crankshaft from the Turbo, giving a displacement of 3,164cc (193.0 cubic inches). The core engine parts were the same for all markets, only the compression ratio and the emissions devices varying. Porsche was moving toward one model for all its markets.

For Rest-of-the-World markets, the compression ratio rose from 9.8:1 to 10.3:1 by using higher crowns to the new forged pistons and a lower roof height for the combustion chamber. The compression ratio was 9.5:1 for the United States, Canada, and Japan. Valves were unchanged from the 911SC, but there were larger port diameters of 40 millimeters (1.56 inches) inlet and 38 millimeters (1.48 inches) exhaust, and cam timing was revised. Fuel remained 93 RON for Rest-of-the-World models or lead-free 91 RON for catalyzed versions. As on the Turbo, no head gasket was used.

Digital Motor Electronics came to the 911 for the 1984 model year, improving performance and reducing fuel consumption by 10 percent.

The new 911 Carrera Rest-of-the-World engine's specific power figure of 73-brake horsepower per liter was the highest since the 2.7 Carrera RS's 78.2 brake horsepower per liter. Overall output was 231-brake horsepower at 5,900 rpm, with maximum torque of 284 Nm at 4,800rpm. The trade-off for the catalyzed engine with its lower compression ratio was 207-brake horsepower at 5,900 rpm and maximum torque of 260 Nm at 4,800 rpm. Australia, Sweden, and Switzerland had special engines tuned for low hydrocarbon emissions and low noise.

For the first time on a 911, the ignition, fuel, and ambient engine parameters were mapped using a microprocessor control unit. The system also measured engine temperature from a ceramic sensor fitted within the cylinder head. This Digital Motor Electronics (DME or Motronic 2) system was the main reason for power increasing on the 3.2 Carreras, in tandem with a 10 percent improvement in fuel consumption. This was due in some part to the over-run fuel cut-off, improved cold starting, and better cold start stabilization.

The fuel-injection system was now termed by Bosch as LE-Jetronic rather than the previous K-Jetronic. The inlet manifold pipework was redesigned to provide charge-boosting resonance to improve the fuel air dynamics. The Motronic system also provided protection against over-revving by cutting the fuel injection at precisely 6,520 rpm, removing the need for a mechanical device in the distributor. Other features of the engine were a more stable idle response to accessory loads and over-run fuel cut-off above 1,200 rpm. No air injection pump was required, and the engine compartment seemed much less cluttered without it.

New heat exchangers (with silencer or muffler) had larger pipework and more efficient silencing. To reduce heat loss, the exchangers were given double-skinned construction. The 930/21 engine for U.S., Canadian, and Japanese engines was fitted with an improved Lambda sensor and a three-way catalytic converter.

The 3.2 engines were the first to be fitted with the "mother of all chain-tensioners," the engine oil-fed hydraulic type. These new tensioners effectively closed the story on the 911's famous weakness. The feed pipes to the tensioners were taken off the external oil supply pipes to each cylinder head bank.

The underside of a Club Sport reveals the Getrag-built G50 gearbox that was introduced for the 1987 model year. The new gearbox offered the durability needed to cope with the engine's increasing torque. Timing chain tensioners had always been a weak point in the reliability of the 911 engine. The new Carrera 3.2 received a new design that used engine oil to maintain hydraulic pressure on the timing chain idler. The new tensioners could be recognized from the outside by the small feed pipes branching from the cylinder head oil supply.

For the 1986 model year, the major engine and transmission parts were guaranteed for five years or 50,000 miles; this will not bother any readers of this book, but it shows Porsche's confidence in the powertrain's reliability. Emissions-equipped models received an upgrade in 1987, when the engine (930/25) was remapped and 95 RON fuel was specified, taking power up to 217-brake horsepower at 5,900 rpm and torque to 265 Nm at 4,800-brake horsepower. A policy statement at the start of the 1987 model year said that all new models would offer the same power whether or not they were catalyzed. By September 1987, 85 percent of new Porsches were delivered with catalytic converters as standard.

Transmission

The decision not to make the new Carrera engine 3.3 liters, which could have been achieved simply by using the Turbo's barrels as well as its crankshaft, was due to the torque limitations of the 915 gearbox. The transmission's durability was extended by fitting a gearbox oil pump and circulating hot oil through a tube-type cooler mounted beside the casing.

For the 3.2 Carrera, fourth and fifth gears were lengthened, becoming 0.966:1 (28:29) and 0.763:1 (29:38), respectively, with a crown wheel/pinion ratio of 8:31. U.S. models used a shorter fifth gear of 0.790:1 (30:38).

In 1987, the 915 was replaced by the Getrag-built G50 five-speed gearbox, with its Borg Warner synchromesh system. The G50 is easily distinguished from the 915 because reverse is to the left and away; whereas, on the older gearbox it was to the right and back. The gear lever was revised, becoming more slender. The main reason for the change was that the 915 gearbox was expensive compared to other units, especially now that it needed its own oil cooling system. The G50 gearbox used on the 3.2 Carrera had a maximum torque capacity of 300 Nm and did not need separate oil cooling. The clutch was enlarged to the 240-millimeter (9.4-inch) size of the Turbo and still used the large rubber damper at its center. The clutch was now hydraulically operated, which made for less tiring operation.

Electrical Equipment and Lighting

The 1984 models were fitted with a larger 92A/1,260-watt alternator with additional cooling guides at its center. A central rear stoplight came to U.S. models in 1986: It started at the top of the window, found a new home at the lower edge in 1987, and returned to the top again in 1988. Rear foglights were integrated into the reflective strip with the reversing lights in 1987. The quartz halogen headlamp power remained a total of 110-watt dipped and 120-watt main beam, but at last the U.S. cars received headlamps that looked like those fitted to the rest of the world's 911s. For some markets, integrated front foglights were fitted below the front bumper line.

Suspension and Steering

The new Carrera carried over the suspension of the outgoing SC, but Boge's new gas dampers became the standard fitting from 1985.

The 1986 models had stiffer anti-roll bars, diameter increasing from 20 millimeters to 22 millimeters at the front and from 18 millimeters to 21 millimeters at the rear. The shock absorbers were uprated, and the rear torsion bars increased in diameter from 24 millimeters to 25 millimeters.

With the introduction of the G50 gearbox, the rear torsion bar tube had to be revised to clear the larger clutch bell housing. The new cast-iron support for the semi-trailing arms used the Turbo's geometry, incorporating anti-squat characteristics.

Brakes

The 304-millimeter (11.8-inch) diameter front brake discs on the 1984 Carrera increased in thickness from 20.5 millimeters (0.80 inch) to 24 millimeters (0.94 inch), giving more air circulation between the faces. At the rear disc thickness rose from 20 millimeters (0.78 inch) to 24 millimeters (0.94 inch) on a 309-millimeter (12.1-inch) diameter. The total pad area was 78 square centimeters (12.1 square inches) for the A-type front calipers and 52.5 square centimeters (8.1 square inches) for the cast-iron M-type rear calipers. The same calipers had been fitted to the outgoing SC.

The Hydrovac servo, of 8 inches diameter, was common with the Turbo. A pressure-limiting valve was introduced into the rear brake circuit and reduced the chances of wheel lock-up under heavy braking. A new brake pad wear sensor was also fitted.

Wheels and Tires

At the time of its introduction, the Carrera's standard wheels were the telephone dial cast-alloy type with five oval holes around the center. The familiar Fuchs alloys were still available as an option (now with locking wheel nuts), and their centers could be ordered in white or platinum as well as black.

There were numerous changes in wheel specification during the life of the Carrera 3.2. From 1984, the standard 15-inch wheel sizes were 6J with 185/70 tires at the front and 7J with 215/60 tires at the rear. An option was 7J at the front (with 205/55ZR tires) and 8J at the rear (with 225/50ZR tires) on 16-inch Fuchs wheels. In 1987, the standard front tires grew to 195/65VR, still on the 6J rims, and in 1988 the standard wheel sizes went to 7Jx15 front and 8Jx15 rear, the Fuchs forged-alloy type replacing the telephone dials. The 16-inch wheels remained an option with the same tire sizes as before, although they were standard on the Club Sport.

For the final model year of the 3.2 Carrera, 1989, the standard wheels were 6Jx16 front and 8Jx16 rear, with 205/55ZR and 225/50ZR tires, respectively.

Carrera Turbo Look

From 1984, Carreras could be ordered optionally with the Turbo Coupe bodyshell, and this was announced as a regular model from September 1985. The specification included the Turbo's flared front and rear wheel wings, tea-tray wing, and front spoiler extension. The Turbo's suspension and brakes, including perforated discs and 917-type calipers, were used without change, as were 7J/9J front and rear wheels. Cornering was improved with the wider track, stiffer rear torsion bars, and a softer rear anti-roll bar. Ride height dropped from 108 millimeters (4.2 inches) to 94 millimeters (3.7 inches). Inside, the only trim options were leather and cloth or leather throughout.

The Turbo Look's extra weight, about 50 kilograms (110 pounds) more than the regular Carrera, affected the acceleration, and the increased frontal area also contributed to the top speed being approximately 12 miles per hour slower, a

Club Sports had (green) Bilstein gas dampers as standard. All Carrera 3.2s were given larger versions of the familiar A-type cast-iron calipers and the brake discs were thicker (at 24 millimeters) than those on the SC.

Most Club Sports were finished in Grand Prix White with these decals on the sides and a small logo on the front lid. The wheel centers were normally color-coded to the decal colors, but white and black centers were available.

Part of the stripped-down specification of the Club Sport was the deletion of the automatic heater control and the return of the older two-lever manual control next to the handbrake. In the absence of electric seat adjustment, the manual levers fore and aft movement are also grouped near the handbrake. Note the shift pattern of the C50 gearbox.

On the Club Sport this carpeted shelf, complete with small oddments pockets below, replaced the normal rear seats. There was no facility for fitting rear loudspeakers to this model

During 1988, a special anniversary model was released to celebrate 25 years of production of the 911, as shown by a factory-fitted dashboard plaque. Anniversary specification could be ordered on any model in the 911 range.

point that explains why some customers specified the turbo engine in the Carrera bodyshell. But the Turbo Look looked good and cost much less than a real Turbo.

The Targa and Cabrio became available in Turbo Look from 1986, the year in which 245/45VR rear tires on 9Jx16-inch Fuchs wheels became a special option. In the U.K., the Turbo-Look model was known as the Carrera with Sport Equipment (SE) for the 1986 model year and the Carrera Super Sport from September 1986.

Carrera Club Sport

Available from September 1987, the Club Sport was a stripped-out Sport Equipment model, the deleted features, including electric windows, electric front seats, rear wiper, central locking, radio (but the windshield antenna remained), passenger sun visor, rear seats, sound insulation (except for engine bay and roofliner), and air conditioning (where fitted as standard). Club Sport models carried the internal option number M637.

The finish inside was not austere; however, the rear seat area had fitted carpeting, and the seat trim was leather and cloth or full leather. A shorter-throw gearshift was fitted, and the alarm system of the regular Carrera was used. Other detail omissions included the automatic heater control, lockable oddments bin, door pocket lids, and the trim panels for the rear bulkhead and sides, while the door trims were simplified. Oddly, items that remained were headlamp washers and (on U.K. cars) electric exterior mirrors.

Although the cars were prepared in Grand Prix White with optional red "Carrera CS" side script, it is known that at least one car in the United Kingdom was finished in red, so left-hand-drive cars in other colors probably exist. All were coupes, except one: a special-order Targa made for a favored German customer who paid an extra DM 7,000 for the privilege. Red wheel centers were normal, but wheels could also be supplied with white or black centers. Where no PVC sealer was applied to the underside, the anticorrosion warranty was reduced from 10 years to 2. For most markets it was deleted, but U.K. cars generally had this treatment.

The claimed weight saving was about 50 kilograms (110 pounds) on the regular Carrera, but only 23 kilograms (51 pounds) on U.K. cars, according to *Motor* magazine. At first Club Sports were given 6Jx15 and 7Jx15 wheels using Pirelli P6 tires in sizes 195/65VR and 215/60VR. Later models received 6Jx16 and 7Jx16 wheels and Dunlop D40 tires in sizes 205/55VR and 225/50VR. Bilstein gas dampers were fitted all round.

The engine was allowed to run to 6,840 rpm as opposed to the standard car's maximum of 6,520 rpm by rechipping the Motronic system and using hollow intake valves. The rev counter was redlined from 6,600 rpm, as opposed to the regular Carrera's 6,200 rpm. Although maximum power was unaffected, the engine tweaks and lighter weight combined to improve acceleration, particularly above 60 miles per hour. The Club Sport could cover 0 to 60 miles per hour in 5.2 seconds compared with the standard car's 5.6 seconds (*Autocar* figures), while top speed rose from 148 to 151 miles per hour.

The Club Sport was discontinued in September 1989 after 340 cars had been delivered. It is believed that only 28 were sold in the United States, with 50 going to Britain.

Anniversary Carrera

For the 1988 model year, an exclusive run of Carreras in all body styles and with special Marine Blue metallic paint was made to celebrate 25 years of production of the 911. By coincidence it also marked the completion during the summer of 1987 (on June 3, to be precise) of the 250,000th 911. The interiors were finished in blue metallic crushed leather with "F. Porsche" signatures on the headrest area of the two front seats. Special silver blue silk velour carpet completed the luxurious interior of the anniversary models, and the short gear lever first seen on the Club Sport was used. The cars carried no model designation on the engine lid. Of the 875 Anniversary Carreras made, 300 went to the United States (120 Coupes, 100 Cabrios, and 80 Targas), 250 were sold in Germany, and 50 went to the U.K. (30 Coupes, 10 Cabrios, and 10 Targas).

Speedster

This model had first been proposed to Peter Schutz when he took over at Porsche in late 1981, but the body style chosen at that time was the Cabriolet. The Speedster prototype was shown at the Frankfurt Show in 1987, and production models went on sale in January 1989, using the Cabrio bodyshell without any additional stiffening. As with the Cabrio, the Speedster could be ordered in most markets with the Slant-Nose or Turbo-Look body styles, but only the latter was sold in Germany and the United States. The Turbo Look accounted for 1,894 of the 2,065 Speedsters made between January and September 1989; 63 right-hand-drive Speedsters were officially imported to the United Kingdom and 823 went to the United States.

Visual distinction was provided by the aluminum-framed windscreen being raked down by 5 degrees and accompanied by frameless side windows. There was a new simplified hood, termed an emergency or temporary hood by the factory to reinforce the message that it was not built to the same high standards of comfort as the Cabrio hood. It was claimed that the Speedster was designed "for friends of open-air motoring." The hood was stowed under a color-coded polyurethane molding that was designed to improve the aerodynamics of the open car but made the rear look awkwardly bulky. Customers were warned that the hood might not be waterproof and were advised that the Speedster should not be taken through a car wash. Before purchases could proceed, buyers were asked to sign a disclaimer that they would accept "a degree of wind noise and water ingress from the seal areas in inclement conditions." A removable (and hand-fitted at the factory) alloy hard top with heated rear window was listed as an option, but it is unclear whether any were delivered to customers.

There really were no frills on the Speedster. The windows and the heater were manually controlled. The seats were dropped to accommodate the lower roofline, although 20-millimeter (0.8-inch) spacers were used at the front of the seats to provide better thigh support. The lower part of each seat was the basic nonelectric version with a Sport seat back fitted, as used on the Club Sport. The rear seats were removed and the area carpeted. The M419 factory option provided a permanently installed storage box with two lockable lids in the rear seat area.

The factory claimed a 70-kilogram (154-pound) weight savings over the Coupe, but on the road it was more like 40 kilograms (88 pounds), a difference that was canceled out on the Turbo-Look version. Quoted performance was 0 to 100 kilometers per hour (0 to 62 miles per hour) in 6.0 seconds, but 0.1 second could be added for the Turbo Look and 0.2 second to either model if a catalytic converter was fitted.

As a tailpiece, this Speedster was the last 911 model to be built in the old Zuffenhausen factory on a bodyshell based on the original 1963 design. The Carrera 4 was built on a new production line.

The Anniversary 911s had various unique features, including metallic blue crushed leather for the seats and an "F. Porsche" signature on the headrest area. This car is owned by Roger Wynne.

The Speedster's large fiberglass hood cover molding hinges backward and remains in place all the time, precluding the fitting of rear seats.

The Anniversary models were painted in Marine Blue Metallic with matching wheel centers.

This Speedster interior shows manual window winders and the smaller sun visors used to suit the lower windscreen.

Production Changes

1984 (Start of E-series)
Engine increased to 3,164cc with longer-throw crankshaft of 3.3 Turbo and Nikasil barrels of 911SC; Bosch Motronic 2 engine management with LE fuel injection (and engine temperature sensing on cylinder head); 10.3:1 compression ratio with higher crown pistons (and 96 RON fuel); off accelerator fuel cut-off above 1,200 rpm, improved idle speed control and Lambda adjustment on U.S., Canadian, and Japanese engines; new cam timing (advanced by 3 degrees); cylinder head gasket deleted; larger inlet (38mm) and exhaust (40mm) ports; hydraulically damped spring chain tensioners fed by engine oil; new heat exchanger design with larger pipe diameters, two-stage silencing (on RoW models) and resonant charge boost air intake manifold; U.S., Canadian, and Japanese engines use 91 RON lead-free fuel, with 9.5:1 compression ratio, using new three-way catalytic converter in place of first silencer (muffler); oxygen sensor now preheated; new final silencer, with 10 percent improved flow rate; engine weight rises from 190kg to 210kg; gear ratios (U.S.): first, 3.181; second, 1.778; third, 1.261; fourth, 1.000; fifth, 0.790; reverse, 3.325; final drive, 3.875. Gear ratios (RoW): first, 3.181; second, 1.833; third, 1.261; fourth, 1.000; fifth, 0.763; reverse, 3.325; final drive, 3.875; sunroof air deflector revised; Turbo's heater controls fitted and in certain markets central locking is standard; 24mm thick brake discs with larger calipers front and rear; brake pressure limiter to prevent panic front wheel locking; brake servo now 8in; motor-driven vacuum assistance for brake servo maintains brake pressure over longer period.

1985 (Start of F-series)
Production actually started on Oct. 1, due to a metal workers' strike in Germany; wing-mounted oil cooler changed from brass tube to matrix type; lower front spoiler has slot to improve oil cooling airflow; gear lever travel shortened by 10 percent; radio antenna now in windshield; windshield washers heated; active carbon filters in breather system prevent escape of fuel vapor; electric adjusted front seats with part leather and cloth or full leather inlay; headrests 40mm taller, backrest release on both sides of seat back.

1986 (Start of G-series)
Swiss models receive more effective silencer; revised shock absorbers and new anti-roll bars; revised rear torsion bars; optional 10 percent (again) shorter gear shift; all models now have the same gear ratios: first, 3.5:1; second, 2.0591; third,

1.409:1; fourth, 1.125:1; fifth, 0.889:1; reverse, 3.325:1; final drive, 3.444:1; front seats lowered by 20mm and with greater adjustment; new dash panel with larger face-level and side window fresh air vents and temperature sensor; new switches and better heat regulation; digital self-seek radio with balance control standard; sun visors receive covered vanity mirrors; Sports seats are a no-cost option.

1987 (Start of H-series)
Motronic system on U.S., Canadian, and Japanese engines remapped (new 930/25 engine code) and fuel grade raised to 95 RON, giving output of 217 brake horsepower (DIN) and maximum torque of 265Nm; front-mounted oil cooler gets thermostatically controlled fan on these models; Australia gets its first unique model, 207 brake horsepower and equipped as previous U.S. models (930/21), with timing retarded to run 91 RON fuel (as opposed to 95); all other RoW models (noncatalyzed) run on 98 RON; Swiss models fitted with rear spoiler (and front chin spoiler) to improve engine compartment air circulation, which had been reduced by an acoustic shield mounted under the engine; additional air-injection pump fitted to Swiss cars (930/26), power as 930/20 RoW engine; all models fitted with Getrag G50 gearbox and hydraulic clutch operation, with these ratios: first, 3.5:1; second, 2.059:1; third, 1.409:1; fourth, 1.074:1; fifth, 0.861:1; reverse, 2.857:1; final drive, 3.444:1; clutch size increased to 240mm diameter; new rear torsion bar housing center section in cast iron; standard front tires now 195/65VR 16; exterior mirror adjustment switch repositioned; seats now adjustable in three planes; headlight beam adjuster mounted on dash; anti-corrosion warranty extended to 10 years; new rear panel has reflective script and foglights; door handle contains "point of light" to assist finding it in the dark; Targas get improved weather sealing with rain gutters; powered Cabrio hood now standard.

1988 (Start of I-series)
Standard telephone dial wheels replaced by 15in diameter 7J front and 8J rear Fuchs forged alloys (with 195/65VR and 215/60VR tires); the following items, previously options, become standard: passenger door mirror, electric passenger seat, central locking, headlight washers, intensive wash for the windshield; emergency crank provided for electric windows; optional eight-speaker plus booster sound package (hi-fi pack), crushed leather upholstery for subsequent mobile phone installation; all brake pads, clutch facings, and seals for engine and gearbox are asbestos free.

1989 (Start of J-series)
Fuchs wheels go up one size all around to 6Jx16in front, 8Jx16in rear; minor change to the fifth-speed gear assembly to reduce noise; anti-roll bars now 22mm front, 21mm rear; car alarm fitted and linked to central locking, marked by flashing red diodes in the lock buttons; optional seat heating for both passenger and driver and a radio with CD player.

Dimensions

Wheelbase
2,271mm.

Track (front/rear)
1,398mm/1,405mm (standard), 1,432/1,500mm (Turbo Look to 1986), 1,434/1,526mm (Turbo Look from 1986).

Length
4,291mm.

Width
1,650mm (standard), 1,829mm (Turbo Look).

Options

The following is a list of equipment options used from the introduction of the 911SC in 1978 through to 1992. Porsche Cars North America is among the references for this listing, which is all that can be obtained from official sources. Regrettably it is not possible to date these options, so this list must also apply to the chapters on the 911SC (1978–1983) and the 3.6-liter Carrera 4 and 2 (1989–1993). Many M numbers were standard for a particular market and will not be shown on the vehicle identification label (VIL). The hundreds of detail options are not shown here, and some M numbers represent a group of options for a particular model.

M09 three-speed Sportomatic; M18 Sport steering wheel with elevated hub; M20 Speedometer with two scales (kph/mph); M26 activated charcoal canister; M030 Sport suspension for Carrera 2 (1992/3); M68 bumpers with impact absorbers; M70 tonneau cover, Cabriolet; M97–99 Anniversary model 1989; M103 adjustment of shock absorber strut; M126 digital radio 1982; M139 seat heating (left); M148 modified engine 930/66; M152 engine noise reduction; M154 control unit for improved emissions; M155 Motronic unit for cars with catalytic converters; M156 quieter silencer; M157 oxygen sensor and catalyst; M158 Radio Monterey (1986) or Reno (1987); M160 Radio Charleston; M167 Bridgestone tires; M176 oil cooler with fan; M185 Automatic two-point rear seat belts; M186 manual rear seat belts; M187 asymmetric headlamps; M190 increased door side strength; M195 prepared for cellular telephone; M197 higher amperage battery (88Ah); M218 license brackets, front and rear; M220 locking differential (40 percent); M240 version for countries with inferior fuel; M261 passenger external mirror, flat glass; M286 high-intensity windshield washer; M288 headlight washer; M298 prepared for unleaded fuel, manual transmission; M326 Radio Blaupunkt Berlin; M327 Radio Blaupunkt Koln; M328 Radio Blaupunkt Bremen; M328 Radio Blaupunkt Symphony; M329/330 Radio Blaupunkt Toronto; M335 Automatic three-point rear seat belts; M340 seat heating (right); M341 central locking; M351 Porsche CR stereo radio/cassette Type DE, manual antenna, loudspeakers; M375 asbestos-free clutch lining; M377/378 combination seat (left/right); M378/380 series seat, electric vertical adjustment (left/right); M383/387 sports seats, electric vertical adjustment (left/right); M389 Porsche CR stereo U.S. radio/cassette, manual antenna, loudspeakers; M391 stone guard decal; M395 light metal wheels 6Jx15in front and 7Jx15 in rear, forged, with 205 and 225 tires; M399 air conditioning without front condenser; M401 light metal wheels; M403 50-year anniversary model (1982); M406 front wheel housing protection (1983–86); M407 rear seats with static belts; M409 sport seats in leather (left/right); M410 sport seats in leatherette/cloth (left/right); M419 rear luggage compartment instead of seats; M424 automatic heating control; M425 rear wiper; M437/438 comfort seats (left/right); M439 cabriolet top, electric operation; M440 manual antenna, two loudspeakers in doors and suppression; M441 electric antenna (right), two loudspeakers in doors and suppression; M443 tinted front and side glass, heated windshield;

M444 Cabriolet; M446 Targa build kit; M451 prepared for radio for sport group; M454 cruise control; M461 electric antenna (right); M462 Sekuriflex laminated windshield; M463 clear windshield; M464 without compressor and tire pressure gauge; M467 external driver's mirror, convex; M468 graduated windshield tint, green side glass; M469 black headlining; M470 without spoilers; M473 with spoilers; M474 Sport shock absorbers; M475 Brake pads without asbestos; M482 Engine compartment light; M483 right-hand drive; M487 connection for foglight from parking light; M490 HiFi sound system; M491 Turbo-Look body; M492 H4 headlights for left-hand traffic; M494 two speakers on rear shelf; M496 black-look external trim, color-coded headlamp rims; M498 without rear model designation; M503 Speedster variant of Cabriolet; M505 Slant-Nose (U.S.A.); M506 Slant-Nose (RoW); M513 lumbar support (right seat); M525 alarm with continuous sound; M526 cloth door panels; M528 passenger side external door mirror, convex; M533 alarm system; M559 air conditioning; M565 safety steering wheel in leather, 380mm diameter; M566 Rectangular front foglights; M567 graduated green tint windshield; M568 tinted windshield and side glass; M573 air conditioning; M577 heated and tinted windshield; M586 lumbar support, left seat; M590 center console; M592 anti-lock brakes (Bosch-Teves); M592 brake fluid warning system; M593 ABS Bosch; M594 ABS Wabco; M602 third brake light, top of rear screen; M605 vertical headlight adjustment; M630 police equipment; M637 Club Sport model; M650 electric sunroof; M651 electric windows; M652 intermittent wipe; M656 manual steering; M659 front foglights (1979); M659 on-board computer; M666 without lacquer preservation and chrome preservation; M673 prepared for lead-sealed odometer; M684 one-piece rear seat; M686 Radio Blaupunkt Ludwigsburg; M688 Radio Blaupunkt Boston; M690 CD player CD10 with radio; M691 CD player (CD01 for 1988, CD02 from 1989) with radio; M701 Slant-Nose; M702 high-performance engine (930/66); M930935/945/947/948 seat covers; M970 floor mats; M974 velour carpet in luggage compartment; M980 seat covering in ruffled leather; M981 all-leather lining; M986 partial leather lining.

Color Schemes

1984 (chart W74-704-2041)
Standard body colors
Guards Red (017), Glacier Blue (32Z), Black (700), Grand Prix White (908), Chiffon White (182).

Special order body colors
Moss Green Metallic (20C), Pewter Metallic (655), Slate Blue Metallic (661), Quartz Gray Metallic (662), Ruby Red Metallic (810), Kiln Red Metallic (811), Zinc Metallic (956), Light Bronze Metallic (966), Platinum Metallic (655).

Fabrics
Leatherette (BPX) in Gray-Beige (4FK), Burgundy (3MK), Cadbury Brown (4RB), Blue (1HH), or Black (435); leather (EXH) in Can-Can Red (80S), Pearl White (8YD), Dark Green (6JD), Champagne (1VD), Burgundy (7LD), Gray-Beige (6FL), Cadbury Brown (4RB), Black (1AJ), or Blue (30B); textured cloth with wavy line pattern (TPU) in Brown (7NU), Blue (30C), Black (70F), Gray Beige (8FU), or Burgundy (5MU); fabric with in-woven diagonal "Porsche" script (TPC) in Black (4CR), Brown (6TR), Gray-Beige (8RR), Blue (5HR), or Burgundy (2LR); checkerboard velour (TPB) in Light Gray/Black (4FJ), Brown/Gray (5RH), Blue/Gray (7GH), or Burgundy/Gray (9LH); pinstripe velour (TPB) in Brown/Beige (3NN), Black/White (7BN), Gray-Beige/White (9FN), Blue/White (8GJ), or Burgundy/White (1MJ).

Carpets
Cut pile velour (TFK) in Light Gray (60A), Brown (40E), Dark Blue (30B), Dark Green (6JD), Black (70E), Gray-Beige (2FL), Can-Can Red (80S), Burgundy (80E), or Champagne (1VD).

1985 (chart VMA7.84, WVK1 00S20)
Standard body colors
Guards Red (027), Black (700), Pastel Beige (S36), Dark Blue (347), Marble Gray (673), Grand Prix White (908).

Identification

Model year	Model	Engine	Gearbox	Chassis numbers	Engine numbers
E-series 1984	911 Carrera	930/20	915/67	WPOZZZ91 ZES 1 00001–4033	63E0000I onward
	Carrera Targa	930/20	915/67	WPOZZZ91ZES140001–1469	63E00001 onward
	Carrera Cabrio	930/20	915/67	WPOZZZ91ZES150001–1835	63E00001 onward
	Carrera Japan	930/21	915/68	WPOZZZ91 ZESI 09501–9717	64E0000I onward
	Carrera Targa Japan	930/21	915/68	WPOZZZ91 ZES 149501–9564	64E0000I onward
	Carrera Cabrio Japan	930/21	915/68	WPOZZZ91 ZES 159501–9577	64E0000I onward
	Carrera U.S.	930/21	915/68	WPOAB091 ES 120001–2282	64E0000I onward
	Carrera Targa U.S.	930/21	915/68	WPOEB091 ES 160001–2260	64E0000I onward
	Carrera Cabrio U.S.	930/21	915/68	WPOEB091ES170001–1191	64E0000I onward
F-series 1985	911 Carrera	930/20	915/69	WPOZZZ91ZFS 1 00001–3529	65F0000I onward
	Carrera Targa	930/20	915/69	WPOZZZ91 ZFS 14000 1–143 5	65F00001 onward
	Carrera Cabrio	930/20	915/69	WPOZZZ91 ZFS 15000 1– 1 583	65F00001 onward
	Carrera Japan	930/21	915/70	WPOZZZ91 ZFS 109501–722	64F00001 onward
	Carrera Targa Japan	930/21	915/70	WPOZZZ91ZFS149501–564	64F00001 onward
	Carrera Cabrio Japan	930/21	915/70	WPOZZZ91 ZFS159501–575	64F00001 onward
	Carrera U.S.	930/21	915/70	WPOAB091 FS 120001–1959	64F00001 onward
	Carrera Targa U.S.	930/21	915/70	WPOEB091 FS 160001–1942	64F00001 onward
	Carrera Cabrio U.S.	930/21	915/70	WPOEB091 FS 170001–1 050	64F00001 onward
G-series 1986	911 Carrera	930/20	915/72	WPOZZZ91 ZGS 1 00001–4031	63G0000I onward
	Carrera Targa	930/20	915/72	WPOZZZ91ZGS140001–1758	63G00001 onward
	Carrera Cabrio	930/20	915/72	WPOZZZ91 ZGS 150001–2358	63G00001 onward
	Carrera Japan	930/21	915/73	WPOZZZ91 ZGS 1 09501–733	64G00001 onward
	Carrera Targa Japan	930/21	915/73	WPOZZZ91 ZGS 149501–579	64G00001 onward
	Carrera Cabrio Japan	930/21	915/73	WPOZZZ91 ZGS 159501–580	64G00001 onward
	Carrera U.S.	930/21	915/73	WPOAB091 GS 120001–2619	64G00001 onward
	Carrera Targa U.S.	930/21	915/73	WPOEB091 GS 160001–1976	64G00001 onward
	Carrera Cabrio U.S.	930/21	915/73	WPOEB091 GS 17000 1–1986	64G00001 onward
H-series 1987	911 Carrera	930/20	950/00	WPOZZZ91ZHS 1 00001–3381	63H00001 onward
	Club Sport	930/20	950/00	WPOZZZ91ZHS105001–081	63H00001 onward
	Carrera Targa	930/20	950/00	WPOZZZ91ZHS140001–1354	64H00001 onward
	Carrera Cabrio	930/20	950/00	WPOZZZ91ZHS150001–1464	64H00001 onward
	Carrera Japan	930/25	950/01	WPOZZZ91 ZHS 1 09501–808	64H00001 onward
	Carrera Targa Japan	930/25	950/01	WPOZZZ91 ZHS149501–579	64H00001 onward
	Carrera Cabrio Japan	930/25	950/01	WPOZZZ91 ZHS 159501–585	64H00001 onward
	Carrera U.S.	930/25	950/01	WPOAB091 HS 120001–2916	64H00001 onward
	Carrera Club Sport U.S.	930/25	950/01	WPOAB091 HS 125001–300	64H00001 onward
	Carrera Targa U.S.	930/25	950/01	WPOEB091 HS 160001–2232	64H00001 onward
	Carrera Cabrio U.S.	930/25	950/01	WPOEB091 HS 170001–2653	64H00001 onward
I-series 1988	911 Carrera	930/20	G50/00	WPOZZZ91 ZJS 100001–3580	63J00001 onward
	Club Sport	930/20	G50/00	WPOZZZ91 ZJS 105001–148	63J00001 onward
	Carrera Targa	930/20	G50/00	WPOZZZ91 ZJS 140001–1281	63J00001 onward
	Carrera Cabrio	930/20	G50/00	WPOZZZ91 ZJS 15000 1–150 1	63J00001 onward
	Carrera Japan	930/25	G50/01	WPOZZZ91 ZJS 1 0950 1–930	64J00001 onward
	Carrera Targa Japan	930/25	G50/01	WPOZZZ91 ZJS 14950 1–586	64J00001 onward
	Carrera Cabrio Japan	930/25	G50/01	WPOZZZ91 ZJS 15950 1–581	64J00001 onward
	Carrera U.S.	930/25	G50/01	WPOAB091JS 120001–2066	64J00001 onward
	Carrera Club Sport U.S.	930/25	G50/01	WPOAB091 JS 12 500 1–302	64J00001 onward
	Carrera Targa U.S.	930/25	G50/01	WPOEB091 JS 160001–1500	64J00001 onward
	Carrera Cabrio U.S.	930/25	G50/01	WPOEB091JS 170001–2116	64J00001 onward
J-series 1989	911 Carrera	930/20	G50/00	WPOZZZ91 ZKS 100001–3532	63K00001 onward
	Carrera Targa	930/20	G50/00	WPOZZZ91 ZKS 140001–1063	63K00001 onward
	Carrera Cabrio	930/20	G50/00	WPOZZZ91ZKS150001–2787	63K00001 onward
	Club Sport	930/20	G50/00	WPOZZZ91ZKS 105001–090	63K00001 onward
	Speedster	930/20	G50/00	WPOZZZ91ZKS 153000–4242	63K00001 onward
	Carrera U.S.	930/25	G50/01	WPOAB091 KS 120001–1156	64K00001 onward
	Carrera Targa U.S.	930/25	G50/01	WPOEB091 KS 160001–0860	64K00001 onward
	Carrera Cabrio U.S.	930/25	G50/01	WPOEB091 KS 170001–1361	64K00001 onward
	Speedster U.S.	930/25	G50/01	WPOEB091 KS 17300 1–823	64K00001 onward
	Club Sport	930/25	G50/01	WPOEB091 KS 125001–007	64K00001 onward

General notes: Chassis numbering Model years are identified by a letter for the 10th character of RoW models or the ninth character of U.S. models, as follows: E 1984, F 1985, G 1986, H 1987, J 1988, K 1989. **Engines** 930/26 was supplied alongside RoW models as a special model for Switzerland from 1985 and Sweden from 1987; 930/25 was supplied to Austria from 1987. 930/26 was as 930/20, plus an air pump and extra noise reduction. **Gearboxes** Note change of designation for G50 gearbox for 1988, from 950 to G50; G50/02 was supplied to Switzerland. **Option** M220 (locking differential) was available on all 1988 G50 gearboxes.

Production Data

Model year	Model	Power (bhp DIN@rpm)	Torque (Nm@rpm)	Compression ratio	Weight (kg)	Number built
1984	911 Carrera	231@5,900	284@4800	10.31	1,160	4,033
	Carrera Targa	231@5,900	284@4,800	10.3:1	1,210	1,469
	Carrera Cabrio	231@5,900	260@4,800	10.3:1	1,210	1,835
	Carrera Japan	207@5,900	260@4,800	9.5:1	1,250	217
	Carrera Targa Japan	207@5,900	260@4,800	9.5:1	1,300	64
	Carrera Cabrio Japan	207@5,900	260@4,800	9.5:1	1,250	77
	Carrera U.S.	207@5,900	260@4,800	9.5:1	1,250	2,282
	Carrera Targa U.S.	207@5,900	260@4,800	9.5:1	1,300	2,260
	Carrera Cabrio U.S.	207@5,900	260@4,800	9.5:1	1,300	1,191
1985	911 Carrera	231@5,900	284@4,800	10.3:1	1,160	3,529
	Carrera Targa	231@5,900	284@4,800	10.3:1	1,210	1,435
	Carrera Cabrio	231@5,900	260@4,800	10.3:1	1,210	1,583
	Carrera Japan	207@5,900	260@4,800	9.5:1	1,250	222
	Carrera Targa Japan	207@5,900	260@4,800	9.5:1	1,300	64
	Carrera Cabrio Japan	207@5,900	260@4,800	9.5:1	1,300	75
	Carrera U.S.	207@5,900	260@4,800	9.5:1	1,250	1,959
	Carrera Targa U.S.	207@5,900	260@4,800	9.5:1	1,300	1,942
	Carrera Cabrio U.S.	207@5,900	260@4,800	9.5:1	1,300	1,050
1986	911 Carrera	231@5,900	284@4,800	10.3:1	1,210	4,031
	Carrera Targa	231@5,900	284@4,800	10.3:1	1,260	1,758
	Carrera Cabrio	231@5,900	260@4,800	10.3:1	1,260	2,358
	Carrera Japan	207@5,900	260@4,800	9.5:1	1,260	233
	Carrera Targa Japan	207@5,900	260@4,800	9.5:1	1,310	79
	Carrera Cabrio Japan	207@5,900	260@4,800	9.5:1	1,310	80
	Carrera U.S.	207@5,900	260@4,800	9.5:1	1,300	2,619
	Carrera Targa U.S.	207@5,900	260@4,800	9.5:1	1,350	1,976
	Carrera Cabrio U.S.	207@5,900	260@4,800	9.5:1	1,350	1,986
1987	911 Carrera	231@5,900	284@4,800	10.3:1	1,210	3,381
	Club Sport	231@5,900	284@4,800	10.3:1	1,172	81
	Carrera Targa	231@5,900	284@4,800	10.3:1	1,260	1,354
	Carrera Cabrio	231@5,900	284@4,800	10.3:1	1,260	1,464
	Carrera Japan	217@5,900	265@4,800	9.5:1	1,260	308
	Carrera Targa Japan	217@5,900	265@4,800	9.5:1	1,310	79
	Carrera Cabrio Japan	217@5,900	265@4,800	9.5:1	1,310	85
	Carrera U.S.	217@5,900	265@4,800	9.5:1	1,250	2,916
	Carrera Targa U.S.	217@5,900	265@4,800	9.5:1	1,300	2,232
	Carrera Cabrio U.S.	217@5,900	265@4,800	9.5:1	1,300	2,653
1988	911 Carrera	231@5,900	284@4,800	10.3:1	1,210	3,580
	Carrera Targa	231@5,900	284@4,800	10.3:1	1,260	1,281
	Carrera Cabrio	231@5,900	284@4,800	10.3:1	1,260	1,501
	Carrera Japan	217@5,900	265@4,800	9.5:1	1,260	430
	Carrera Targa Japan	217@5,900	265@4,800	9.5:1	1,310	86
	Carrera Cabrio Japan	217@5,900	265@4,800	9.5:1	1,310	81
	Carrera U.S.	217@5,900	265@4,800	9.5:1	1,250	2,066
	Carrera Targa U.S.	217@5,900	265@4,800	9.5:1	1,300	1,500
	Carrera Cabrio U.S.	217@5,900	265@4,800	9.5:1	1,300	2,116
	Club Sport	231@5,900	284@4,800	10.3:1	1,172	148
	Club Sport U.S.	217@5,900	265@4,800	9.5:1	1,210	21
1989	911 Carrera	231@5,900	284@4,800	10.3:1	1,210	3,532
	Carrera Targa	231@5,900	284@4,800	10.3:1	1,260	1,063
	Carrera Cabrio	231@5,900	284@4,800	10.3:1	1,260	2,787
	Speedster	231@5,900	284@4,800	10.3:1	1,210	1,242
	Carrera U.S.	217@5,900	265@4,800	9.5:1	1,250	1,156
	Carrera Targa U.S.	217@5,900	265@4,800	9.5:1	1,300	860
	Carrera Cabrio U.S.	217@5,900	265@4800	9.5:1	1,300	1,361
	Speedster	217@5,900	265@4800	9.5:1	1,210	823
	Club Sport	231@5,900	284@4800	10.3:1	1,172	83
	Club Sport U.S.	217@5,900	265@4800	9.5:1	1,210	7

General notes The restoration workshop produced a handful of Slant-Nose Carrera conversions between 1984 and 1987: one in 1984, two in 1985, one in 1986, and five in 1987. For the 1988 model year, the Slant-Nose became a production model but only on the Turbo. The 1987 remapped 930/2S engine for the U.S.A. (214bhp DIN) is more frequently quoted with its SAE maximum power of 217bhp. The Club Sport (M637) was discontinued in September 1989. On the subject of weights, there was a large difference between factory homologation weights and the dry weight of equipped cars. Different markets offered different levels of basic equipment, and others (especially U.S., Japan, and Canada) had extra emissions equipment. For instance, the homologation weight of the 1984 model was 1,207kg, but this rose to 1,280kg ready for sale in Germany. The quoted ex-factory weight of the same model was 1,160kg. Quoted weight should be treated as a guide only.

Special order body colors

Garnet Red Metallic (822), Crystal Green Metallic (33N), White Gold Metallic (S39), Prussian Blue Metallic (33X), Moss Green Metallic (20C), Iris Blue Metallic (33P), Nutmeg Brown Metallic (492), Meteor Metallic (961), Silver Metallic (936).

Fabrics

Leatherette as 1984, excluding Gray-Beige (4FK) but with addition of Gray-Green (4JX); leather as 1984 excluding Gray-Beige (6FL) but with addition of Gray-Green (SJX), Wild Buffalo (dark brown, SNW) and Ocean Blue (6GX); checkerboard velour deleted for 911; pinstripe velour (TPB) in Brown/White (3NN), Black/White (7BN), Blue/White (8GJ), Burgundy/White (1 MJ), or Gray Green/White (3JV); pinstripe (narrow) flannel (TPC) in Black (8BF), Brown (2TF), Gray-Green (9JF), Blue (6GF), or Burgundy (1 MF); fabric with in-woven diagonal "Porsche" script, more prominent than 1984 (TPC), in Black (2CZ), Brown (INZ), Blue (6HZ), Burgundy (SLZ), or Gray-Green (1 JK); Cabrio hoods in Black, Dark Brown, Dark Blue, Burgundy, or Gray-Green.

Carpets

As with 1984, except Gray-Green (8JK) replaces Gray-Beige and White (2YN) added—a good color for a car carpet.

1986

Standard and special order body colors as with 1985.

Fabrics

Leatherette as 1985, but with Gray-Beige (4FK) reinstated; leather as 1985, but with Gray-Beige (6FL) reinstated; pinstripe velour as 1985, but with addition of Gray-Beige/White (9FN); pinstripe flannel and "Porsche" script fabric as with 1985, but including Gray-Beige (SUY) in the latter.

Carpets

As with 1985, but with Gray-Beige (2FL) reinstated.

1987 (chart VMAP6/86, WVK102721)
Standard body colors

Guards Red (027), Black (700), Summer Yellow (10W), Caramel Beige (499), Carmine Red (80F), Grand Prix White (908), Dark Blue (347), Turquoise (21M).

Special order body colors

Lagoon Green Metallic (3SY), Granite Green Metallic (699), Nougat-Brown Metallic (40B), Espresso Brown Metallic (40D), Diamond Blue Metallic (697), Marine Blue Metallic (3SV), Silver Metallic (980), Cassis Red Metallic (80D), Venetian Blue Metallic (3SU).

Fabrics

Leatherette (BPX) in Linen (4WX), Burgundy (3MK), Mahogany (1 MX), Black (435), Gray-Green (4JX), or Blue (1 KX); leather (YDX) in Burgundy (7LD), Mahogany (2LX), Brown (4RB), Black (1AJ), Blue (7JX), Gray-Green (SJX), Linen (7VX), Plum Red (1MC), Silver-Gray (3VC), Caramel (4UC), Venetian Blue (7KC), or Champagne (1VD); pinstripe velour (TPB) in Black/White (7BN), Mahogany/White (6LN), Blue/White (8GJ), Burgundy/White (1 MJ), Gray-Green/White (3JV); pinstripe flannel (TPC) in Mahogany (9LF) Anthracite (8BF), Gray-Green (9JF), Blue (6GF), or Burgundy (1MF); fabric with in-woven diagonal "Porsche" script as 1986, but less Brown and add Mahogany (4MR); Cabrio hoods in Black, Mahogany, Blue, Burgundy, or Gray-Green.

Carpets

Cut pile velour (TFK) in Mahogany (SMF), Blue (3KF), Linen (2XF), Burgundy (80E), Black (70E), Gray-Green (8JK), Champagne (1VD), Plum Red (4MM), Silver-Gray (7VM), Caramel (SUM), or Venetian Blue (3KM).

1988 (chart VMAP7/87, WVK102720)
Standard and special order body colors

As with 1987.

Fabrics and carpets

Special materials available for 25-year anniversary model, painted in Marine Blue Metallic (3SV); ruffled leather (YDS 8HF) in Blue Metallic with "Ferry Porsche" signature on the headrest area of the two front seats; silk velour carpet (TLV 6HM) in Silver Blue.

The 911 Carreras (964) (1989–1993)

Ian King's Carrera 4 Targa shows the new design of front bumper and side skirt, with a much more squared-off lower edge to the 911's classic curves. This car is fitted with five-spoke Cup Design wheels.

When recession hit in the late 1980s, the yuppies deserted Porsche in droves. The 3.2 Carrera suddenly seemed to be rather outdated as the competition, especially from Japan, targeted the sports car market that Porsche had dominated for so long. In 1987, 911 Carrera sales had slipped back to around 17,000. At the end of that year Schutz was gone, replaced by well-trusted Porsche finance man Heinz Branitzski. He was briefed to find Porsche a new direction—again.

Porsche's problems were compounded by the fact that its loyal customers, who had previously bought a 911 because it was something special and not likely to be seen in every town center in the land, had deserted the marque too. Branitzski's task was to reestablish the trust of the core customers and somehow take the company forward from a much reduced trading position. He had a difficult job. In the last year of the 3.2 Carrera, 1989, just less than 7,000 were made. There was a cold wind blowing at Porsche.

Management instability continued as Porsche plunged into recession on a scale that the company was not prepared for. In March 1990, another new chief executive officer, Arno Bohn, formerly of the Nixdorf computer business,

Evolution Outline

August 1989: The Carrera 4 was introduced as a new four-wheel-drive 911 model, along with a restyle of the bodyshell, a twin spark 3.6-liter engine (250-brake horsepower), a coil spring over shock absorber suspension, and ABS brakes.

October 1989: The Carrera 2 is announced (rear-wheel drive only); Tiptronic automatic transmission is launched at same time.

August 1991: The Turbo-Look body style for the Carrera 2 Coupe and Cabriolet is introduced.

October 1991: The Carrera 2 RS is introduced with 260-brake horsepower and up to 170 kilograms lighter than Carrera 2.

August 1992: Porsche presents RS America (entry-level Carrera 2) for North America and America Roadster (Turbo-Look Cabriolet Carrera 2).

October 1992: The Carrera 2 Speedster is launched.

February 1993: Carrera 2 Speedster production starts, and the 911 Celebration (30 years of the 911) is introduced.

December 1993: The Carrera 2 and 4 are discontinued, the Targa is deleted, and the 911 (993) Carrera is introduced in Coupe and Cabriolet forms.

Mike King's Carrera 2 Tiptronic, again fitted with the attractive Cup Design wheels.

In standard form for the first three years of production the Carrera 4 used these new seven-spoke alloy wheels, with 205/55 front tires and 225/50 rear tires. Considerable road noise was transmitted into the cabin because tire pressures were high.

was given the task of rescuing the company. There are stories of bitter boardroom battles over the direction Porsche should take in its struggle to survive. There were several director-level resignations, and Bohn gained a reputation for being outspoken in his conflict with the controlling Porsche and Piech families. By September 1992, he too was gone and was replaced by former Production Director Wendelin Wiedeking, then aged 39.

Wiedeking's declared objective was to slash Porsche's cost base by 30 percent by 1995. From the moment he took over, Herr Wiedeking had to counter continuous external comment that the firm was up for sale. This was strenuously rejected at every turn, but it was clear that some major surgery was going to be necessary on a company that had grown complacent of its position. This would appear not to have been the most conducive environment from which to stage a recovery, but Wiedeking was to lead a whirlwind of change.

The new broom started sweeping. In 1993 alone, the workforce was reduced by 15 percent, and by 1994 nearly 40 percent of the original management had been laid off. Many new initiatives improved productivity. Wiedeking's production training brought massive dividends, which started with Japanese specialists introducing state-of-the-art *kaizen* (constant improvement) production methods. The savings in production were startling: The new 1994 Carrera took 40 hours less to build, quality improved by 15 to 20 percent, the amount of space needed to assemble each vehicle was reduced by 21 percent, and the stock inventory—such a drain on the company's liquidity—by 43 percent. Business did indeed improve, turning around the record loss of 239 million D-marks in 1992–1993 on the strength of both cost savings and rising sales.

The recovery was led by the new 993, but the 964 played its part. At the start of the 1994 model year the 993 was available only in two-wheel-drive coupe form, and 3,690 964s were sold during the model year: Carrera 2 Speedsters,

Cabriolets, Carrera 4s, and Turbos. But 16,693 993s were sold, too, demonstrating forcefully how the new model had captured the imagination of the marketplace in a way the 964 had not. It was a very different picture from 1993, when a total of just 12,500 Porsches were sold.

Production of the 964 ceased in spring 1994, with completion of orders for the Turbo. The end of the 964 also marked the passing of the Speedster, as this model was not a feature of the 993 range.

Let us return to 1989 and the new Carrera 4, because this was the car that

The Cabriolet progressively ate into the Targa's share of the 911 market, to the extent that by 1993 the Targa had virtually disappeared. This 1993 Cabriolet shows off the new Classic Gray hood color for that year.

was to win back Porsche's loyal customers, to show them that owning a 911 was indeed something special. With its back to the wall, the company resolved to fight its way out of trouble with the one major asset that had hauled it back from the brink in previous hard times: the engineering team at Weissach.

That Porsche's engineers managed to pull still more innovations from the 911 ideas pile in the late 1980s is astonishing, but the extravagant 959 program had given them a healthy reserve of technology to draw upon. The 959 was a wonder car with many technological marvels of industry-leading standard, but Porsche did not make as much as it might have with the car. The 283 959s were all presold, and by the time they were delivered to a booming market they seemed grossly underpriced. A buoyant gray market sprung up around the 959, for a speculative owner who paid some £180,000 could resell immediately for anything up to £500,000—and someone reputedly paid $1,000,000 in Japan.

None of this speculative gain went to Porsche, but it was an obvious move for the cash-strapped company to cream off some of the 959's technology into a new range of 911s, the Carrera 4 and Carrera 2. There was a new factory, too, for the strikingly painted (in shades of pink) body assembly plant at Zuffenhausen would build the latest 911s. To these models would fall the task of keeping Porsche afloat until the new direction could fire the excitement of those much sought new customers.

The Carrera 4 introduced an electrically operated rear spoiler (above) that deployed automatically above 50 miles per hour and retracted when speed fell below 6 miles per hour. In the wake of the Carrera 4, the Carrera 2 was introduced (below) early in 1990 to replace the old Carrera 3.2. More sporting than the four-wheel-drive model, it was modified to great effect by the factory's racing department.

Officially announced in November 1988 but leaked to the press as much as a year earlier, the Carrera 4 was a significant development for Porsche. Whereas all previous 911s were part of a continuous development stream that could be traced back to 1963, the Carrera 4 was 87 percent new, and as such it should be judged the first stage of the second generation. As had happened so many times, the changes on the four-wheel-drive Carrera 4 were understated by the factory. The bits that remained unchanged were those that everyone could see: roof, front wings, front compartment lid, doors, and seats, and of course, that famous profile. Inevitably the word *facelift* crept into press reports by the less well-informed, but anyone who looked closely could see that the "87 percent new" tag had real credibility. The engine, suspension, brakes, and transmission were all new. Under the skin, the 911 had been truly transformed. The changes were major enough for the car to be given a new internal factory designation of

964. The joke on the cynical press—there were many at the time because it was fashionable to knock Porsche in 1989—was that there were still those who talked about the "wayward handling" of the rear engine design. For normal road use, the 911 had been tamed long before.

The Carrera 2 followed early in 1990, replacing the 3.2 Carrera. The new two-wheel-drive 911 used most of the Carrera 4's equipment, but with a simpler and lighter transmission. With the basic models of the second generation established, Porsche then set about widening the appeal of the 911 in the way that had proved successful in the later years of the 3.2 Carrera. The Turbo Look, the Speedster, and another Anniversary model (marking the 911's 30th birthday) enhanced a range that had to take the company through its worst-ever trading situation in the period 1991 to 1993. Deliveries of the Carrera 4 and Carrera 2 ran out in 1993, to be replaced with the 993 model.

Bodyshell

The structure of the Carrera 4 was entirely new. It was made, as previously, from hot-zinc-dipped steel, but considerable efforts had been made to improve manufacturing efficiency by using highly automated methods. In terms of the bodyshell generally, it had been important to retain the classic 911 profile, yet to improve the aerodynamics and the styling. These goals were achieved elegantly with new front and rear bumpers, combined with a much smoother, enclosed underbody and a movable rear spoiler.

The bumpers were made from deformable thermoplastic supported on an aluminum subframe. For U.S. models, the subframes were carried on telescopic dampers to provide "collision recovery" ability. For Rest-of-the-World models, the supports were simple deformable structures. The driving lights were styled into the new bumpers, so that changes of line in the bodyshell profile were less abrupt than on the earlier models. At the rear, the exhaust tailpipe exited on the right-hand side, the opposite to the 3.2 Carrera.

The rear spoiler was a particularly neat solution to the potential conflict between retaining the classical 911 shape yet providing improved stability at higher speeds. The spoiler was raised by an electric motor when the car exceeded 50 miles per hour (80 kilometers per hour) and retracted when speed fell below 6 miles per hour (10 kilometers per hour). Since the spoiler was housed in a larger opening in the engine cover, cooling was improved when the car was stationary. The moving spoiler might not have been as effective aerodynamically as a whale-tail, but it was successful from the visual point of view.

Aerodynamic improvements were applied to most details of the bodyshell. The gap between the top of the rear window glass and the roof was reduced. The front windshield was glued into a much lower profile rubber seal, which in turn was glued to the bodyshell. The rising drip rails next to the windshield were reduced in size. The oil cooler was still in the right front wing, ahead of the wheel, but aligned differently to benefit from air ducted into the wheel arch from under the bumper, hot air being ducted out just ahead of the front wheel. The condenser for the air conditioning system (where one was fitted) was placed in the same manner in the left front wing.

The Carrera 4 bodyshell was shared by the Carrera 2, which was announced a year later, in October 1989, in Coupe, Targa, and Cabrio forms. Sales of the Targa model, however, were dwindling, and the Carrera 2 would be the last 911 to be offered with this style of open motoring. For the 1992 model year the Turbo-Look Cabrio was also offered for the Carrera 2. From the 1993 model year, all models carried the chassis number on the A-pillar, so that it was visible from outside the car. This was in the interests of better security.

Body Trim

The Carrera 4 was notable in having little superfluous body trim. New plastic sill extensions squared off the sides of the car, but other trim—including door mirrors and windshield wipers—was carried over from the 3.2 Carrera. The sunroof received a new wind deflector at the leading edge, while the addition of the movable spoiler required the rear wiper to be mounted through the window glass instead of on the engine lid.

The heating system was effectively completely new, the new undertray incorporating new ducting and servo-operated fans to reduce temperature fluctuations. The new design also took account of air conditioning, although this remained an option. The revised heating and ventilation went a long way to providing the 911 with a contemporary climate control equivalent to other luxury —and water-cooled—GT cars. The system was further improved for 1992, and at the same time the Turbo-Look Cabrio received the automatic control of the closed models. From 1993, the air conditioning refrigerant was CFC free.

Interior Trim

The higher central driveshaft tunnel for the four-wheel-drive system was the only obvious difference between the old 3.2 Carrera and the new Carrera 4. New door loudspeakers were fitted and new trim choices were available (see Color Schemes on pages 117–118). A footrest was also provided alongside the clutch for the first time on a 911. On right-hand-drive models, the front compartment lid release lever moved conveniently to the driver's side.

From the 1990 model year, driver and passenger air bags were fitted for specific markets and became standard across the left-hand-drive range from April 1991. Right-hand-drive cars were equipped with a driver's air bag from 1993. When a passenger air bag was fitted, the glovebox moved to a new position below the dashboard. For the 1991 model year, a time delay on the interior light and new rear seat back releases (with a button on the top of the seat back) were introduced.

Dashboard and Instruments

The main dash was carried over from the outgoing 3.2 Carrera, but there were detail revisions. All the instruments were revised in appearance from the earlier Carrera and were backlit. Most changed were the oil level and oil pressure gauges, which now had "external" indicator needles, meaning that the needles no longer extended from behind a hidden pivot. The gauges also included an array of 13 warning lights, which finally ensured that even the most longstanding 911 driver was forced to look in the handbook to find out what they all meant.

Apart from new trim choices and door loudspeakers, the only significant change in this Carrera 4's interior architecture compared with the old Carrera 3.2 is the higher central tunnel necessary for the four-wheel-drive system.

The instruments were totally updated for the new models (above). The figures and indicator needles were now backlit at night, and the oil combination gauge now contained an array of warning lights. This car does not have the air bag steering wheel. The instruments continued to be developed (below), and by 1992 the clock even carried its own complement of warning lights. The speedometer contained a shift indicator on Tiptronic models.

The factory said the Carrera 4 was 87 percent new under the skin, and here's some of the evidence. The luggage compartment has a completely different layout, with the plastic fuel tank now moved up and back to accommodate the front differential below, the fuse panel moved to the left-hand rear of the compartment, and the new ABS equipment under the cover to the rear of the battery.

A 7,600-rpm rev counter was fitted, and the speedometer was calibrated to 180 miles per hour or 300 kilometers per hour. New climate controls, mounted in the middle of the dash, were taken from the 944 series.

The dashboard was carried over to the new Carrera 2 but obviously without the controls for the four-wheel-drive transmission. The Carrera 4 had the differential lock control mounted on the center console ahead of the gear lever.

From the 1990 model year, Tiptronic-equipped cars had an onboard computer that gave the driver the following information: journey distance on fuel remaining, daily kilometer total, average fuel consumption, digital speed read-out, average journey speed, and outside air temperature. Also from 1990, the position of the electrically operated rear spoiler could be manually controlled by a switch on the center console, although the speed-controlled movement remained.

Luggage Compartment

The luggage compartment was reshaped and reduced in size to accommodate the Carrera 4's front differential and driveshaft assemblies. For the same reason, fuel tank capacity was reduced from 85 liters (18.70 Imperial gallons, 22.46 U.S. gallons) to 77 liters (16.94 Imperial gallons, 20.34 U.S. gallons), including a reserve of 10 liters (2.20 Imperial gallons, 2.64 U.S. gallons). A new option from 1993 was a 92-liter tank (20.24 Imperial gallons, 24.31 U.S. gallons) for those who wanted extended range.

The Carrera 4 and Carrera 2 shared a new 3.6-liter engine developing 250-brake horsepower. A notable feature of the new models was the distinctive whine, like the sound of a jet aircraft turbofan, made by the revised curved-blade cooling fan while cruising.

Engine

The Carrera 4 engine, and subsequently that of the Carrera 2, was termed the M64/01 and had a capacity of 3,600cc (219.6 cubic inches). It developed 250-brake horsepower at 6,100 rpm and maximum torque of 310 Nm at 4,800 rpm for all markets.

It was a design goal for the Carrera 4 that its performance should exceed that of the 3.2 Carrera, so power had to be increased to compensate for the weight of the four-wheel-drive equipment. Increased capacity was achieved by enlarging the bore from 95 millimeters (3.70 inches) to 100 millimeters (3.90 inches) and the stroke from 74.4 millimeters (2.90 inches) to 76.4 millimeters (2.98 inches). The cylinder heads used ceramic port liners: ceramic is a poor conductor of heat, and in this application it reduced the transfer of heat from the exhaust gas to the cylinder head. The cylinder heads ran up to 40 degrees Centigrade cooler in the region of the exhaust ports, allowing the deletion of the sodium-cooled exhaust valves that had been present from the first 911s. Sodium cooling, however, was now used on the intake valves in order to allow heat to transfer from the head to the valve and so help cold starting. It also reduced noise between valves and followers when cold.

New forged pistons with dished crowns ran in slightly conical cylinders so that the cylinder walls became perfectly parallel when the engine was hot. The two center cylinders carried anti-knock sensors, each one connected to the adjacent cylinders by a metal strap to detect the onset of detonation. The crankcase was revised to accommodate the wider spaced cylinder head bolt attachments and a new, lighter crankshaft was used (but with all major bearing dimensions carried over from the 3.2-liter engine) with a vibration damper at the pulley drive end. A new 12-blade cooling fan was driven at the same 1.6:1 ratio as on the 959. The crank drove the cooling fan in the familiar way, but now with a belt different from that driving the alternator.

A twin-spark ignition system with double distributors (the second one was driven by a small toothed belt from the first) allowed the ignition timing to be retarded by 6 degrees compared with the 3.2 engine. This, in turn, allowed the compression ratio to increase to a standard 11.3:1 for all markets, despite a decrease in the octane requirement from 98 to 95 RON. These improvements were made possible by a revised Motronic program. A new two-stage resonant intake manifold ensured good low-speed response.

A primary objective of the new engine was to reduce noise, and the cam timing chain tensioners were completely redesigned for this purpose. Considering one side only, the new hydraulic tensioner bears onto the rear of a large polyamide lever, which is pivoted at the other end of its length. The end of the lever, which is shaped to bear onto the trailing part of each double-row chain, also carries a mounting for a connecting rod to a second (also pivoting) chain ramp on the other side of the chain. This way the tensioner works on both the driven and driving lengths of the chain.

The engine oil cooler, present on all previous 911s, was deleted, and the oil radiator in the right-hand front wing was enlarged accordingly. The intake system for the new engine was completely new, using pulsed air theory to ensure the best filling of the cylinders. The new Motronic injection used sequential fuel injection, which was timed on crankshaft position and controlled by parameters such as engine temperature, engine speed, and oxygen sensing (Lambda) in the exhaust. The Motronic system also controlled any tendency for the engine to predetonate by retarding the spark in 3-degree steps when using low-grade fuel or under load.

The big breakthrough with the Carrera 4 was that it truly became a car for all markets. Every engine had the same power and torque, whether or not it was fitted with a three-way catalytic converter. This alone says a lot about the clever design of the converter-equipped exhaust system. The catalyst itself was all-metal (with no ceramic core) and so was more compact. All Carrera 4s had an active charcoal filter to absorb vapor from the fuel tank.

From 1993, all Porsche models leaving the factory were filled with Shell TMO full synthetic engine oil.

Transmission

A prototype four-wheel-drive Cabrio study had been shown at the 1981 Frankfurt Show, and the 959 had pioneered four-wheel drive in production at Porsche. The

Great attention was paid to the aerodynamics of the Carrera 4. A full-length undertray to the rear of the engine not only helped airflow but also contributed to lower noise levels. Note the NACA duct below the gearbox area.

Two new rotary controls were found on the Carrera 4 center console (top). The left-hand switch is a manual over-ride for deploying or retracting the automatic rear spoiler, while the right-hand one allows the center and rear differentials to be locked in poor weather condition. Tiptronic was introduced to the Carrera 2 (above) as the next-generation automatic transmission for Porsches. On the left-hand side of the gate the driver had the choice of clutchless (and intelligent) manual shifting or a fully automatic regime. Moving the lever to the right-hand side of the gate offered a push/pull shift option.

Carrera 4's transmission was much simpler than that on the 959, however, and owed more to the system used on the Paris-Dakar four-wheel-drive cars of 1984.

The five-speed gearbox was known as the G64/00 and was derived from the G50 used on the 3.2 Carrera. The drive to the front wheels was taken from the front of the gearbox, via a center epicyclical differential that divided the torque transmitted from the engine to the front (31 percent) and back (69 percent) wheels. A rigid torque tube containing a propeller shaft and the gear linkage took the drive to the front axle, where a front differential distributed drive to the wheels. The rear wheels were driven from the center differential via a shaft through a hollow gearbox output shaft to another differential. The slip of both differentials was controlled by multi-plate clutches. Control of the differentials was electronic and linked to the ABS sensors in each wheel, so that the correct amount of torque could be split between each axle or each wheel if slip was detected. The center and rear differentials could also be locked manually—for traction in extreme conditions—by means of a "traction" switch in the center console; this locking facility would disengage above 25 miles per hour. For the Swiss market, a variant with longer fourth and fifth speeds (G64/01) was used to meet local noise control requirements.

The transmission of the new Carrera 2 was based on the G50 design, with changes to the ratios. The 9:31 ratio of the crown wheel and pinion was unchanged from the 3.2. On export models to the United States, Canada, Japan, and Australia, fourth and fifth gears were shortened (32:36 from 35:38 for fourth, 37:33 from 38:33 for fifth), mainly for noise reasons. This gearbox was known as the G50/01, with Switzerland again receiving its own G50/02 variety.

For the 1990 model year, a double mass flywheel containing a rubber damper was fitted. This was termed ZMS (*Zweimassenschwungrad*) in technical documentation. The new flywheel assembly reduced the transmission of low-speed torsional vibration from the engine to the gearbox.

Tiptronic dual-function transmission was introduced with the Carrera 2 at the start of 1990. This transmission, the result of a joint study by ZF and Bosch, had four speeds selectable entirely automatically or in a semi-automatic sequential mode. The gearbox was described as "intelligent" in that a computer calculated the right gear for the loading on the transmission. The other feature—and the big improvement over previous automatic gearboxes—was its ability to give ratio changes without interruption of the driving torque, termed by the factory as a power-flow change.

The Tiptronic selector offered the driver a gear shift with two operating planes. In the first plane a conventional P-R-N-D-3-2-1 automatic shift was available, but if the lever was moved to the second plane (to the right) the driver had a sequential "adaptive" shift. Pushing the lever forward would change to a higher gear, and pulling it back would change to a lower gear. If the car's speed did not match the desirable speed range for that ratio, the control unit would retain the shift command until the appropriate moment by assessing vehicle speed, accelerator actuation speed, engine speed, and lateral and longitudinal acceleration. The system was intended to prevent unwanted gear shifts in corners and to be responsive to "sporting" driving by sensing fast accelerator movements.

Despite all the hype about its electronic brains and so on, performance of the Tiptronic was down on a manual Carrera 2, 0 to 62 miles per hour (0 to 100 kilometers per hour) taking 6.6 seconds as opposed to 5.7 seconds. But let that not detract from the Tiptronic; it has been an outstanding improvement in automatic transmission technology, and its value is in its flexibility for town and country driving.

The Tiptronic system for the United States and Canada was improved for the 1992 model year with a revised 9:32 final drive ratio and with the addition of the Keylock/Shiftlock control system to prevent accidental selection of an incorrect ratio. This was extended to Tiptronic models for all markets the following year.

Electrical Equipment and Lighting

The alternator on the Carrera 4 was uprated to 1,610-watt/115-amp and charged a 72Ah battery. The new front deformable bumper had integrated driving lights and foglights. The new headlamps were sealed-beam units, and all markets (except right-hand drive and France) now had the same lights. At the rear, the old style of taillight was broadly retained, but the lenses were raked with the line of the rear body rather than presenting a vertical face. The rear foglamps were integrated into a new reflector strip fitted under the engine lid. The number plate lamps were now fitted in the bumper molding, above the number plate.

Suspension and Steering

The Carrera 4 suspension front and back was completely new and marked the end of torsion bars on the 911. The front differential and driveshafts meant there simply was not space for them. The MacPherson strut principle was maintained at the front, with concentric coil springs over the struts and aluminum lower arms. The new front suspension allowed a degree of front and back movement that had not been possible with the torsion bar arrangement, and this helped to subdue cabin noise on rough surfaces. Negative scrub radius (the 3.2 Carrera had positive scrub) was included in the front suspension geometry. This reflected the contribution of the new ABS to wheel stability under braking and gave the Carrera 4 a degree of automatic steering correction when the front wheels began to slip. A 20-millimeter front anti-roll bar replaced the outgoing 3.2 Carrera's 22-millimeter bar. The front suspension on the Carrera 2 was largely identical to the Carrera 4, except for the absence of driveshafts. The increased weight on the front axle was the main reason for the introduction of power steering on this 911, using the proven rack-and-pinion design.

At the rear the Turbo's cast-aluminum semi-trailing arms were used, with coil springs acting concentrically outside the existing shock absorbers. Rubber mountings allowed some wheel movement to give roll steer in cornering. Rear anti-roll bar size dropped from the 3.2 Carrera's 21 to 20 millimeters (or 19 millimeters on the Tiptronic). The rear suspension was common to Carrera 4 and Carrera 2.

Brakes

The brakes on the Carrera 4 were completely new, although derived from those on the 928 S4, and were linked to Bosch ABS (Anti-Block System). The brake servo acted in the same way to reduce the effort to move the master cylinder piston, but additional control was placed on the outlet, which included the ABS control unit. A separate hydraulic pump charged a pressure accumulator, which charged the control unit to provide energy to counter brake pedal force and provide the ABS function to each wheel. An ABS sensor was provided for each front

The front suspension discarded the 911's time-honored torsion bars and adopted conventional coil springs over the shock absorbers. A significant redesign of the front chassis was necessary to accommodate four-wheel drive.

The Carrera 2 RS arrived in late 1991. With no concessions to touring comfort, this car was modified to perform. The suspension was lowered 40 millimeters from standard, instantly giving the car a purposeful stance.

The Carrera 2 RS is barely suitable for road use. The Spartan interior includes lightened trim and racing bucket seats that are uncomfortable on long journeys. Revised door trims have canvas pulls and manual windows.

wheel, and there was a further one for the rear wheels. Under heavy braking, the rear brake pressure would be eased to prevent locking, as on the 3.2 Carreras. As brake pedal pressure was increased and the front wheels began to lock, the ABS would reduce the braking pressure through the control unit.

Brake disc sizes were 298 millimeters (11.6 inches) front and 299 millimeters (11.6 inches) rear—a minute difference!—on both Carrera models. The discs had four-piston aluminum calipers all round. The pistons were of unequal size on each face, with the front primary pistons being sized at 40 millimeters (1.56 inches) diameter and the secondary ones at 36 millimeters (1.40 inches). The rear calipers were smaller, with 30-millimeter (1.17-inch) and 28-millimeter (1.09-inch) diameter pistons. Cooling air for the front brakes was ducted from the twin horizontal slots under the front number plate.

Wheels and Tires

The looks of the 1989 Carrera 4 were set off by new seven-spoke, smoothly styled, slightly convex-faced alloy wheels, known as Club Sport wheels. Wheel and tire sizes were the same as the standard issue on that year's 3.2 Carrera, namely 6Jx16-inch front wheels with 205/55ZR tires and 8Jx16-inch rear wheels with 225/50ZR tires. Bridgestone RE71 tires were the preferred factory fit.

From the start of the 1992 model year, both the Carrera 4 and 2 received new "Cup Design" wheels. Derived from the Carrera Cup racing series, these attractive five-spoke alloy designs were unchanged in size and used the same tires.

Carrera 2 RS

Born out of the successful Carrera Cup racing series, the "second-generation" Carrera 2 RS was a sports model with little concession to comfort and was announced at the Geneva Motor Show in March 1991. The output of the rechipped 3.6-liter engine was increased to 260-brake horsepower at 6,100 rpm, with maximum torque of 325 Nm at 4,800 rpm. Pistons and cylinders were claimed to be matched and a sports flywheel lightened by 7 kilograms was used. The engine mounts were solid rubber and only a single cooling fan drive was used; 98 RON fuel was required and a low-rating 36-amp/hour alternator was fitted.

The standard form of the new RS was the Sport (or Lightweight), claimed by the factory to weigh 1,230 kilograms (2,712 pounds). Besides this basic model, three variants of the RS were offered: the Carrera Cup (option M001, for the racing series), the Touring (option M002), and the Competition (option M003, another racing version with small differences over the Carrera Cup model). We shall not discuss the two racing versions here, but a description of how the Touring model differed comes later.

The Sport was a stripped-out version with the sunroof, electric mirrors, electric seats, central locking, alarm, and electric windows removed, and the wiring loom to support these items was also largely removed. Recaro sports seats with only fore and aft adjustment were fitted, and these had seat belts color-coded to the body. There were no rear seats, this area being carpeted and having the RS logo on the firewall. There were simple door trims with door pull straps and manual window winders. There was provision only for a two-speaker radio system, and the side windows used thinner glass (3 millimeters instead of 4.7 millimeters). There was no interior sound insulation. Options were a leather-covered steering wheel with extended center hub, deletion of rear model designation, and a basic stereo/cassette at no extra cost.

Special seam welding was used on the bodyshells, and the wing edges were rolled to enable larger wheels to be fitted. Underbody sealer was deleted, and the body corrosion warranty was only three years as a result. Only the Space-Saver tire was covered by elementary carpeting in the front compartment, which also had a master switch, a 92-liter (20.24 Imperial gallons, 24.31 U.S. gallons) fuel tank, and an aluminum lid. The rear bumper was a new lightweight design, with the number plate lamps either side of the plate. Manually adjusted Turbo-style exterior mirrors were fitted.

The bodyshell was lowered by 40 millimeters (1.56 inches), and stiffer springs and shock absorbers were used. This was not a car to use for touring. The understeering nature of the car was increased by using a 24-millimeter (0.94-inch) diameter front anti-roll bar, up 4 millimeters (0.16 inch) on the Carrera 2. The standard car's steel front hubs were replaced by aluminum ones, and an adjustable rear anti-roll bar was fitted, reduced to 18 millimeters (0.70 inch) from the Carrera 2's 20 millimeters (0.78 inch). The rear suspension was modified to change the roll steer effect of the standard car and the spring plates allowed more negative camber of approximately 1 degree all around. Ball-type joints were used for the shock absorber top mountings front and rear. A cross-brace was fitted in the front compartment between the front shock absorber top mountings.

Brakes were from the Turbo at the front and from the Carrera Cup racer at the rear, the latter of 299 millimeters (11.66 inches) diameter and 24 millimeters

Available in the United States from 1992, the RS America was a reduced specification Carrera 2 rather than a high-performance special. It has driver and passenger air bags as standard, hence the revised steering wheel.

The engine of the RS America was the standard 250-brake horsepower Carrera 2 unit. Note the air conditioner compressor pipes leading directly out of the engine compartment to the remotely mounted condenser. The mechanism for the moving electric spoiler of the regular Carrera 4 and Carrera 2 models had displaced the condenser from its previous position under the engine lid grille.

(0.94 inch) thickness. The two-stage ABS was readjusted to provide better recovery during hard use.

The Cup Design magnesium alloy wheels were 7.5Jx17 front and 9Jx17 rear with 205/50ZR and 255/40ZR tires, respectively. No steering servo was fitted to left-hand-drive models. The G50 gearbox had closer ratios, with a higher final drive ratio of 3.444:1 and stronger synchromesh than the Carrera 2. The gear lever was shortened and moved close to the driver. A limited slip differential was standard.

The roadgoing RS variant was the Touring model (option M002), which weighed around 1,300 kilograms (2,866 pounds). This better-equipped RS came with a stereo/cassette, central locking, soundproofing, electric windows, and the rear panel trim found on the Carrera 2 (but no rear seats). It had Carrera two-door panels, sports seats with electric height adjustment, and the thinner side glass. It came with the aluminum front compartment lid, the 10-year body warranty (it had underbody protection), and the Carrera 2's wiring harness. Its options were headlamp washers, heated seats, electric sunroof, full interior climate control, a nontinted windshield, or a tinted windshield with a dark green upper edge.

Performance of the Sport was impressive, with a factory-quoted maximum speed of 162 miles per hour (261 kilometers per hour) and a 0- to 62-mile-per-hour (0- to 100-kilometer-per-hour) time of 5.4 seconds. The RS was not sold in the United States because its weight-saving thin glass and lack of door beams did not comply with federal regulations. Porsche's objective was to start production in the summer of 1991 and to make at least 1,000 units by the end of the year in order to qualify the car for the racing Group N/GT class. However, a total run of 2,051 cars was made to the end of the 1992 model year, of which 76 were Touring versions. But these figures should be treated with caution as there are discrepancies in the records. For the record, 120 Carrera Cup cars were built in 1991 and 113 in 1992.

As with all Carrera 4 and Carrera 2 models, the RS America has no bumper over-riders (right). The bumper is flexible, but it is necessary to park carefully to avoid scraping the paint. The fixed rear spoiler used on this model is the one previously seen on the 3.2 Carrera. The RS America does not have rear seats (far right), but unlike the Club Sport model of 1987 this model has doors to the storage boxes under the shelf.

RS America

This model was manufactured solely for the U.S. and Canadian market-place in 1992–1993. The concept of the RS America was similar to that of the European RS, but driver-reaction in the United States seemed to fall well short of the ecstatic reception given in Europe to the new Lightweight.

The first impression is that many of the weight-saving measures of the European RS were used on the RS America, but the key to understanding the difference was that the RS America sold for about $10,000 less than a regular Carrera 2; whereas, the European

RS sold for about $20,000 more. There was a significant amount of detail difference because the European RS was a homologation special for racing; whereas, the America was a low specification variant of the regular model.

The RS America saved weight by losing the air conditioning, power steering, electric sunroof, and rear seats. Sound insulation was removed from the rear firewall and the rear quarter panels. A lightweight fixed whaletail spoiler replaced the moving rear spoiler of the standard car. Inside the electric windows stayed, but the lightweight door trims, with door pulls, from the European RS were used. A storage compartment replaced the rear seats. In the front, lightweight fabric replaced the pile carpeting of the Carrera 2.

A sports suspension package was fitted (the same M030 option that was available for the Carrera 2), and the aluminum alloy Cup Design wheels were 7Jx17 with 205/50ZR tires at the front and 8Jx17 with 255/40ZR tires at the rear. Anti-roll bar sizes were 22 millimeters (0.86 inch) front and 20 millimeters (0.78 inch) rear.

Unlike the RS, the RS America used the standard 250-brake horsepower (DIN) engine. The factory's 0- to 62-mile-per-hour (0- to 100-kilometer-per-hour) time was 5.4 seconds and the top speed was 162 miles per hour (261 kilometers per hour). Weight was 1,340 kilograms (2,955 pounds) compared with 1,398 kilograms (3083 pounds) for the Carrera 2. Some 240 RS America models were sold before the start of the 1993 model year (in August 1992). These all carry the 1993 "P" designator in their chassis numbers, however, with engine numbers retaining the 1992 "N" designator.

America Roadster

This was a Turbo-Look Cabrio for the 1992 model year with the Carrera 2's normally aspirated 3.6-liter engine. It came complete with Cup Design wheels, as did all 1992 models. It had the fully automatic folding hood of the standard Cabrio and could be ordered with manual or Tiptronic transmission. Brakes were the Turbo's cross-perforated discs with a diameter of 322 millimeters (12.56 inches) at the front and 299 millimeters (11.66 inches) at the rear. The standard car's anti-roll bars were changed to 21 millimeters (0.82 inch) front and 22 millimeters (0.86 inch) rear, except that the rear bar was reduced to 21 millimeters (0.82 inch)

The Speedster returned in 1993 on the Carrera 2 chassis. Customers were not obliged to have body-color wheels, as here, but with the Speedster one was making a loud statement anyway.

The Speedster interior featured a color-coded instrument surround and Recaro bucket racing seats.

A limited-edition 911 (below) for the road was the RS3.8. Developed from the Carrera 2 RS, this 300-brake horsepower sprinter was a homologation special for GT racing in 1993. Note the biplane wing and the horizontal splitter protruding from the front spoiler. To celebrate the 30th anniversary of the 911 in 1993, a commemorative run of Carrera 4s with the Turbo bodyshell was produced. Apart from special paint, the main external distinguishing feature is this "30 Jahre" style of 911 logo (below left) on the engine lid.

when Tiptronic was specified. Factory figures gave performance as 0 to 62 miles per hour (0 to 100 kilometers per hour) in 5.5 seconds and a top speed of 158 miles per hour (254 kilometers per hour). A total of 250 cars were made.

Carrera 2 Speedster

Announced in October 1992, the new Speedster was based on the Carrera 2. The changes from the Coupe were based around the shortened windshield and simplified hood concept seen on the 1989 model. Interestingly, the Speedster was not offered from its introduction in Turbo Look, which had been far and away the most popular version in 1989.

Inside, the bucket Recaro seats from the RS were used, the backs of these being color-coded to the exterior body. Optionally, Sports seats that were electrically adjustable for height or the Carrera 2 multi-function seats with heating could be specified. Also color-coded inside were the door pull straps, the gear lever and handbrake boots, and the instrument mounting facia.

As before, the Speedster was well-equipped and was available in five-speed manual or Tiptronic forms. The standard Cup Design wheels were 6Jx17 front (with 205/55ZR tires) and 8Jx17 rear (with 225/50ZR tires), and these could be ordered with body coloring as well. The hood design benefited from improved windshield locks. Manually adjustable external mirrors from the Carrera 2 RS were used. Although a run of 3,000 Speedsters was planned for 1993, only 936 were actually built. Unlike the 1989 Speedster, the 1993 model had unique chassis number identification (see page 117).

911 Celebration

This model was a limited-edition Carrera 4 with the Turbo-Look bodyshell. However, the running gear remained standard Carrera 4, so these cars are not full Turbo-Look models, with the Turbo brakes and suspension.

The Celebration was introduced in March 1993 on the anniversary of 30 years of continuous production of the 911. The specification was like the 1993 Carrera 4 but with special paint and an interior featuring full leather and "30 Jahre 911" badges. It came with a 92-liter fuel tank (20.24 Imperial gallons, 24.31 U.S. gallons) and a stylized 911 badge on the engine cover with its underline embossed with the words "30 Jahre." The number of these cars manufactured was 911.

RS 3.8

The RS 3.8 was a limited-edition series that was intended to qualify the car for GT racing in 1993. These Weissach-built cars (about 100 were made) were distinguished by their large, adjustable biplane rear wing on a full Turbo-Look bodyshell. The engine (M64/04) had a capacity of 3,746cc and was not turbocharged. It produced 300-brake horsepower at 6,500 rpm and maximum torque of 360 Nm at 5,250 rpm. The compression ratio was 11.0:1 and Bosch Motronic 2.1 engine management was used. The Speedline 9Jx18 front wheels were fitted with 235/40ZR Dunlop tires, the 11Jx18 rears with 285/35ZR tires. Weight was reduced to 1,140 kilograms (without fuel), enabling 0 to 62 miles per hour (0 to 100 kilometers per hour) acceleration in 4.9 seconds and a top speed of 170 miles per hour (274 kilometers per hour).

Production Changes

1989 (Start of K-series)

Engine capacity 3,600cc with 100mm bore and 76.4mm stroke; sodium-filled 42.5mm intake valves, hollow 49mm exhaust valves; engine oil capacity reduced to 12 imperial pints (11.4 liters); new free-flow (all-metal) catalytic converter with low noise silencer (muffler); G64/00 five-speed gearbox, driving through torque-splitting center epicyclical differential; ratios as follows: first, 3.5:1; second, 2.118:1; third, 1.444:1; fourth, 1.086:1; fifth, 0.868:1; reverse, 2.857:1; final drive, 3.444:1; driveshaft forward to front differential (in torque tube) and rearward through hollow shaft in gearbox to rear differential; center differential linked to Bosch ABS provides four-wheel drive with torque sensing at each wheel; brakes are 298mm/28mm front and 299mm/24mm rear; new underbody with center tunnel to accommodate torque tube, new heating, and ventilation system; speed-controlled electrically operated rear spoiler; new front and rear bumpers, detail body changes to improve aerodynamics; coil spring suspension all around; new 77-liter fuel tank and front suspension changes shape of luggage compartment; asbestos-free materials now used on all models.

1990 (Start of L-series)

Two-mass flywheel lowers interior noise levels; 10-speaker fitment; headlamp height adjustment standard; new option of onboard computer, giving outside temperature, fuel consumption, and speeds, with read-out integrated into rev counter; Carrera 4 now available in Targa and Cabrio (with electrically operated roof) forms; Carrera 2 replaces 3.2 Carrera, based on Carrera 4 but rear-wheel-drive only, with same power, suspension, and brakes; available from launch as Coupe, Targa, or Cabrio; Carrera 2 offered with Tiptronic automatic gearbox; final drive ratios 3.444:1 (manual) or 3.667:1 (Tiptronic).

1991 (Start of M-series)

Air bags standard for driver and passenger on left-hand-drive cars from April 1991; interior light delay switch introduced on all models; new seat back release buttons on seat top; new control unit for the central locking allows doors to be locked and front luggage compartment then to be opened (and armed again after closing); sports suspension pack available for Carrera 2 (new shock absorbers, springs, and front anti-roll bar); manual gear ratios altered slightly to first 3.5:1, second 2.059:1, third 1.407:1, fourth 1.086:1, fifth 0.868: 1; new Tiptronic ratios of first 2.479:1, second 1.479:1, third 1.000:1, fourth 0.728:1, final drive 3.667:1

1992 (Start of N-series)

The Carrera 2 RS, RS America, and Turbo-Look Cabrio introduced for new model year; on Carrera 4 and 2, new Cup Design wheels replace seven-spoke CS design; new style external mirrors; new interiors.

1993 (Start of P-series)

Carrera 2 Speedster introduced; 911 Celebration model; otherwise no significant changes.

Dimensions

Wheelbas: 2,271mm. **Track (front/rear):** 1,379mm/1,374mm.
Length: 4,250mm. **Width:** 1,651mm.

Options

See listing in Carrera 3.2 (1984–1989) chapter (page 100).

Color Schemes

1989 (charts VDA 7/88, WVK 10720)

Standard body colors

Guards Red (80K), Black (700), Linen Gray (60M), Apricot Beige (548), Murano Green (22C), Grand Prix White (908), Dark Blue (347).

Identification

Model year	Model	Engine	Gearbox	Chassis numbers	Engine numbers
K-series 1989	Carrera	M64/01	G64/00	WP0ZZZ96ZKS40000 1– 2068	62K00001 onward
	Carrera 4 U.S.	M64/01	G64/00	WP0AB096KS45000 1–1117	62K00001 onward
L-series 1990	Carrera 4	M64/01	G64/00	WP0ZZZ96ZLS400001– 8329	62L00001 onward
	Carrera 4 Targa	M64/01	G64/00	WP0ZZZ96ZLS410001–1299	62L00001 onward
	Carrera 4 Cabrio	M64/01	G64/00	WP0ZZZ96ZLS420001–3411	62L00001 onward
	Carrera U.S.	M64/01	G64/00	WP0AB296LS450001–2117	62L00001 onward
	Carrera Canada	M64/01	G64/00	WP0AB096LS459001–9080	62L00001 onward
	Carrera 4 Targa Canada	M64/01	G64/00	WP0BB296LS4600001–0158	62L00001 onward
	Carrera 4 Targa U.S.	M64/01	G64/00	WP0BB096LS469001–9061	62L00001 onward
	Carrera /4 Cabrio U.S.	M64/01	G64/00	WP0CB096LS470001–0673	62L00001 onward
	Carrera 4 Cabrio Canada	M64/01	G64/00	WP0CB096LS479001–9061	62L00001 onward
	Carrera 2	M64/01	G50/03	As Carrera 4	62L00001 onward
	Carrera 2 Tiptronic	M64/01	G50/01	As Carrera 4	62L00001 onward
	Carrera 2 U.S.	M64/01	G50/01	As Carrera 4	62L00001 onward
M-series 1991	Carrera 4	M64/01	G64/00	WP0ZZZ96ZMS40000 1–7840	62M00001 onward
	Carrera 4 U.S.	M64/01	G64/00	WP0AB296MS410001–1608	62M00001 onward
	Carrera 4 Targa	M64/01	G64/00	WP0ZZZ96ZMS430001–1196	62M00001 onward
	Carrera 4 Targa U.S.	M64/01	G64/00	WP0BB296MS440001–0746	62M00001 onward
	Carrera 4 Cabrio	M64/01	G64/00	WP0ZZZ96ZMS450001–3886	62M00001 onward
	Carrera 4 Cabrio U.S.	M64/01	G64/00	WP0CB296MS460001–2207	62M00001 onward
	Carrera 2	M64/01	G50/03	WP0ZZZ96ZMS400001–7840	62M00001 onward
	Carrera Cup	M64/01	G50/03	WP0ZZZ96ZMS409001–120	62M00001 onward
N-series 1992	Carrera 4	M64/01	G64/00	WP0ZZZ96ZNS400001–04844	62N00001 onward
	Carrera 4 U.S.	M64/01	G64/00	WP0AB296ZNS420001–0715	62N00001 onward
	Carrera 4 Targa	M64/01	G64/00	WP0ZZZ96ZNS430001–0597	62N00001 onward
	Carrera 4 Targa U.S.	M64/01	G64/00	WP0BB296ZNS440001–0211	62N00001 onward
	Carrera 4 Cabrio	M64/01	G64/00	WP0ZZZ96ZNS450001–2885	62N00001 onward
	Carrera 4 Cabrio U.S.	M64/01	G64/00	WP0CB296ZNS460001–0992	62N00001 onward
	Carrera 2	M64/01	G50/03	WP0ZZZ96ZNS400001–04844	62N00001 onward
	Carrera 2 RS	M64/03	G50/10	WP0ZZZ96ZNS490001–1992	62N80001 onward
	Carrera 2 RS America	M64/01	G50/05	WP0AB296PS418001–18298	62N00001 onward
P-series 1993	Carrera 4	M64/01	G64/00	WP0ZZZ96ZPS40000 1–3249	62P00001 onward
	Carrera 4 U.S.	M64/01	G64/00	WP0AB296PS420001–0520	62P00001 onward
	Carrera 4 U.S. (718)	M64/01	G64/00	WP0AB296RNS420001–0280	62P00001 onward
	Carrera 4 Targa	M64/01	G64/00	WP0ZZZ96ZPS430001–0419	62P00001 onward
	Carrera 4 Targa U.S.	M64/01	G64/00	WP0BB296PS440001–0137	62P00001 onward
	Carrera 4 Targa U.S. (718)	M64/01	G64/00	WP0BB296RS440001–0081	62P00001 onward
	Carrera 4 Cabrio	M64/01	G64/00	WP0ZZZ96ZPS450001–1414	62P00001 onward
	Carrera 4 Cabrio U.S.	M64/01	G64/00	WP0CB296PS460001–0600	62P00001 onward
	Carrera 4 Cabrio U.S. (718)	M64/01	G64/00	WP0CB296RS460001–0138	62P00001 onward
	Carrera 2	M64/01	G50/03	WP0ZZZ96ZPS400001–3249	62P00001 onward
	Carrera 2 U.S.	M64/03	G50/05	As Carrera 4	62P80001 onward
	Carrera 2 Tiptronic	M64/01	A50/02	As Carrera 4	62P50001 onward
	Carrera 2 Tiptronic U.S.	M64/01	A50/03	As Carrera 4	62P50001 onward
	Carrera 2 RS America	M64/01	G50/05	WP0AB296PS418001–450	62P00001 onward
	Carrera 2 RS America (718)	M64/01	G50/05	WP0AB296PS418001–068	62P00001 onward
	Speedster	M64/01	G50/03	WP0AB296PS418001–509	62P00001 onward
	Speedster U.S.	M64/01	G50/00	WP0AB296PS418001–427	62P00001 onward
	Carrera RS 3.8	M64/04	G50/10	WP0ZZZ96ZPS497001–129	62P85001 onward

General notes: Manual gearbox The Carrera 4 gearbox (G64/00) was the same for all markets except Switzerland (G64/01). From 1991, the Carrera 4 gearbox for Taiwan was G24/02. On the Carrera 2, the Swiss gearbox was G50/02 with a longer fourth and fifth gear (for less noise). The Carrera 2 gearbox (also with optional limited slip differential) was G50/03 (or G50/04 for Switzerland). Gearboxes carried serial numbers (e.g., G5005 1 0 00001): the first five digits refer to the gearbox type, here G50/05; the next digit refers to whether a limited slip differential (lsd) is fitted (l or 2 = yes, 0 = no), with type 1 referring to the optional C2 40 percent unit and type 2 to the C2 RS 20–100 percent unit. **Tiptronic** Engines from 1991 were in the series 62M50001 onward; the Tiptronic gearbox type number was A50, with serial numbers in the series A50011 001945 onward. The 1991 Tiptronic was A50/01 only, but for 1992 there was A50/02 for RoW cars (serial numbers start at A5001) or A50/03 for U.S. and Taiwan (serial numbers start A5003). **Carrera 2 RS** 1992 basic version was the Sport/Lightweight/Basic model. Options on this were Carrera Cup (M001), Touring (M002), or Competition (M003). The chassis numbers shown above for the RS are only the production series not build numbers (see page 114). The 1992 Carrera Cup cars had chassis numbers starting at WP0ZZZ96ZNS499001; M003 versions were assigned chassis numbers starting with WP0ZZZ96ZNS498001. There is conflict in the numbering for the 1992 RS types, so treat the data presented here with caution. The 1992 RS America was option number M504. **Miscellaneous** 1990 U.S. Carreras were delivered with air bag. Canadian examples without air bag are shown with a 9 as the 13th character in the chassis number (instead of a 0). The 1993 Speedster is option M503 on the Cabrio chassis. U.S./Canada models after May 1993 were listed as 1994 (R-series) models.

Production Data

Model year	Model	Power (bhp DIN@rpm)	Torque (Nm@rpm)	Compression ratio	Weight (kg)	Number built
1989	Carrera 4	250@6,100	310@4,800	11.3:1	1,450	2,068
	Carrera 4 U.S.	250@6,100	310@4,800	11.3:1	1,450	1,117
1990	Carrera 2/4	250@6,100	310@4,800	11.3:1	1,350/1,450	3,957
	Carrera 2/4 Targa	250@6,100	310@4,800	11.3:1	1,400/1,500	322
	Carrera 2/4 Cabrio	250@6,100	310@4,800	11.3:1	1,400/1,500	895
	Carrera 2/4 U.S.	250@6,100	310@4,800	11.3:1	1,350/1,450	1,317
	Carrera 2/4 Canada	250@6,100	310@4,800	11.3:1	1,350/1,450	80
	Carrera 2/4 Targa U.S.	250@6,100	310@4,800	11.3:1	1,400/1,500	158
	Carrera 2/4 Targa Canada	250@6,100	310@4,800	11.3:1	1,400/1,500	61
	Carrera 2/4 Cabrio U.S.	250@6,100	310@4,800	11.3:1	1,400/1,500	673
	Carrera 2/4 Canada	250@6,100	310@4,800	11.3:1	1,350/1,450	61
1991	Carrera 2/4	250@6,100	310@4,800	11.3:1	1,350/1,450	7,840
	Carrera 2/4 U.S.	250@6,100	310@4,800	11.3:1	1,350/1,450	1,608
	Carrera 2/4 Targa	250@6,100	310@4,800	11.3:1	1,400/1,500	1,196
	Carrera 2/4 Targa U.S.	250@6,100	310@4,800	11.3:1	1,400/1,500	746
	Carrera 2/4 Cabrio	250@6,100	310@4,800	11.3:1	1,400/1,500	3,886
	Carrera 2/4 Cabrio U.S.	250@6,100	310@4,800	11.3:1	1,400/1,500	2,207
1992	Carrera 2/4	250@6,100	310@4,800	11.3:1	1,350/1,450	4,844
	Carrera 2/4 U.S.	250@6,100	310@4,800	11.3:1	1,350/1,450	715
	Carrera 2/4 Targa	250@6,100	310@4,800	11.3:1	1,400/1,500	597
	Carrera 2/4 Targa U.S.	250@6,100	310@4,800	11.3:1	1,400/1,500	211
	Carrera 2/4 Cabrio	250@6,100	310@4,800	11.3:1	1,400/1,500	2,885
	Carrera 2/4 Cabrio U.S.	250@6,100	310@4,800	11.3:1	1,400/1,500	992
	Carrera 2 RS	260@6,100	325@4,800	11.3:1	1,250	2,051
	RS America	250@6,100	310@4,800	11.3:1	1,340	298
1993	Carrera 2/4	250@6,100	310@4,800	11.3:1	1,350/1,450	3,249
	Carrera 2/4 U.S.	250@6,100	310@4,800	11.31	1,350/1,450	520
	Carrera 2/4 U.S. 718[1]	250@6,100	310@4,800	11.3:1	1,350/1,450	280
	Carrera 2/4 Targa	250@6,100	310@4,800	11.3:1	1,400/1,500	419
	Carrera 2/4 Targa U.S.	250@6,100	310@4,800	11.3:1	1,400/1,500	137
	Carrera 2/4 Targa U.S. 718[1]	250@6,100	310@4800	11.3:1	1,400/1,500	81
	Carrera 2/4 Cabrio	250@6,100	310@4,800	11.3:1	1,400/1,500	1,414
	Carrera 2/4 Cabrio U.S.	250@6,100	310@4,800	11.3:1	1,400/1,500	600
	Carrera 2/4 Cabrio U.S. 718[1]	250@6,100	310@4,800	11.3:1	1,400/1,500	138
	RS America	250@6,100	310@4,800	11.31	1,340	450
	RS America 718[1]	250@6,100	310@4,800	11.3:1	1,340	68
	Speedster	250@6,100	310@4,800	11.3:1	1,350	509
	Speedster U.S.	250@6,100	310@4,800	11.3:1	1,400	427

General notes

U.S. models are frequently quoted with a maximum power output of 247-brake horsepower, but this refers to the SAE net horsepower as opposed to the German standard DIN figure. U.S./Canada models after May 1993 were listed as 1994 (R-program) models.

Numbered notes

1. Option M718 refers to a 1993 midyear specification change.

Special order body colors

Forest Green Metallic (22E), Cognac Brown Metallic (40L), Coral Metallic (81 K), Baltic Blue Metallic (37B), Slate Gray Metallic (22D), Velvet Red Metallic (81 L), Diamond Blue Metallic (697), Linen Gray Metallic (55), Silver Metallic (980), Stone Gray Metallic (693).

Fabrics

Leatherette (BPX) in Linen Gray (4WX), Burgundy (3MK), Blue (1KX), Mahogany (1MX), Black (43S), or Cashmire Beige (7RT); leather (YDX) in Burgundy (7LD), Mahogany (2LX), Venetian Blue (7KC), Black (1AJ), Blue (7JX), Cashmire Beige (2WH), Velvet Red (4MT), Linen Gray (7VX), Silk Gray (5VT), Slate Gray (2WT), or Caramel (4UC); pinstripe velour (TPC) in Linen Gray/White (4WJ), Black/White (7BN), Mahogany/White (6LN), Blue/White (8GJ), Burgundy/White (1MJ), or Cashmire Beige/White (4TN); multi-color studio check (TPD) in Black (2VV), Mahogany (8XV), Blue (9JV), Burgundy (1MV), Linen Gray (6UV), or Cashmire Beige (5TC); fabric with in-woven diagonal "Porsche" script (TPC) in Black (2CZ), Cashmire Beige (7TH), Mahogany (4MR), Blue (6HZ), Burgundy (5LZ), or Linen Gray (5WZ); Cabrio hoods in Black, Mahogany, Blue, or Burgundy.

Carpets

Silk velour (TFK) in Mahogany (5MF), Blue (4KV), Linen Gray (2XF), Burgundy (8MD), Black (5FV), Slate Gray (3WT), Cashmire Beige (8UT), Velvet Red (9MT), Silk Gray (1VT), Caramel (5UM), or Venetian Blue (3KM).

1990 (charts WVK 102020, WVK 103815)

Standard body colors

As 1989 plus Marine Blue Metallic (35V).

Special order body colors

Satin Blue Metallic, Oak Green Metallic, Venetian Blue Metallic, Violet Blue Metallic, Cassis Red Metallic, Tahoe Blue Metallic, Granite Green Metallic, Turquoise Metallic, Lagoon Green Metallic, Zermatt Silver Metallic.

Fabrics Same as 1989.

Carpets Same as 1989.

1991 (charts VMK 8/90, WVK 127410)

Standard body colors

Guards Red* (80K), Black* (700), Rubystone Red* (82N), Maritime Blue* (38B), Grand Prix White* (908), Signal Green (22S), Mint Green (22R).

Special order body colors

Cobalt Blue Metallic (37U), Oak Green Metallic (22L), Polar Silver Metallic* (92E), Slate Gray Metallic (22D), Black Metallic (738), Horizon Blue Metallic (37X), Midnight Blue Metallic* (37W), Coral Red Metallic (82H), Amethyst Metallic* (38A), Amazon Green Metallic (37Z).

* Indicates colors available on Carrera 2 RS.

Fabrics

Leatherette (BPX) in Classic Gray (5WH), Cobalt Blue (5ZF), Light Gray (3ZT), Magenta (9WX), Black (43S), or Cashmire Beige (7RT); Leather (YDS) in Classic Gray (6XL), Light Gray (8ZL), Black (8YR), Cobalt Blue (9YL), Cashmire Beige (4YU), Magenta (6YL), Sherwood Green (J25), Carrera Gray (D35), or Matador Red (M05); multi-color studio check (TPD) in Black (2VV), Classic Gray (9WT), Cobalt Blue (9YD), Magenta (1 MV), Light Gray (6UV), or Cashmire Beige (5TC); fabric with in-woven diagonal "Porsche" script (TPC) in Black (2CZ), Cashmire Beige (TH), Light Gray (7TH), Classic Gray (6WC), Cobalt Blue (7ZK), or Magenta (9YC)

Carpets

Silk velour (TLV) in Classic Gray (4XR), Light Gray (6YR), Magenta (8WZ), Cobalt Blue (4ZN), Black (5FV), Matador Red (M33), Cashmire Beige (8UT), Carrera Gray (D13) or Sherwood Green (J23),

1992 (chart WVKI2742192)

Standard body colors

Black (A1), Guards Red (G1), Grand Prix White (P5), Rubystone Red (G4), Maritime Blue (F2), Signal Green (M1), Mint Green (N4).

Metallic body colors

Blue (Z8), Amazon Green (N7) Amethyst (F9), Slate Gray (09), Horizon Blue (F4), Coral Red (G7), Oak Green (N9), Cobalt Blue (F6), Midnight Blue (F8), Polar Silver (A8).

Special order body colors

Satin Blue Metallic (50), Marine Blue Metallic (56), Cassis Red Metallic (52), Violet Blue Metallic (57), Granite Green Metallic (53), Tahoe Blue Metallic, Lagoon Green Metallic (54), Turquoise Metallic (59), Zermatt Silver Metallic (55).

Special body colors for Turbo-Look

(chart WVK126910 10/92)
Raspberry Red Metallic (with Red interior), Wimbledon Green Metallic (with Green interior), Lavender Blue Metallic (with Gray interior).

Fabrics

Multi-color studio check in Blue, Light Gray, Cashmire Beige, Classic Gray, Light Gray, or Cobalt Blue; other Porsche fabrics unchanged; leather in Black, Light Gray, Cashmire Beige, Light Gray, or Cobalt Blue; custom leather in Matador Red, Carrera Gray, Sherwood Green; Cabrio hoods in Black, Dark Blue, Cobalt Blue, or Magenta.

Carpets

Same as 1991.

1993 (charts WKV 127 42093, VMK 8/92)

Standard body colors

Same as 1992, excluding Rubystone Red.

Special order body colors

Same as 1992, excluding Metallic Coral Red, but with addition of Violet Blue Metallic (57), Wimbledon Green Metallic (B5), Raspberry Red Metallic (A7), and (in early 1993) Speed Yellow.

Fabrics

Same as 1992, but Cabrio hoods now include Classic Gray.

Carpets Same as 1991.

The 911 Turbo (1975–1993)

If any one model of Porsche 911 comes to the mind of the proverbial man-in-the-street, then it is an image of a black Turbo, crouched low on wide wheels clothed with big wing extensions. The Turbo conjures up fantasies of raw power and elegance, of high automotive technology and style. In 1974, in post-oil-crisis Europe, it was a bold and courageous statement of defiance about the future that delighted the automotive industry and Porsche's customers alike.

The Turbo's pedigree and its character were faultless. Turbocharging had made its name on Porsche racing cars with the Can-Am 917-10s and 917-30s of 1972–1973. These huge open sports cars, with flat-12 turbocharged engines developing up to 1,100-brake horsepower, had crushed their opposition.

The road car's origins can be traced back to a prototype 911 study shown at the 1973 Paris Salon. A year of intensive development followed, during which the company agonized internally about whether such a powerful car had a place on roads, which were, at that time of the Middle

East oil crisis, restricted to meager speed limits. But Ernst Fuhrmann's leadership gave the Turbo a clear direction, and in October 1974, the new production model was unveiled. Code-numbered 930 internally, the Turbo was instantly given the status of company flagship and demonstrated new

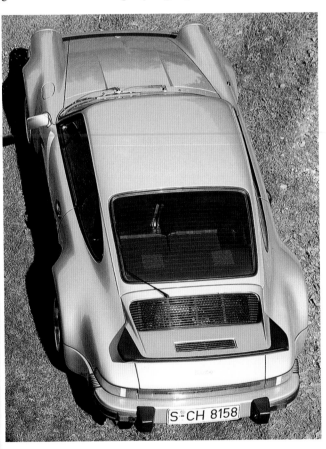

The Turbo's dramatically flared wheel arches and large rear spoiler caught the imagination of enthusiasts the world over. This is an early production car from 1974.

Evolution Outline

October 1974: The 3.0 Turbo is announced with 260-brake horsepower (U.S. models 245-brake horsepower from 1975), extended wheel arch flares and tea-tray spoiler, and a four-speed gearbox.

October 1976: The Martini limited edition is introduced.

August 1977: A 3.3-liter model (300-brake horsepower or 265-brake horsepower for U.S.) is introduced with an intercooler and 917 brakes.

July 1979: The Turbo is discontinued in the United States.

August 1982: Improvements are made to the exhaust to reduce air pollution and noise.

August 1985: The engine is upgraded with Motronic engine management; production resumed for the United States with the Turbo SE/930S (Slant-Nose) limited edition. The Turbo is now available in Targa and Cabriolet forms.

October 1988: The G50 five-speed gearbox is introduced.

July 1989: The Turbo is discontinued.

March 1990: A new Turbo is announced, using the Carrera 2 chassis (3.3 liters with 320-brake horsepower).

October 1992: The engine is enlarged to 3.6 liters (360-brake horsepower).

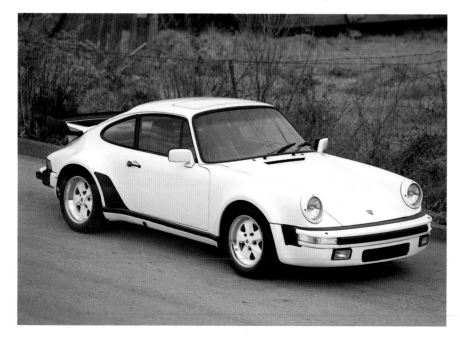

Alan Stein's lovely U.K.-specification 3-liter 911 Turbo (above). The right-hand-drive version did not become available until September 1975, so it featured all the 1976 model year benefits such as a zinc-coated bodyshell and new electrically operated door mirrors. Jim Boyden's 1986 U.S. Turbo (below) is a fine example of the car that was re-introduced to the American market after an absence of six years.

levels of 911 luxury and technology. Incidentally, the original official designation for the car was 911 Turbo, not 930 Turbo.

The marketing people initially wanted the Turbo to be a stripped-out lightweight, expecting demand to be as strong as that seen previously with the 1973 Carrera RS. Like the RS, the Turbo was playing its part in the racing homologation game, the original plan having been to build a series of 500 over the allowed period of two years. The salesmen keenly sold the early Turbos on the basis that the model would remain a limited edition, but with all the development involved it seems unlikely that Fuhrmann and his directors shared this view. In any case, the Turbo's popularity was such that the planned 500 production run was more than doubled. The Turbo's future was ensured.

The Turbo featured a completely reworked flat-six engine of 3 liters, and introduced a whole new set of design margins. At a stroke, this countered some suggestions that, in growing from 2 liters to 2.7 liters, the original engine was fully stretched and conceding some of its original reliability. The 3-liter was a superb engine and laid the foundation for Porsche's 911 engine programmers right through to the present day.

The new engine turned out to have immense marketing power. It became a real status symbol to have that little word *Turbo* on your rear deck, and this fashion subsequently spread right across the motor industry. Yet for all the hype, in bare statistical terms, the Turbo's overall performance was not much better than that of the Carrera RS. This was due to the difficulty of spinning the wheels under hard acceleration (to obtain 0- to 60-mile-per-hour times), the ratio gaps in the four-speed gearbox, and the car's extra weight. The 2.7 Carrera with 210-brake horsepower returned a maximum speed of 140 miles per hour (225 kilometers per hour) and went to 60 miles per hour in 6.3 seconds. The Turbo with 260-brake horsepower managed 153 miles per hour (246 kilometers per hour) and reached 60 miles per hour in 6.1 seconds.

Torque was much improved as well, the peak rising from 255 Nm at 5,100 rpm to 343 Nm at 4,000 rpm. The curve was less peaky, and this allowed the engineers to justify only four speeds in the redesigned gearbox. At the time, Porsche told its customers that the engine could pull so strongly from low revs that five speeds were simply unnecessary. As an aside, the presence of the turbo in the exhaust actually made the 911 quieter. The new 3-liter engine, with many improvements over the sometimes not-as-dependable 2.7-liter unit, also proved to be very reliable.

But what really set the Turbo apart was its looks, which were quite unlike those of any other production 911. With a deep front air dam, large rear spoiler, and heavily flared wheel arches front and back, the car looked fantastic. Porsche was playing to the exclusivity market with the Turbo in a way that it had not dared contemplate before.

For 1978, the engine capacity was increased to 3.3-liters, and the Turbo received the brakes it should have had from the start (early cars are noticeably underbraked). The engine upgrade seemed a big step at the time, but history shows it to have been simply another stage in the relentless enlargement of the flat-six. The 3.3-liter Turbo was hailed by *Motor* in 1978 as the quickest production road car it had ever tested. The Turbo progressively acquired all the most

By 1986 the rear spoiler was deepened (above) on its underside to allow the intercooler to exhaust through the engine grille. As a point of detail, the new U.S. cars were no longer termed "Turbo Carreras." The body warranty was extended to 10 years on 1986 models. Robin Duckitt's 1989 car (below) is a U.K.-specification limited edition built as a final batch before what was expected to be the Turbo's permanent demise. This car, typical of the customizing work performed by Porsche during the late 1980s, features the rear wings of the Slant-Nose model, but with conventional headlamps and a deep front skirt. A new Turbo, however, had arrived within a year.

Derived from the Carrera 2, the new 3.6-liter Turbo of 1993 had a 360-brake horsepower engine that delivered shatteringly quick performance.

The whaletail spoiler was derived from the design used on the 1973–1974 3-litre RS. The 1975 model has a small secondary engine cooling grille, a style that was used only for one year.

So much heat was generated in the engine compartment, particularly at standstill, that the secondary engine cooling grille was enlarged for 1976.

modern technical, environmental, and comfort features, and usually received them ahead of the regular 911 range.

Magazine road tests leading up to 1980 clearly carry the message that the 3.3 Turbo was probably going to be the last and the very best of the 911 line. Fuhrmann was seriously thinking about the end of the 911 series and was not inclined to keep shoveling money into development of a separate Turbo model. It was for this reason that Porsche called a halt to Turbo sales to the United States and Japan at the end of 1980. This was to Canada's gain because it received the more powerful European-specification Turbo from 1981.

But the Turbo would not lie down, especially in Europe. Eventually in 1986, the 930 made it back to the United States, at least partly compensating for the fact that federal laws had kept the sensational 959 off America's highways. Even the Turbo's second demise in 1989 was strongly challenged by its ardent fans. The discontinuation of the Turbo that year was much over-sold by dealer salesmen. They said it was the last chance to buy one and cleared their showrooms and lost a lot of respect from regular buyers in the process because a new-shape Turbo was rolled out at the 1990 Geneva Salon. Many buyers of the old model had thought they were getting a last-of-the-line landmark in 1989. The new model was on sale by the end of 1990.

The new Turbo with the Carrera 2 shape developed 320-brake horsepower from its 3.3-liter engine. When the capacity was stretched to 3.6 liters in 1993, however, performance became nothing short of sensational. Two 3.6-liter versions were available. The standard model with 360-brake horsepower yielded a maximum speed of 175 miles per hour (282 kilometers per hour) and 0 to 62 miles per hour (0 to 100 kilometers per hour) in 4.8 seconds. Then there was the 381-brake horsepower Turbo S, with a maximum speed of 180 miles per hour (290 kilometers per hour) and a 0- to 62-mile-per-hour (0- to 100-kilometer-per-hour) time of just 4.66 seconds—and these are factory figures, which have always been traditionally conservative.

The text that follows only describes new Turbo fittings or differences from the standard 911 of the same model year.

Bodyshell

The 911 Turbo was developed from the H-program (1975 model year) 911 Coupe bodyshell, the impetus behind its revised body shape being aerodynamic development. The front and rear spoiler combination first seen on the 3.0 RS was refined for road use, significantly reducing positive lift at front and rear. But the new wide wing extensions were bad news aerodynamically: The Turbo's frontal area was greater, and so the penetration of the car through the air was poorer when compared to the slim bodyshells of models like the 2.7 Carrera or the 911S.

No one, except perhaps the aerodynamicists, worried too much about this when the car had an extra 50 brake horsepower and looked so good.

From September 1975, when the first right-hand-drive cars became available in the U.K., the Turbo was covered by the new six-year anti-corrosion warranty on the basic load-bearing platform, for which zinc-coated steel panels were used throughout.

From 1978, the whaletail rear spoiler gave way to a tea tray—and there is a difference! The tea tray had a larger area in plain view and was slightly higher in elevation than the whaletail, in order to accommodate the new air-to-air inter-cooler under the central grille area. The tea tray was easily spotted from the side by the upturned lip around its rear and side edges.

In 1986, the anti-rust warranty was lengthened to 10 years as with the other models. This year also saw the availability of the Turbo in Targa form, and the option of the uprated Turbo 930S in the United States or Turbo SE in the U.K. The Turbo could be ordered in Cabrio form as well from September 1987, and any of the three body styles could now be specified in a Slant-Nose version.

At the Geneva Motor Show in March 1990, the new Turbo was launched with the new 911 shape (internal code number 964) first seen on the Carrera 4. The 1991 model year Turbo (as it became) was fitted with a different rear tea-tray spoiler, but no additional front lip spoiler was necessary. The deformable front and rear bumper panels and smooth undertray were the same as on the Carrera 4. The 3.6 Turbo was announced in October 1992 and was available only in coupe form. It was said that the additional torque would not be suitable for the Cabriolet.

Body Trim

The original Turbo in standard form shared with the 2.7 Carrera the new black-look to the windows, door handles, and wipers, completely eliminating chrome from the car's trim and complementing the aggressive character that the changed body shape suggested, but chrome trim remained an option. As final styling touches, the headlamp rims were color-coded and the front parts of the wide rear wheel arches were accented by black protective decals that were supposedly there to stop stone chips, but they also told everyone that these 911s were that little bit different. The rear spoiler included a small grille in the high-pressure top section, to feed air to the cooling blower and to help with cooling the engine compartment when at a standstill. The main grille supplied the air conditioning condenser.

Aside from the obvious bodywork differences, Turbos could be identified by a small "Turbo" script or "Turbo Carrera" on American models on the lower central section of the engine cover. Headlamp washers, foglamps, rear wiper, tinted glass, and an electric sunroof were standard. The Turbo shared the 80-liter fuel tank that had been introduced on the previous year's G-program models. From 1976, an electrically heated and adjustable driver's door mirror was fitted.

The Turbo was the first model to receive new shape external mirrors and a bonded-in windshield in 1990.

Interior Trim

The emphasis was on luxury with the original Turbo. The standard package contained the automatic climate control by Behr, leather seats with tartan inlay, special carpets, stereo/cassette with four speakers (normally an option), and

For 1978 the whaletail gave way to the tea tray, which had one large grille on its upper surface.

The dual functions of the tea-tray grille can be seen with the engine lid raised: The air-to-air intercooler connected into the engine intake manifold is on the left, while the air conditioning condenser on the right is mounted directly to the grille itself.

This 1986 Turbo has a replacement front air dam, complete with opening for a supplementary oil cooler and integrated mountings for driving lights.

These large intakes in the rear wings of this 1989 car were copied from those of the racing 935, but they were more for appearance than function on the road cars.

The first Turbos had the full luxury treatment, featuring a new tartan inlay to the leather seats, a four-speaker stereo with speakers in the doors, and an automatic heater control.

The smart Burgundy interior of this 1986 U.S. Turbo features that year's ventilation improvements, with larger face and side window vents and a new switchgear presentation.

The Turbo's power was nothing special at low revs, but then it arrived all in a rush, that little needle flicking around the dial as the car surged forward. The boost gauge did not become standard on Turbos until the 1977 model year.

extra sound deadening. The rear fan used to improve heater performance on the standard 911 was deleted on the Turbo due to lack of space. Later improvements, which generally led the normally aspirated models, are given in the data section (pages 132–134).

All the refinements introduced on the Carrera 4 and Carrera 2 were given to the 1991 model year Turbo, including the new center console and underdash glove compartment.

Dashboard and Instruments

Differences from the normal 911 were minimal: A smaller three-spoke steering wheel was fitted and the rev counter read to 7,000 rpm instead of 8,000 rpm. Surprisingly, a boost gauge was not fitted to the Turbo until the 1977 model year. At the same time, the heater controls were lit, a seat belt warning light was added, and the handbrake lever mechanism was improved.

Engine

The engine (coded 930/50) was developed from the Carrera RS 3.0 unit. Its capacity of 2,994cc was achieved with larger barrels of 95-millimeter (3.70-inch) bore, but the 70.4-millimeter (2.75-inch) stroke was unchanged.

A single KKK Type 3LDZ exhaust-driven turbocharger ran to a maximum speed of between 80,000 and 100,000 rpm and delivered maximum boost of 0.8 bar. An all-new induction/exhaust system was designed for the turbocharger and wastegate installation. The turbo was installed after the heat exchangers, upstream of the silencer (muffler), and fed from both cylinder banks.

An aluminum crankcase with wider-spaced cylinder head studs was used to suit the larger Nikasil barrels with shrouded stud passages, and there were new stronger forged-alloy pistons on the existing rods and crank. Compression ratio was reduced from 8.5:1 to 6.5:1, but with the turbo at maximum boost the computed ratio became 11.7:1. The pistons were cooled by oil squirters from below, and this cooling requirement, plus the need to maintain a high oil flow through the turbocharger bearings, resulted in the crankcase oil circulation and scavenge pumps being increased in size by 8 millimeters (0.13 inch) and oil capacity growing to 13 liters. The scavenge pump, driven from the end of the left camshaft, returned oil to the main oil tank.

The camshaft housing design was simplified, and the cams now ran in four bearing journals instead of three. There were new cylinder heads with smaller ports (relative to the 2.7 Carrera), and milder cam timing gave better low speed throttle response. The valve-included angle was reduced by 2 degrees 15 minutes, but the valves themselves were the same size as on the RS 3.0 at 49 millimeters (1.91 inches) inlet and 41.5 millimeters (1.62 inches) sodium-cooled exhaust. Fuel of 96 RON was required, but it could be lead-free. Sparks were generated using new breakerless ignition, and fuel was controlled from Bosch K-Jetronic injection, fitted with a larger air throttle valve of 110 millimeters instead of 85 millimeters. The throttle valve area contained the vacuum bleed for the new brake servo. The Turbo was also fitted with a faster-running cooling fan, achieved by using different pulleys. The European engine was 32 kilograms (71 pounds) heavier than the 2.7-liter unit.

Cars for the United States, Canada, and Japan were fitted with thermal reactors fed by a camshaft-driven air pump. Exhaust gas recirculation was also used from 1977 to reduce emissions. The emissions hardware resulted in a maximum power figure of 245-brake horsepower, 15-brake horsepower lower than the Rest-of-the-World level.

For the 1976 models, a by-pass valve in the intake manifolding reduced the ferocity of the "kick" in the back when the accelerator was floored. Previously, around 3,500 rpm had been the threshold of a rocketlike ignition sequence, but now the power came in more progressively, more like an express train, from below 3,000 rpm.

The Turbo engine had its first major upgrade in 1978, going to 3.3 liters. Bore and stroke were increased to 95 millimeters (3.71 inches) and 74.4 millimeters (2.90 inches), respectively, and the main bearings and con rod "big ends" were also enlarged. Compression ratio was raised to 7.0:1. An air-to-air intercooler, located just under the main engine lid grille area, reduced charge air temperature by 50 to 60 degrees Centigrade and, together with the other changes, resulted in a maximum output of 300-brake horsepower, up by 40-brake horsepower. Torque increased, too, to 412 Nm at 4,000 rpm. The new rubber-center clutch design also seen on the 911SC that year resulted in the engine being moved back by 30 millimeters (1.17 inch), which shows how much better the handling had become since the mid-1960s. Also like the new 911SC, every 1978 Turbo was fitted with an air pump to reduce exhaust emissions. All U.S. Turbo models had thermal reactors, but Californian cars also had an additional vacuum control to retard the ignition timing at full load and so reduce emissions further; this extra vacuum control became standard across the U.S. range in 1980.

Progressive improvements to the Turbo engine in 1983 and 1986 were aimed at reduced emissions and noise, the latter dropping by a claimed 25 percent (from 82 dB to 79 dB) on the logarithmic decibel scale. In 1983, maximum torque was edged up to 432 Nm at 4,000 rpm with improvements to the Bosch K-Jetronic fuel injection and the ignition: The injection had a new warm-up regulator and capsule valve in the fuel distributor, while the ignition distributor now had a double vacuum advance/retard and temperature compensation. The revised engine (930/66) had a new exhaust system, with the wastegate exhaust now going directly to atmosphere and the exhausts finishing as a pair of tailpipes on the left side. For the 1986 model year, the engine was heavily revised again (930/68) to bring it in line with worldwide emissions legislation. This was made

The tidy luggage compartment of a 1986 U.S. Turbo (above): The aftermarket brace between the tops of the MacPherson struts is a well-proven modification to stiffen the front structure of a 911, thereby reducing wheel camber change during hard cornering. When stripped of its carpets (below), the luggage compartment of the 3.6 Turbo shows how carefully every component has been packaged. The front strut brace is now standard.

Twin exhaust tailpipes were first seen on the 1983 Turbos when the wastegate exhaust was taken directly to atmosphere.

possible by the new mapped Digital Motor Electronics (DME, or Motronic, as it became known) developed by Bosch. Equipped with this new motor, the Turbo went on sale again in the United States.

The 1991 model year Turbo was still 3.3 liters, but offered 320-brake horsepower at 5,750 rpm and a stunning 450 Nm of torque at 4,500 rpm. It featured a revised resonant air intake system with passages designed for minimum flow loss as well as being matched to a new exhaust. The remapped Bosch Motronic system resulted in more power, better fuel consumption, and improved emissions. The intercooler was enlarged by a claimed 50 percent in terms of air volume, and there was a bigger turbocharger with a new impeller for low-speed response and 0.7 bar maximum boost. All markets had all-metal (and very compact) three-way closed-loop catalytic converters, the converter and silencer fitted to the wastegate forming the left-side exhaust outlet. The main silencer had increased volume and was now positioned longitudinally on the right-hand side of the engine, with its own outlet on the left. New for the Turbo were hydro-bushings for the engine mountings to reduce internal vibration, and cabin noise was also reduced by a dual mass flywheel.

A turbocharged version of the 3.6-liter engine from the Carrera 4 and Carrera 2 was introduced for the spring of 1993. It used the crankshaft, rods, crankcase, camshaft assemblies, and barrels from the Carrera 2, but the pistons and the camshafts themselves (with increased lift and greater overlap) were new. Unlike the Carrera 2 engine, only a single spark plug per cylinder was used, for space reasons.

The first turbo installations were fairly simple compared with what came later. The large duct on the left (complete with wastegate below) is the charge air feed, and the boosted charge returns from the turbo in the other large duct adjacent to it. The turbo itself is mounted below the engine compartment metalwork between the heat exchangers and final silencer.

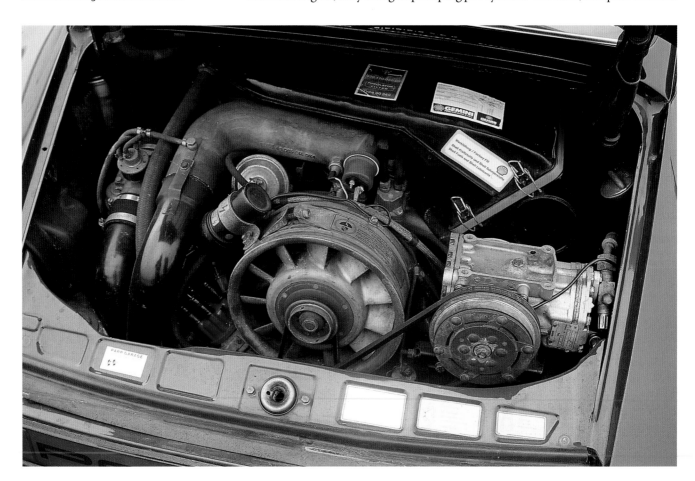

The previous model's early Motronic injection ignition system was retained. Compared with the 3.3-liter engine, the compression ratio was increased from 7.0:1 to 7.5:1, and maximum boost went up to 0.85 bar. Power rose from 320-brake horsepower to 360-brake horsepower, and Porsche claimed fuel consumption was unchanged, if not better.

Transmission

There was an all-new four-speed gearbox (coded 930/30) for the original Turbo, designed so that the new, deeply finned gearbox casing in aluminum (it had been magnesium) was within the same physical envelope as the 915 gearbox. It was designed with a maximum torque capacity of 442 Nm, a reasonable margin on the 1975 engine's output of 343 Nm. The gear wheels themselves were wider and stronger than the 915 gears. An option was a final drive gear set (the 930/32 gearbox) to balance the drive ratio when optional 225/50 tires were fitted. The standard final drive was 4.222:1; the option was 4000:1.

The busy engine compartment of a 1986 U.S. Turbo: The horizontal radiator is the air-to-air intercooler, placed after the turbocharger in the high-pressure duct to the intake plenum. The intercooler reduces the temperature of the charge air and noticeably improves engine power as a result.

The clutch diameter was increased from 225 millimeters (8.78 inches) to 240 millimeters (9.36 inches) and gave increased pedal pressure, but in 1977 an over-center "assister" spring reduced pedal effort. In 1978, a new rubber-centered clutch was fitted, while the pressure plate and clutch housing were made from cast iron to improve strength. The new clutch hub eliminated gear chatter at engine idle, but time would show that this clutch design was not very reliable.

In 1989, the Turbo was offered for the first time with a standard five-speed gearbox, based on the new G50 design that had been announced in 1986 for the 3.2 Carrera. The new 1991 model with the Carrera 4 bodyshell carried over this five-speed gearbox, but with revised ratios and the more precise gear shift mechanism seen on the Carrera 2. It also used the double-mass ZMS flywheel introduced on the Carrera 4 and 2 the same year. The limited slip differential became standard on the new 1991 model and was the same type as used on the Carrera 2 RS, namely with as little as 20 percent locking factor under acceleration and up to 100 percent lock-up on over-run. The 1993 model used the same G50/52 gearbox as the 1991–1992 models.

Electrical Equipment and Lighting

The 1975 Turbo was launched with a 12-volt/66-amp/hour battery (88-amp/hour optional) with a Bosch 980-watt alternator. Alternator output was raised twice, to 1,050 watts/75 amps in 1982 and to 1,260 watts/90 amps (with a standard 88-amp/hour battery) in 1989. Automatic cabin heat regulation was introduced, using heat sensors in the exhaust and cabin. As on the atmospheric models, the headlamps were H4 with a rating of 60 watts (main beam) and 55 watts (dipped). The heated rear window had two-stage operation.

For the 1991 model year, the Turbo received the onboard computer given to the Tiptronic the previous year. By 1993, the battery was 75 amp/hours and the alternator capacity was 1,610 watts/115 amps.

By 1986 the sealed-beam Hella headlamps fitted to U.S. cars were available with the more powerful H4 filaments.

A mud-spattered 1975 Turbo rear end shows off its Bilstein shock absorber and the engine's lower valve covers newly strengthened by added ribbing. The brake calipers look far too humble for the performance of the car. The Turbo did not receive suitably powerful brakes until the 1978 model year.

Suspension and Steering

The Turbo's suspension setup was derived from that of the 3.0 RSR. At the front, there was increased negative camber and reduced castor, making the steering heavier. The front crossmember was cast aluminum and the front suspension had anti-dive geometry, created by raising the rear mounting of the lower wishbones. The front track (on 7-inch rims) was increased by 60 millimeters (2.34 inches). The front anti-roll bar was the old 18-millimeter (0.70-inch) diameter design used on the 1973 911 models, but a new one-piece bar of 20 millimeters (0.78 inch) was adopted in 1977, and this increased to 22 millimeters (0.86 inch) for 1985. For the new 964 Turbo of 1991, the front anti-roll bar was reduced to 21 millimeters, staying at that size for the 3.6-liter Turbo. Rear anti-roll bar size from 1975 was 18 millimeters, but from the 1985 model year this was increased to 20 millimeters. For the 964-based Turbo, for 1991, the rear anti-roll bar stayed at 20 millimeters, increasing to 22 millimeters for the 3.6-liter model. Bilstein gas shock absorbers were used all round.

The geometry of the 1975 model rear semi-trailing arms was changed to reduce squat under acceleration and the track (on 8-inch rims) increased by 120 millimeters (4.68 inches). These semi-trailing arms were now sand-cast aluminum, and the rear wheel bearing carriers were designed to take bearings from the 917 sports racer. Front torsion bar size was 19 millimeters (0.74 inch), the same as the regular 911s. Rear torsion bar diameter was 26 millimeters (1.01 inch), but in 1989 the size increased to 27 millimeters (1.05 inches). Anti-roll bar diameter started at 18 millimeters (0.70 inch) in 1975, went to 20 millimeters (0.78 inch) in 1985, but returned to 18 millimeters (0.70 inch) in 1989. When the new 964-based Turbo model appeared, the standard Carrera 2 suspension was uprated with stiffer springs and shock absorbers. Steering was power-assisted for the first time on a Turbo with damping.

The 1991 model steering was servo-assisted and higher-geared. The suspension was also heavily revised, adopting a coil spring over damper layout with MacPherson struts at the front and semi-trailing arms at the rear. The rear swingarms had toe angle correction in movement to improve stability in a straight line or when changing direction rapidly, particularly when the throttle was closed in a corner.

Brakes

If the original Turbo's looks and engine received all the development attention, the brakes took a few years to catch up. Although the prototype used cross-drilled and ventilated discs from the 917 sports racing cars at front and rear, it was felt that the long-term reliability of these racing-developed items was insufficiently understood (there had been cracking problems between the drilled holes) to include them on a production car. The brakes for the first Turbo, therefore, were carried over from the 2.7-liter Carrera and used S-type aluminum front calipers and M-type cast-iron rear calipers.

The 917-derived brakes were eventually seen on the 3.3-liter Turbo in 1978 and were the largest so far used on a production 911. The new discs were 304-millimeter (11.86-inch) diameter and 32-millimeter (1.25-inch) thick at the front, and 309-millimeter (12.05-inch) diameter and 28-millimeter (1.09-inch) thick at the rear. They were mounted on aluminum hubs and used four-piston aluminum calipers with heavy finning to help cooling. The new brakes gave the 3.3-liter Turbo huge reserves of stopping power.

A brake servo reduced pedal effort for left-hand-drive markets for 1977, and this improvement was carried over to right-hand-drive models in 1978. The ratio of the servo was increased from the original 2.5:1 to 3.0:1 on 1985 models, on which a new brake master cylinder contributed to reducing pedal effort by nearly 25 percent.

ABS anti-lock braking was introduced on the 1991 model Turbo with the adoption of the chassis derived from the Carrera 4. Brake disc diameter changed on the 1991 models to 322 millimeters (12.68 inches) front and 299 millimeters (11.77 inches) rear. The brakes fitted to the 1993 Turbo broke new ground in that Brembo, the manufacturer, was able to paint the calipers in a striking, heat-resistant red paint.

Wheels and Tires

The 1975 models began with Fuchs forged-alloy 15-inch wheels with deep black centers, sizes being 7J front and 8J rear. Production Turbos were generally fitted at first with Dunlop tires in 185/70VR front and 215/60VR rear sizes, but early press cars and U.K. models had Pirelli CN36 tires in the same sizes. Spacers increased the wheel offset front and rear. In the United States, these tires gave a legal bumper height, but elsewhere Pirelli's new low-profile Cinturato P7 tires were a popular option because they had more grip and lowered the center of gravity of the car by 18 millimeters (0.70 inch), but P7s did not last as long. The P7s, specified at 205/55VR front and 225/50VR rear, became standard in 1976; in 1977, 16-inch wheels were fitted and used the same tire profiles.

Rear tire pressures were raised in 1978 from 2.4 bar (34-pound psi) to 3.0 bar (43-pound psi) to compensate for the engine being moved back and putting an extra 30 kilograms (66 pounds) on the rear wheels. The pressure rise increased the "pyong" sound on poor roads. By 1987, the 16-inch wheels were carrying 205/55VR tires at the front on 7J rims, while at the back 245/45VR tires rode on 9J rims.

The 1991 model Turbo used 17-inch Cup Design wheels with 7J front and 9J rear rims, tire sizes being 205/50ZR and 255/45ZR. Unusually, the potential buyer of the 1991 Turbo had three choices for tires: first Bridgestone and then Pirelli and Yokohama were approved for use. The 1993 model Turbo was fitted with three-piece Cup-style wheels made by Speedline. These came in 8Jx18 and 10Jx18 sizes with 225/40ZR and 265/35ZR tires.

The 3.6 Turbo runs on special 18-inch Speedline wheels. The 8J front rims carry 225/40 tires and the 10J rears have 265/35 tires, an incredibly low profile.

The wide wings on this 1976 model housed big 7Jx15 front and 8Jx15 rear Fuchs wheels and spacers increased the track. The tires on these first Turbos were usually Pirelli CN36s with 185/70front and 215/60 rear sizes, which met U.S. bumper height requirements.

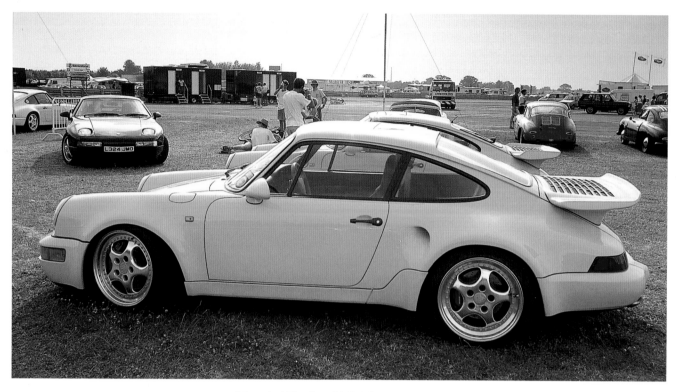

The 1987 Turbo Slant-Nose derived its front profile from the 935 racer, but pop-up headlamps were added. Early customized Slant-Nose cars lacked pop-up headlamps, having the lights mounted below the bumper line.

Martini Turbo (1976)

A Martini Turbo was built for the British Motor Show in October 1976. The car was finished in Grand Prix White with racing sponsor Martini's well-known light blue, dark blue, and red stripes applied. The show car had special Fuhrmann seats that were claimed to be to an orthopedic design with padded blocks of red, white, and blue leather, but these were too expensive for production models. The British Motor Show car also had special velour carpet and leather-trimmed accessories.

The Martini Turbo, in fact, was never a series production model or even a special edition, but the stripes could be ordered as an option (M42) for Grand Prix White models, whether mainstream 911SCs or Turbos. The suspension and engine were the same as on regular 1977 model year Turbos. Of approximately 200 Turbos delivered worldwide with the stripes, half went to the United States.

Turbo SE Slant-Nose (1986–1987)

The Slant-Nose was built initially as a special order conversion (*Sonderwunschen*) by the repair shop in Zuffenhausen. There is some evidence of a first conversion a year earlier, but records suggest the first new car was delivered on July 16, 1981 (VIN: 93ZBS000619). The Slant-Nose only received official option status (M506) in 1986 (for the 1987 model year) as a special limited edition under the newly titled Porsche exclusive program. In the U.K., the Turbo with Special Equipment (Turbo SE) was available as an official option from early 1986, while in the United States the official option model—called the 930S—was not available until March 1987.

Early Slant-Nose custom models had the headlamps in the front air dam, but from 1982 pop-up headlamp versions started to appear (the first was delivered on July 6) and became the standard offering for the 1985 model year. Behind the headlamp covers, on the wing top surfaces, were vents that allowed high-pressure air to escape from the wheel arch interiors when the car was at speed. The rear wings featured strongly styled air intakes ahead of the wheels. Side skirts, body color-coded Fuchs wheels, and a special front spoiler with integrated driving lights completed the exterior body customizing. The S used the same wheel tire sizes as the 1986 Turbo.

The interior was in full leather and came with air conditioning and special electrically adjustable and heated Recaro seats. The controls for these seats were initially on a console on the top side of the seat, not on the sides as on the regular electrically adjustable seats. The custom leather dash panel featured a squared-off version of the instrument pod oval and a color-coded leather steering wheel.

The 1992 3.3-liter Turbo S was a limited edition of just 80 cars. The chassis specification was broadly similar to the Carrera 2 RS but different in detail. Engine output of 380-brake horsepower gave 0 to 62 miles per hour (0 to 100 kilometers per hour) acceleration in just 4.7 seconds.

Engine power was raised to 330-brake horsepower at 5,500 rpm, but maximum torque of 431 Nm at 4,000 rpm was the same as the 1986 Turbo. The power increase came from higher lift cams, a revised exhaust system, higher boost pressure, and a larger intercooler. A larger oil cooler was mounted under the front bumper line.

Production numbers of the Sondenvunsch (special order conversion) Slant-Nose Turbo models were as follows: 1981, 1; 1982, 38; 1983, 35; 1984, 34; 1985, 44; 1986, 52; and 1987, 33. Figures for the production Slant-Nose Turbo are given in the main Production Data table (see page 134).

Turbo S (1992–1993)

Shown as a study at the 1992 Geneva Salon, the special edition Turbo S was made to order, and 80 cars were built. The car could be ordered in any color, but seemed to be most eye-catching in yellow. The output of the 3.3-liter engine was increased to 381-brake horsepower at 6,000 rpm, and maximum torque was 490 Nm at 4,800 rpm.

The study was an experimental lightweight in the style of the Carrera 2 RS, and the Turbo S had similar interior treatment. There were Recaro bucket seats, fabric door pulls, and wind-up windows. Rear seats and radio were deleted, thin side and rear window glass was used, and the electrical harness was lightened. External features included a one-piece whaletail rear spoiler, air intake scoops in the front bumper in place of driving lights, and air intakes in each rear wing for the brakes. The doors, rear engine lid, and front luggage compartment lid were in plastic composite. The prototype carried "IMSA Supercar Champion" decals. The dry weight was 1,290 kilograms (2,844 pounds), approximately 190 kilograms (419 pounds) less than the standard Turbo.

The suspension was stiffened and new brakes and calipers were used. Speedline three-piece wheels of 8Jx18 front and 10Jx18 rear were fitted with Pirelli P Zero tires with sizes of 235/40ZR and 265/35ZR, respectively.

The cars are 10 years apart, but the badge script has not changed. The finish is bright on the 1976 car and matte black on the 1986 car.

This early right-hand-drive Turbo owned by Alan Stein looks purposeful with its wide haunches.

Production Changes

February 1975

Production starts, with first U.K. right-hand-drive cars available September 1975; engine designated 930/50; Nikasil barrels, forged-alloy pistons, aluminum crankcase; compression ratio 6.5:1; cylinder head valve sizes were inlet 49mm and exhaust 41.5mm (sizes later to be adopted for 1978 SC); cooling fan (245mm diameter) ratio increased from 1.3:1 to 1.67:1 to run faster and deliver more air; 96 RON fuel in 80-liter fuel tank; gear ratios (930/30 gearbox) are first, 2.250; second, 1.304; third, 0.893; fourth, 0.656; reverse, 2.437; final drive, 4.000 (or 4.222 in United States); standard RoW final-drive ratio of 4.000 with 15in wheels fitted, but option for 4.222 when 16in wheels used; aluminum S-type calipers (78sq cm swept-disc area) front, cast-iron M-type (52.5sq cm) rear; ventilated disc diameter 282mm front and 290mm rear, thickness 20.5mm front and 20mm rear.

1976

Six year anti-corrosion warranty; new electric door mirror; by-pass valve for turbo, plus maximum boost increased to one bar; Pirelli P7 205/50VR 15 front and 225/50VR 15 rear tires; 16in wheels optional with final drive ratio 4.222; note the Turbo did not use the five-blade cooling fan adopted on 1976 911 models.

1977

Electrical pressure switch gives boost read-out to new gauge mounted within rev counter; twin fuel pumps, modified pressurized fuel accumulator; Hydrovac brake servo (7in) fitted to LHD cars; additional spring reduces clutch effort; 16in Fuchs alloy wheels standard and final drive ratio now standardized at 4.222; first/second gear synchromesh revised and differential assembly strengthened with two planet wheels instead of four; one-piece front anti-roll bar and two-piece spring plates to allow ride height adjustment; two-stage rear window heater; new center console and revised heater/fresh air controls (as 911SC).

1978

New 3.3-liter engine (930/60); 95mm bore and 74.4mm stroke gives 3,299cc; turbo intercooler mounted over engine; new crankshaft (better dynamic balance) with larger main bearings (bearings 1 to 7 up from 57mm to 60mm diameter, bearing 8 up from 31 mm to 40mm), different connecting rod end bearings (narrower, but diameter up from 52mm to 55mm) and shorter connecting rods (by 0.7mm); head gaskets deleted; 97 RON fuel (or 91 RON unleaded for United States with recommendation for 96 RON if driving hard); unequal length cylinder barrel fin layout to balance air cooling from top to bottom of barrel; larger oil pump (pressure port increased from 43mm to 51 mm, scavenge port from 58mm to 80mm); flywheel mounting bolts increased from six to nine on a diameter of 70mm (was 44mm); cooling fan drive ratio now 1.8:1; new anti-clockwise rotating breakerless Capacitative Discharge Ignition (CDI); air conditioning condenser repositioned to front of car; lighter and larger turbo; air injection pump driven from end of left camshaft; 930/60 engine is 23kg heavier than original 930/50; rubber-centered clutch means engine moves back 30mm (and needs larger bell housing); gear ratios (930/34 gearbox) are first, 2.000; second, 1.304; third, 0.893; fourth, 1.600; reverse, 2.437; final drive, 4.222; weight distribution now 37/63 front/rear; rear tire pressures up from 2.4 bar to 3.0 bar: 917 pattern brakes with cross-drilled discs and four-piston alloy calipers (94sq cm pad swept area); disc diameter increased to 304mm front and 309mm rear, thickness to 32mm front and 28mm rear; larger Hydrovac servo (8in), and now fitted to RHD cars; 80-liter fuel tank.

1979

All changes as for 911SC (see page 87).

1980

Turbo discontinued in United States and Japan; RoW models get two exhaust outlets and new brass tube oil cooler.

1981

Alternator rating increased to 1,150W; other changes as for 911SC (see page 88).

1982

Fuchs alloy wheels have highly polished rims to highlight their black centers; other changes as for 911SC (see page 88)

1983

New engine designation of 930/66; completely revised exhaust system, with wastegate exhaust now going direct to atmosphere; power unchanged, but maximum torque rises from 410Nm to 431Nm; K-Jetronic fuel injection has detail changes, with new warm-up regulator and capsule valve in fuel distributor; 98 RON fuel; new ignition distributor with double-vacuum advance/retard and temperature compensation (all injection/ignition changes for low emissions); two boost fans to improve footwell warming (and cooling) at low engine speeds.

1984

Minor safety and comfort changes; anti-theft locking wheel nuts; new interior fabrics with Porsche script; brake pad wear indicators; heating with three-speed fan; alternator rating reduced to 1,100W; new pressure-fed timing chain tensioners.

1985

From October 1984 because of industrial action; radio antenna in windshield; electrically heated washer nozzles; seats slide electrically, now heated and with taller (by 40mm) head restraints; central locking standard; four-spoke steering wheel, shortened gear lever; leather-covered door handles and storage compartment lid; sports seats are no-cost option, with electric height adjustment only; larger brake master cylinder; anti-roll bars increase to 22mm front and 20mm rear; fuel tank now 85 liters.

1986

Turbo re-introduced to U.S. market, 930/68 engine with Digital Motor Electronics (DME) linking exhaust sensors, etc., to injection and ignition; equipped with catalytic converter and Lambda (oxygen) sensor, 95 RON unleaded fuel; all noise and pollution accessories now make engine weight 269kg; for RoW markets new clean DME engine is 930/66; DME associated injection system known as LE-Jetronic; rear wheels now 9Jx16in with 245/45VR tires (front stays at 7Jx16in with 205/55VR tires); front seats lower; restyled dash with larger fascia fresh air vents; sun visors have covered vanity mirrors.

1987

Rear reflector panel has integrated foglights and includes Porsche script; seats fully adjustable electrically; headlight beam adjustable from dash; perforated discs get beveled holes to assist with heat dissipation; gear ratios (all markets) are first, 2.25; second, 1.3043; third, 0.8928; fourth, 0.5250; reverse, 2.437; final drive, 4.222.

1988

Turbo now available as Targa and Cabrio; passenger door mirror and eight-speaker hi-fi installation standard in all markets; electric windows can be raised by emergency manual crank.

1989

Alarm fitted as standard, activates when doors are locked; five-speed G50 gearbox standard (and hydraulic clutch) with ratios (all markets) of first, 3.154; second, 1.789; third, 1.259; fourth, 0.957; fifth, 0.755; reverse, 2.437; final drive, 3.444; larger rear torsion bars, revised anti-roll bars (22mm front, 18mm rear), firmer shock absorbers; brake, clutch and engine/gearbox seals are asbestos-free; Turbo discontinued September 1989.

1991

Turbo relaunched September 1990 (first shown March 1990), RHD cars delivered from early 1991; new two-wheel-drive only Turbo with Carrera 4 Coupe body (type 954) revisions but with usual flared wheel arches and tea-tray rear spoiler; 3.3-liter engine with resonant intake manifold, revised exhaust system, bigger turbocharger and larger intercooler; Maximum boost now 0.7 bar (was 0.8); revised injection and Motronic control; dual mass flywheel; two (left and right) exhaust tailpipe outlets; transmission still five-speed G50 (built by Getrag) with Borg-Warner synchromesh, standard limited slip differential, improved gear shift; smaller external electrically operated mirrors; new 17in Cup Design wheels of 7J front (with 205/50ZR tires) and 9J rear (with 255/40ZR tires); stronger semi-trailing arms; anti-roll bars now 21mm front 22mm rear; disc diameter 322mm front, 299mm rear; four-piston calipers (85sq cm pad swept area) have asbestos-free pads and wear indicators; space saver spare tire is 155-15 size to clear new brake discs; driver/passenger air bag standard for selected markets (including U.S.); standard features include air conditioning, onboard computer with digital boost indicator; backlit instruments.

1992

No major changes to specification.

1993

3.5-liter engine with 100mm bore and 75.4m stroke; compression ratio increased to 7.5:1; 350bhp at 5,500rpm, maximum torque 520Nm at 4,200rpm; stronger clutch and limited slip differential (same as used on Carrera 2 RS); two-spring clutch pedal action; three-piece Speedline wheels of 8Jx18in front (with 225/40ZR tires) and 10Jx18in rear (with 255/35ZR tires); tires are Yokohama A008P; bodyshell lowered 20mm (except U.S.); 12 percent stiffer springs; locked rear axle control bearing deletes toe-change characteristic found on Carrera 2; Turbo S front brakes with red painted calipers all around; driver air bag standard for all markets; 1,510W alternator with 12V/175Ah battery; fuel tank 77 liters (optional 92 liters); "Turbo" logos on wheel hubcaps; chromed "Turbo 3.5" on engine cover and embroidered onto rear firewall carpet; kph speedometers now read to 320 (was 300), mph speedos stay at 180; air conditioner now uses CFC-free refrigerant.

Dimensions

Wheelbase

2,251mm (from 1975), 2,271mm (from 1990), 2,272mm (from 1993).

Identification

Model year	Model	Engine	Gearbox	Chassis numbers	Engine numbers
1975	930	930/50	930/30	9305700001–9305700284	6750001 onward
1976	930	930/50	930/30	9306700001–9306700644	6760001 onward
	930 U.S.	930/51	930/30	9306800001–9306800530	6860001 onward
1977	930	930/52	930/33	9307700001–9307700695	6770001 onward
	930 U.S.	930/53	930/33	9307800001–9307800727	6872001 onward
1978	930	930/60	930/34	9308700001–9308700735	6780001 onward
	930 Japan	930/62	930/34	9308709501–9308709561	6782001 onward
	930 U.S.49[1]	930/61	930/34	9308800001–9308800461	6880001 onward
	930 California	930/63	930/34	9308800001–9308800461	6881001 onward
1979	930	930/60	930/34	9309700001–9309700820	6790001 onward
	930 Japan	930/62	930/34	9309709501–9309709532	6791001 onward
	930 U.S.49[1]	930/64	930/34	9309800001–9309801200	6890001 onward
	930 California	930/63	930/34	9309800001–9309801200	6890001 onward
1980	930	930/60	930/34	93A0070001–93A0070840	6700001 onward
	930 Japan	930/65	930/34	93A0070001–93A0070840	6708001 onward
1981	930	930/60	930/34	WP0ZZZ93ZBS050001–698	6710001 onward
	930 Canada	930/60	930/34	WP0JA093BS050001–0063	6710001 onward
1982	930	930/60	930/34	WP0ZZZ93ZCS000001–938	67C000I onward
	930 Canada	930/60	930/34	WP0JA093CS050001–0089	67C000I onward
1983	930	930/66	930/34	WP0ZZZ93ZDS000001–1015	67D000 1 onward
	930 Canada	930/66	930/34	WP0JA093DS05000 1–0065	67D0001 onward
1984	930	930/66	930/34	WP0ZZZ93ZES000001–0804	67E0001 onward
	930 Canada	930/66	930/34	WP0JA093ES050001–0077	67E000I onward
1985	930	930/66	930/34	WP0ZZZ93ZFS000001–1063	67F0001 onward
	930 Canada	930/66	930/34	WP0JA093FS050001–0085	67F0001 onward
1986	930	930/66	930/36	WP0ZZZ93ZGS000001–1158	67G000I onward
	930 Canada	930/66	930/37	WP0JA093GS050001–0088	67G0001 onward
	930 U.S.	930/68	930/37	WP0JB093GS050001–1424	67G0001 onward
1987	930	930/66	930/36	WP0ZZZ93ZHS000001–0720	67H0001 onward
	930 Canada	930/66	930/36	WP0JA093HS050001–088	67H0001 onward
	930 U.S.	930/68	930/36	WP0JB093HS050001–5000	68H0001 onward
	930 Cabrio	930/66	930/36	WP0ZZZ93ZHS020001–0142	68H0001 onward
	930 Cabrio U.S.	930/68	930/36	WP0EB093ZHS070001–0183	68H0001 onward
	930 Cabrio Canada	930/66	930/36	WP0EA093HS075001–0183	68H0001 onward
	930 Targa	930/66	930/36	WP0ZZZ93ZHS010001–0069	68H0001 onward
	930 Targa U.S.	930/68	930/36	WP0EB093ZHS060001–0087	68H0001 onward
	930 Targa Canada	930/66	930/36	WP0EA093HS065001–0087	68H0001 onward
	930 S-N[2]	930/66	930/36	WP0ZZZ93ZHS050001–0087	68H0001 onward
	930 S-N Targa[2]	930/66	930/36	WP0ZZZ93ZHS060001–0087	68H0001 onward
	930 S-N Cabrio[2]	930/66	930/36	WP0ZZZ93ZHS070001–0087	68H0001 onward
	930 S-N U.S.[2]	930/68	930/36	WP0EB093HS050001–0087	68H0001 onward
	930 S-N Targa U.S.[2]	930/68	930/36	WP0ZZZ93ZHS060001–0087	68H0001 onward
	930 S-N Cabrio U.S.[2]	930/68	930/36	WP0ZZZ93ZHS070001–0087	68H0001 onward
1988	930	930/66	930/36	WP0ZZZ93ZJS000001–0677	67J0001 onward
	930 Targa	930/66	930/36	WP0ZZZ93ZJS01000I–0136	67J0001 onward
	930 Cabrio	930/66	930/36	WP0ZZZ93ZJS020001–0247	68J0001 onward
	930 NA[3]	930/68	930/36	WP0JB093JS050001–0701	68J0001 onward
	930 Targa NA[3]	930/68	930/36	WP0EB093JS060001–0141	68J0001 onward
	930 Cabrio NA[3]	930/68	930/36	WP0EB093JS070001–0591	68J0001 onward
	930 S-N[2]	930/68	930/36	WP0ZZZ93ZJS000001–0591	68J0001 onward
	930 S-N Targa NA[2]	930/68	930/36	WP0EB093ZJS01000I–0591	68J0001 onward
	930 S-N Cabrio[2]	930/66	930/36	WP0EA093JS020001–0591	68J0001 onward
1989	930	930/66	G50/50	WP0ZZZ93 KS000001–857	67K0051–1103
	930 Targa	930/66	G50/50	WP0ZZZ93KS010001–115	67K0051–1103
	930 Cabrio	930/66	G50/50	WP0ZZZ93KS020001–244	67K0051–1103
	930 NA[3]	930/68	G50/50	WP0JB093KS050001–639	67K0051–1232
	930 Targa NA[3]	930/68	G50/50	WP0EB093KS060001–109	67K0051–1232
	930 Cabrio NA[3]	930/68	G50/50	WP0EB093KS07000 1–600	67K0051–1232
1991	964T	M30/69	G50/52	WP0ZZZ96ZMS470001–2298	61 M00001
	964T U.S.	M30/69	G50/52	WP0AA296 M S480001–674	61M00001
1992	964T	M30/69	G50/52	WP0ZZZ96ZNS4 70001–836	61N00001
	964T U.S.	M30/69	G50/52	WP0AA296NS480001– 309	61N00001
1993	964T	M64/50	G50/52	WP0ZZZ96ZPS4 70001–650	61P00001
	964T U.S.	M64/50	G50/52	WP0AC296RS480001– 288	61P00001

General notes

Engines 930/54 was the 1977 Turbo engine for Japan (as 930/53); 930/62 was the 1978–1979 engine for Japan; 930/64 was the 1979 model run-out for the U.S.; 930/65 was the 195kw 1980–1982 engine for Japan (as 930/64).

Miscellaneous 1988 onward Cabrios carry a "Cb" suffix to chassis number; some number sequences refer to the production series allocated to a particular model and so will not align with the actual number of a specific model built; 964T refers to the new Turbo built on the Carrera 2/4 chassis.

Numbered notes 1. U.S. 49 refers to non-California U.S. specification for "49 States." 2. S-N refers to Slant-Nose. 3. NA refers to North American specification (U.S. and Canada).

Production Data

Model year	Model	Power (bhp DIN@rpm)	Torque (Nm@rpm)	Compression ratio	Weight (kg)	Number built
1975	930	260@5,500	343@4,000	6.5:1	1,140	284
1976	930	260@5,500	343@4,000	6.5:1	1,195	644
	930 U.S.	245@5,500	343@4,000	6.5:1	1,195	530
1977	930	260@5,500	343@4,000	6.5:1	1,195	695
	930 U.S.	245@5,500	343@4,000	6.5:1	1,195	727
1978	930	300@5,500	412@4,000	6.5:1	1,300	735
	930 U.S.	265@5,500	395@4,000	7.0:1	1,300	461
	930 Japan	265@5,500	395@4,000	7.0:1	1,300	61
1979	930	300@5,500	412@4,000	7.0:1	1,300	820
	930 U.S.	265@5,500	395@4,000	7.0:1	1,300	1,200
	930 Japan	265@5,500	395@4,000	7.0:1	1,300	32
1980	930	300@5,500	412@4,000	7.0:1	1,300	840
1981	930	300@5,500	412@4,000	7.0:1	1,300	698
	930 Canada	300@5,500	412@4,000	7.0:1	1,300	63
1982	930	300@5,500	412@4,000	7.0:1	1,300	938
	930 Canada	300@5,500	412@4,000	7.0:1	1,300	89
1983	930	300@5,500	432@4,000	7.0:1	1,300	1,015
	930 Canada	300@5,500	412@4,000	7.0:1	1,300	65
1984	930	300@5,500	432@4,000	7.0:1	1,300	804
	930 Canada	300@5,500	412@4,000	7.0:1	1,300	77
1985	930	300@5,500	432@4,000	7.0:1	1,300	1,063
	930 Canada	300@5,500	412@4,000	7.0:1	1,300	85
1986	930	300@5,500	432@4,000	7.0:1	1,335	1,158
	930 Canada	300@5,500	412@4,000	7.0:1	1,335	88
	930 U.S.	282@5,500	390@4,000	7.0:1	1,335	1,424
1987	930	300@5,500	432@4,000	7.0:1	1,335	720
	930 Targa	300@5,500	432@4,000	7.0:1	1,335	69
	930 Cabrio	300@5,500	432@4,000	7.0:1	1,335	142
	930 Canada	300@5,500	412@4,000	7.0:1	1,335	88
	930 U.S.	282@5,500	390@4,000	7.0:1	1,335	1,605
	930 Targa U.S.	282@5,500	390@4,000	7.0:1	1,335	87
	930 Cabrio U.S.	282@5,500	390@4,000	7.0:1	1,335	183
	930 S-N U.S.[1]	282@5,500	390@4,000	70:1	1,335	200
1988	930	300@5,500	432@4,000	7.0:1	1,335	677
	930 Targa	300@5,500	432@4,000	7.0:1	1,335	136
	930 Cabrio	300@5,500	432@4,000	7.0:1	1,335	242
	930 US	282@5,500	390@4,000	7.0:1	1,335	701
	930 Targa U.S.	282@5,500	390@4,000	7.0:1	1,335	141
	930 Cabrio U.S.	282@5,500	390@4,000	7.0:1	1,335	591
	930 S-N	300@5,500	432@4,000	7.0:1	1,335	18
	930 S-N U.S.[1]	282@5,500	390@4,000	7.0:1	1,335	278
1989	930	300@5,500	432@4,000	7.0:1	1,335	857
	930 Targa	300@5,500	432@4,000	7.0:1	1,335	115
	930 Cabrio	300@5,500	432@4,000	7.0:1	1,335	244
	930 U.S.	282@5,500	390@4,000	7.0:1	1,335	639
	930 Targa U.S.	282@5,500	390@4,000	7.0:1	1,335	109
	930 Cabrio U.S.	282@5,500	390@4,000	7.0:1	1,335	600
	930 S-N	300@5,500	432@4,000	7.0:1	1,335	32
	930 S-N U.S.[1]	282@5,500	390@4,000	70:1	1,335	147
1991	964T	320@5,750	450@4,500	7.0:1	1,470	2,288
	964T U.S.	320@5,750	450@4,500	7.0:1	1,470	674
1992	964T	320@5,750	450@4,500	7.0:1	1,470	836
	964T U.S.	320@5,750	450@4,500	7.0:1	1,470	309
	964T S[2]	381@6,000	490@4,800	7.0:1	1,470	80
1993	964T	360@5,500	520@4,200	7.5:1	1,470	650
	964T U.S.[3]	360@5,500	520@4,200	7.5:1	1,470	288

Numbered notes

1. S-N refers to Slant-Nose.
2. S indicates special edition Turbo S.
3. 1993 U.S. Turbo 3.6 production total includes midyear specification change models (M718).

Track (front/rear)
1,432mm/1,500mm (from 1975), 1,434mm/1,525mm (from 1985), 1,442mm/1,488mm (from 1993).

Length
4,318mm (from 1975), 4,250mm (from 1990), 4,275mm (from 1993).

Width
1,829mm (from 1975), 1,775mm (from 1990), 1,755mm (from 1993).

Color Schemes

1975
Body colors: As 911 (see page 76).
Interiors
The new Turbo was offered with a new range of interior fabrics for the seat centers termed "Tartan Dress" (999.551.081.40) in MacLaughlan (red, 8AB), Black Watch (green, 2AC), or Dress Mackenzie (brown/beige, 4AD); these could be matched with red, black, or brown-beige leather; alternatively full leather could be specified.

1976
Body colors: Same as 911 (see page 76).
Interiors
Unchanged, but Tartan Dress now offered across the whole; 911 range.

1977
Body colors
Same as 911 (see page 76).
Interiors
Grained leatherette (999.551.012.40) and light basketweave leatherette added for the Turbo, in Black (7AU), Lobster (8AU), or Cork (5AU); pinstripe velour (see 911) join Tartan Dress fabrics and offered in Black/White, Lobster/Black, or Cork/Black.

1978
Body colors
Same as 911 (see page 88).
Interiors
Leather color options now Lobster (8AH), Cork (5AH), Black (7AG), Blue (3AG), Yellow (IAG), Light Green (2AP), Light Red (8AT), or White (9AG); fabrics were pinstripe or Tartan Dress, as 1977; velour pile carpets in Lobster, Cork, Black, Yellow, or Light Red to match the other materials.

1979
Body colors: Same as 911SC (see page 89).
Interiors
Turbo now offered only with leather (no leatherette), colors as 1979 911SC (see page 89); cloths as are 1978; new cut-pile velour carpets as 1979 911SC.

1980
Body colors: Same as 911SC (see page 89).
Interiors
Checkerboard velour and textured fabric offered in same range as 1979 911SC (see page 89), leather unchanged from 1979.

1981
Body colors: Same as 911SC (see page 89).
Interiors
Berber tweed fabric joins others (as 1980 SC).

1982 onward
Body colors and interiors all as 911 of same model year (see pages 89, 101–102, and 118).

Chapter 9

The 911 Carrera, GT, and Turbo (993) (1993–1998)

The 993 was the fourth generation of 911, making striking improvements in the three critical areas of sports car appeal: looks, power, and handling. It turned around Porsche's fortunes from 1994, becoming the best-selling 911 ever.

If the Carrera 2 and 4 had turned around the core Porsche customers during the recession of the early 1990s and got them buying again, then the new Carrera—identified both internally at Porsche and externally as the 993—re-invented the concept of the 911 and opened up a whole new market. The result proved to be the right car at the right time for Porsche. From the moment of launch in late 1993, the factory struggled to keep up with demand.

Whatever the economic position of the company at the start of the decade, no one could accuse Porsche of being

Evolution Outline

December 1993: The 993-bodied 911 is introduced with 272-brake horsepower, a 3.6-liter engine, and a multi-link rear suspension.

August 1994: The new Carrera 4 with transmission is 50 percent lighter than the 964 type. Tiptronic transmission is available for rear-wheel-drive Carreras.

February 1995: The Carrera RS with 300-brake horsepower, followed by new 993 Turbo with 408-brake horsepower engine, twin turbochargers, and six-speed gearbox.

September 1995: The 911 Targa and Carrera 4S (wide-body) is announced.

September 1996: The wide-bodied Carrera S (rear-wheel drive) is introduced.

September 1997: The 911 Carrera Coupe (996) replaces the rear-wheel-drive 993 Coupe and Cabriolet.

March 1998: The 911 Carrera Cabriolet (996) is introduced.

Off-roading in the Carrera 4! Using one of the lightest four-wheel-drive systems, and assisted by the traction-controlling automatic brake differential (ABD), the Carrera 4 accelerated faster than the two-wheel-drive model, even on firm ground.

The ever-popular Cabriolet followed the coupe in spring 1994. The clean, fulsome lines of the rear were accentuated by a narrower light strip for the 993.

complacent. There was dynamism in the development of the 911 that had not been seen since the progress of the early cars in the late 1960s and early 1970s. The car that headlined that new surge was the 993, a 911 that made every earlier 911 look positively dated.

The 993 was a major investment in the short term for Porsche, born of the high priority to inject the 964 models with wider appeal while consolidating sales to core customers. The 993's task was to sustain the company's recovery from the difficult years of recession until the start of the wholly new model range due in 1996–1997. This it did famously.

Porsche's strategy meant the 993 had to combine typical 911 features—high performance and aggressive character—with the kind of improvements that would win new customers from the refined sports saloons offered by the likes of Mercedes and BMW. Consequently, the big effort went into reducing ride harshness and interior noise.

The fourth distinct generation of 911, the 993, was said to be 80 percent new when it was announced. It was a claim that had been made before, notably on the 968, and often observers had been left asking what had really changed and just what "80 percent" actually meant. Porsche had no intention of making this mistake again. The 993 made striking steps forward in the three critical areas of sports car appeal: looks, engine, and handling.

First impressions were startling. No other car in the price range conveyed the same static presence that gripped you with simultaneous feelings of retro and high technology, performance and dependability. Briton Tony Hatter had conceived a new visual interpretation of the 911 that injected adrenaline into the lines of the 964, which looked almost bland by comparison. Design department head Harm Lagaay called the new appearance "muscular," and, indeed, the 911 gave the impression of being on steroids.

The Targa, a refreshingly innovative new concept for an old Porsche favorite, lost the dated look of the earlier model and was easily mistaken for a coupe from some angles. Prominent in this view are the new design of "concave" spoke two-piece wheels.

Once in the driving seat, the familiar 911 cockpit seemed much the same. The engine remained at 3,600cc (219.6 cubic inches), but an extra 22-brake horsepower not only compensated for the car's additional 20 kilograms (44 pounds), but improved performance all round. Acceleration to 62 miles per hour (100 kilometers per hour) was 0.1 second better, at 5.6 second, and top speed rose to 168 miles per hour (270 kilometers per hour), up 6 miles per hour (10 kilometers per hour) on the 964 model.

The effort to improve the ride and handling ensured the real joy of the 993 was to be discovered when you were on the move. There was an immediate realization that, at any speed, the car was altogether quieter and less anxious in the cabin. There was also less susceptibility to bump and

This is a 1997 Carrera S, which combined the Turbo chassis and rear-wheel-drive transmission to produce a supremely confident package.

thump over poor road surfaces. This was a new kind of comfort in a 911, and it was easy to understand why drivers who had never considered the car before might be tempted. There was more.

The real treat came when you pushed this 911 through a series of demanding bends, even in the wet. With earlier 911s, tire improvements had obscured many of the 911's original tail-happy vices, but in the right (or is it wrong?) conditions, it was still possible to provoke the characteristic power-off tail-slide. This unfriendly behavior was a product not only of the rearward weight bias but also the semi-trailing arm rear suspension. For the 993, the engineers came up with a completely new multi-link suspension derived from the Weissach axle first seen on the 928. It was a significant and costly change to make, but the result was a 911 with virtually no handling vices and vastly superior ride quality. When you lifted in the middle of a rain-soaked corner to avoid that errant wild animal, the new 911 did not automatically unleash an unwelcome scare as the car swapped ends and dispatched you into the scenery. To provoke the 993 into any sort of tail slide now demanded fairly violent action from the driver.

The windshield wiper location was revised so that each wiper covered some 80 percent of the glass area. It was considered too expensive to recess the pivots below the bonnet line.

By August 1995, the 993 was the only model range offered by Porsche. The towel had been thrown in on the struggle to keep interest alive in the four-cylinder 968 and V-8-powered 928 ranges. Not for the first time the future of Porsche rested squarely on the 911's shoulders and, happily, the early success of the 993 was sustained. Even the Targa reemerged alongside the Coupe and Cabriolet. The new Targa caught a wave of excitement in much the same way as had the fresh styling of the Coupe. It was a new concept for an open-roofed fixed-head car.

Another surprise, and an indication that the 993 had indeed successfully penetrated new markets, was the popularity of the Tiptronic automatic transmission option. Even outside the United States, where automatics have always been popular, Tiptronics were accounting for up to 60 percent of 993 sales in the big cities. This was a very different picture to the old days of Sportomatic—and a testament to the aggravation of driving in conditions of ever increasing congestion.

The 1995 Carrera RS addressed the constant niche demand for a hard-edged, no-compromise 911. By virtue of its multi-link rear suspension and 300 brake horsepower, the new Carrera RS was far more accomplished than the 964 models. It will rate among the most desirable of hot-rod 911s in years to come. While not being all that suited to everyday traffic, an RS cannot be bettered for fun at the racetrack.

In 1995, the Turbo returned. For a car used to being described in superlatives, this new version was as outstanding as one could imagine. The 408 brake horsepower from its twin-turbo engine was nothing less than racing car performance in a car that offered complete luxury and real refinement.

For the 1997 model year, the 993 was showing no signs of needing replacement. Including the Turbo, there were eight different versions to choose from. Even on the introduction of the new 911 (the 996) in September 1997, a waiting list remained for the older rear-wheel-drive model. But while the rear-wheel-drive 993s ceased production by the end of 1997, the all-wheel-drive and Turbo 993s were planned to continue in production for the remainder of the 1998 model year (until July 1998).

Horst Marchart, executive vice-president in charge of research and development, had said that survival requires change. He considered that the modern sports car should always be influenced by modern technology not restrained by traditional solutions, and so the 996 made a dramatic break with 911 heritage: It was water-cooled for improved cylinder head cooling and to reduce acoustic noise. It was larger and more comfortable than the 993. It was a Porsche for the new century.

It has been said the 911 is like the proverbial carpenter's hammer. It has had three new heads and four new handles, but it is still the same hammer. The water-cooled 911s are indeed wonderful cars that win many hearts in our technology-conscious age. But it is a human failing to be sentimental. While the concept of a water-cooled 911 is perhaps appropriate for its time, it can be difficult for enthusiasts to contemplate.

Time will tell whether the water-cooled cars will challenge the 993's status as arguably the greatest sports car of the twentieth century.

Bodyshell

At first glance, the body of the 993 appeared to be nothing more than a makeover on the 964 Turbo. But there was much more to the new appearance than the pronounced wheel-arch flares. Following the example started by the 968, there had been considerable effort to replace the previous straight lines of the 964 with, in the industrial designer's vocabulary, "softer" lines. This trend would reach its peak with the later 996 model. Referring to the 964 Turbo wings as looking like "big lips" around the wheels, Harm Lagaay considered the bulges on the 993 to be more muscular, and by inference more smoothly integrated. Along with new, lower head lamps, the frontal appearance of the 993 seemed more aggressive.

The 993 was the first 911 to require significant changes to the body-in-white, mainly to accommodate the mountings for the subframe that carried the multilink suspension. The only body parts carried over from the 964 were the roof and bonnet. There were revised door beams for improved side impact protection and simplified operation of the door mechanisms. The changes resulted in a bodyshell that was said to be 20 percent stiffer with no increase in weight. The shell was still hot-dip galvanized and the 10-year warranty against rust perforation was maintained. Water-based paints were now used entirely, even for the metallic colors.

The rubber seals that located the windshield were reduced in size, increasing the glass area and improving aerodynamics. Rear side windows were bonded to the outside, reducing wind noise, while new seals reduced the force necessary to shut the doors.

The 993 was available initially only in Coupe form, but the Cabriolet followed in March 1994. The real surprise came with the return of the Targa for the 1996 model year.

The new Targa design retained the overall shape and character of the 911 while featuring an electrically operated glass panel that could slide backward. The Targa was based on the same body-in-white as the Cabriolet, with additional strengthening around the windshield frame. The new variant was only 30 kilograms (66 pounds) heavier than the Coupe. The new roof design owed nothing to the earlier Targas, having better all-round visibility while achieving increased roll-over protection. In line with the general refinement of the 993, the Targa was notable for its low wind noise, not a strong point of the old Targa!

The feeling inside the Targa was much more open, because there was indeed more glass. Thermally insulated, the glass contained a special UV filter to help keep inside temperatures under control on hot, sunny days. If you did not like direct sun, a roller blind would glide across the opening at the touch of a switch. The whole design was extremely elegant, both in appearance and operation, and as a result new Targas commanded a premium over the Coupe. Memories of the old and chunky-looking Targas faded fast.

Body Trim and Fittings

The front valence was heavily revised to reflect the new style that had first been adopted with the 968, using more flowing break lines where it attached to the wings. As well as significantly larger inlets on the front, small side air exits on either side acted as invisible spoilers ahead of the front wheel profiles, reducing drag at higher speeds.

At the rear, the policy of greater integration of the valence was continued, with accommodation for the twin exhaust outlets and a less pronounced bumper than on the 964. The attention to drag reduction was further evident at the top of the rear window, where a small lip prevented flow breakaway over the recess, and again under the car, where a new underbody sheath was claimed to give the 993 a

The Targa's roof was thermally insulated and filtered ultra-violet light. The elegance of the design is evident, particularly in the absence of the old rain gutters of the coupe and the new form of the rear side window. The opening glass slid back under the rear window at the touch of a switch to provide open-air motoring. The panel in front of the sliding roof opened forward to prevent wind buffeting inside the car.

The interior received new fabrics and colors, as well as revised door trims and rear side trims. This is a 1997 model coupe in opulent Boxster Red leather. By this time the 911 was winning customers from the more comfort-oriented sports saloons such as BMW and Mercedes. The Cabriolet featured a wind-break (below) behind the front seats to ensure wind-in-the-hair motoring did not become too wild.

degree of ground effect. The new engine cover incorporated a movable spoiler that integrated more closely to the cover when closed.

The improvement to detailing was a highlight of the 993's new specification. Of note were the new electrically operated door mirrors and the color-coded door handles, both items first used on the 968. The windshield wiper location was revised, with the pivots placed closely together and providing improved sweep of the glass. The pivots were still exposed; it would still have been too expensive to modify the body-in-white to recess these.

The Cabriolet soft-top was significantly stiffer than on the 964 model. The Cabrio also introduced an optional wind deflector behind the front seats. This reduced air turbulence and noise and also gave some protection to luggage behind the seats.

Interior Trim

A new interior design was offered for the 993, including new colors and fabrics. There were new door and rear side trims to complement the updated appearance. The electrically controlled front seats were revised with a new seam pattern and improved upper thigh support. For those in chilly climates, seat heating was available as an option.

The 911 has always had to make the best out of a heating system based around the air-cooled engine. Consistency of heat delivery has been the main problem, especially when the engine is cold. The 993's heating was improved with the adoption of a revised electronically controlled heating unit, which included an integrated particle filter. The filter improved the interior environment by capturing particles down to a size of 0.005 millimeter, which screens out most flower pollens. Air conditioning was a factory option (standard in some markets) and featured a new "max cold" control position.

The heated rear window now had automatic time control, and the driver had two levels of heating (de-ice and de-fog). After 12 minutes the de-ice circuit switched off automatically, while the de-fog was switched off manually. There was a new type of switch for the external mirror control, located on the door just inside from the driver's mirror.

Dashboard and Instruments

The dashboard was an evolution of the 964 layout, reflecting the new interior colors, but with driver and passenger air bags standard for all markets.

The standard radio fit from the factory was the Blaupunkt Bremen RCM43 radio/cassette player, with a CD player on the options list. Also on the options list was a newly developed 10-speaker system that was fully integrated into the standard fittings. This included an ISO-watt amplifier, woofers in the doors, a tweeter below each of the knee bolsters, and a pair of two-way speakers on the parcel shelf. Automatic sound regulation was possible with the addition of an optional digital sound processing (DSP) unit fitted in the driver's door armrest. Also optional was an onboard computer that gave read-outs of fuel consumption. Theft protection, as delivered from the factory, improved with the integration of the central locking and alarm with an engine immobilizer.

Luggage Compartment

The shape of the luggage compartment was largely unchanged from the 964, having a capacity of 123 liters. A notable design feature was that the Space-Saver spare wheel contributed to the energy-absorbing capability of the car in a frontal impact. It was mounted below and in front of the plastic fuel tank, which held 74.S liters (16.4 Imperial gallons, 19.7 U.S. gallons) of super unleaded (98 RON) fuel. A 92-liter (20.2 Imperial gallons, 24.3 US gallons) version was available as an option.

Engine

The 993 engine remained at 3,600cc (219.6cu in) but was some 10 percent more powerful than the 964 version. Maximum power rose to 272-brake horsepower at 6,100 rpm and maximum torque to 330 Nm (243 pound feet) at 5,000 rpm. Compression ratio remained at 11.3:1, and fuel consumption was claimed to be about the same.

Internal improvements included lighter pistons and connecting rods and a strengthened crankshaft. The 993 engine now used many lightweight materials, including magnesium for the cooling fan, oil pump housing, and timing chain housings. Plastic was used for the intake system, cooling and heating ducting, valve covers, and vacuum reservoir.

Induction system airflow sensing was by the hot film method and the Bosch engine management system was upgraded to version M2.10, with knock regulation and control of the sequential, multi-point fuel injection. An important improvement that would lead to reduced servicing costs was the introduction of hydraulic valve adjustment. The exhaust system now had dual exit pipes and separate catalytic converter cores downstream of the individual heat exchangers,

The 3. 6-liter engine gained another 22-brake horsepower. Despite weighing an extra 20 kilograms, the 993 delivered better all-round performance than the 964. The improved 1996 models (left) used a Varioram induction system and larger valves to produce 285-brake horsepower from the last full-scale production version of the air-cooled boxer "six."

as well as a central gas mixing unit. This layout improved pressure losses in the system and reduced noise.

From the 1996 model year the engine was upgraded with Varioram induction technology and larger intake and exhaust valves. Maximum power increased to 285-brake horsepower at 6,100 rpm and maximum torque to 340 Nm (251 foot-pounds) at 5,250 rpm.

First seen on the 1995 Carrera RS, Varioram was a Porsche-patented design that altered the length of the inlet pipe according to engine revolutions, so improving the volumetric efficiency at different engine speeds. In the mid-range, it was claimed Varioram increased torque over the 272-brake horsepower engine by as much as 40 Nm (29 foot-pounds). Fuel consumption and exhaust emissions were also reduced because of the more efficient combustion. Up to 5,000 rpm the pipes are almost double the length of the pipes in the earlier 993. As engine revolutions increase beyond 5,000 rpm, a sliding sleeve on each bank of intake pipes, operated by intake vacuum, shortens the intake pipe length in two stages. Above 5,800 rpm both cylinder banks are interconnected to ensure best volumetric efficiency.

Transmission

Two transmission options were offered with the 993, manual and Tiptronic. As noted earlier, the reworked automatic option proved to be very popular. The shift program was revised to cope with the increased torque and power of the engine and was enhanced with a feature that enabled sensing of varying road resistance (uphill or downhill). In automatic mode, a downshift could now be prompted by braking, ensuring the right ratio was available to accelerate away again. Tiptronic was only available on the two-wheel-drive models.

Tiptronic S, available as a no-cost option for the 1995 Tiptronic models, gave the driver the choice of shifting in the manual mode either using the floor-mounted lever or using rocker switches integrated into the steering wheel. As with the other Tiptronics, the gear selected was indicated at the base of the speedometer.

The manual transmission on the 993 was new and offered six forward speeds. Shifting effort was reduced some 40 percent on the 964 gearbox by new double-cone synchromesh on first and second gears. As a result of a comprehensive weight reduction effort on the internals, the new gearbox weighed the same as the five-speed 964 unit. Lightening measures included hollow-boring the pinion shaft and fitting the back of the crown wheel with forged pockets. The gearbox housing was a thin-wall aluminum pressure casting with wall thickness reduced by up to 2 millimeters (0.08 inch) on the previous casing. From the 1995 model year, a new hydraulic-assisted clutch system lowered the clutch force and reduced pedal travel.

The automatic brake differential (ABD) option, available for manual 993s, prevented a single wheel spinning under acceleration on differing grip surfaces. The system used the ABS sensors on each rear wheel to detect wheelspin on acceleration. The control unit then applied selective braking through a high-speed hydraulic actuator on the specific rear brake circuit, effectively introducing an intelligent limited slip differential. A control lamp on the combined dial told the driver when this was in operation. The system cut out above 70 kilometers per hour (44 miles per hour).

For the start of the 1995 model year an entirely redesigned four-wheel-drive model was announced. Claimed to be one of the lightest four-wheel-drive systems available, it weighed half that of the 964 variant, while friction losses were reduced by the same amount. The 993 Carrera 4, as a result, came out 30 kilograms (66 pounds) lighter overall than the 964 version.

ABD was standard on the new Carrera 4 and linked to the drive to the front axle. When a rear wheel slipped, a viscous clutch automatically directed increased drive torque to the front axle. ABD also compensated for the difference in rotation speeds between the front and rear wheels when cornering. An asymmetric rear axle differential lock applied a 25 percent locking effect to a spinning rear wheel on acceleration and 40 percent when on over-run. This latter feature was another counter-measure to the traditional lift-off oversteer tendency of the 911, since the lock promoted stabilizing understeer should the throttle be abruptly lifted halfway through a bend.

The extent of the improvements on the Carrera 4 were enough for it to enjoy a 0.1-second advantage on 0- to 100-kilometer-per-hour (62.5-mile-per-hour) acceleration over the two-wheel-drive version, despite a 50-kilogram (110-pound) weight penalty. Top speed of the two models was identical.

Electrical Equipment and Lighting

The new headlamps of the 993 were perhaps its most startling visual feature. They achieved far better lighting—the claimed improvement was approaching 50 percent—than was available on the 964. Each lamp unit used poly-ellipsoid technology and H1 bulbs for dipped-beam coverage. High-beam light intensity was increased using a variable focus reflector. Variable focus lamp design is based on a concept where the focal length of the reflector is calculated for every point on the reflector surface. The reflector, rather than the lens unit, therefore produces the required light distribution. As a result, the lens units look completely different from the earlier ones, having a clear glass area where the lens refracting elements used to be. As before, however, individual high-pressure jets kept the glass clean.

Removing the headlamp assemblies was a simple task. A lever inside the luggage compartment released the unit, allowing it to be removed from the front. There were no cables or other clips to be disconnected. This made bulb changing very simple, while the new design also permitted simple changing of the dipped beam direction.

The driving lights, turn indicators, and foglights were located as a unit in the front valence. The foglights also used ellipsoid technology.

The revised styling at the rear resulted in a narrower reflector band and taillights. The taillight units were smaller than before since the central reflector now incorporated the reversing as well as the rear foglights. Teflon film prevented splashed water entering the light units in each rear wing.

The new six-speed gearbox brought an improved shift and better synchromesh on first and second gear.

Poly-ellipsoid headlamps gave the 911 an altogether different appearance by day and by night. The reflector, rather than the glass lens, produced the required light distribution. The whole lamp unit can be removed by moving a lever inside the luggage compartment.

Porsche's lightweight-stable-agile (LSA) design provided the 993 with new multi-link rear suspension—a major change under the surface.

The brakes on the 993 were outstanding, featuring cross-drilled and ventilated discs and four-piston calipers. ABS 5 helped ensure the wheels did not lock up when the pedal was pressed too hard.

Suspension and Steering

The most significant revision on the 993 over previous 911s was the scrapping of the semi-trailing arm rear suspension and its replacement with a multi-link arrangement. Called an LSA (lightweight-stable-agile) axle by Porsche, this had geometry derived from the Weissach rear axle first used on the front-engined 928.

The Weissach rear geometry provided a degree of roll-steer, with the outer wheel toeing-in (up to 2 degrees) during cornering and reducing the possibility of liftoff oversteer. The most obvious improvements from the driver's perspective were in cornering stability and body roll, while the degree of squat under acceleration was reduced. The 993 indeed proved to be far less susceptible to lift-off oversteer and more stable during rapid lane changes.

The rear axle looked similar to the dual wishbone layout often used on racing cars. The arms were cast aluminum and fitted inboard to a cast-aluminum two-piece subframe, which in turn attached through four rubber bushings to the bodyshell. Springing was by coils over gas pressure shock absorbers, with the units attached direct to the bodyshell. The new arrangement provided a much smoother ride, as well as a manufacturing benefit. The whole engine and suspension assembly could be built before installation into the car.

The front suspension was an improvement of the existing MacPherson strut system, with increased castor and negative scrub radius. Almost every front suspension component was redesigned, saving 3 kilograms (6.6 pounds) on the weight of the whole axle, and improvement of ride comfort was made a priority. The steering action was lighter, and a new elastic track rod design reduced the transmission of road vibration back to the steering wheel.

Sport suspension was available as an option and featured shorter, stiffer springs, and anti-roll bars together with harder dampers.

Brakes

The improvements introduced to the 993's brakes began just beyond the pedal, with a new linkage through the vacuum servo that gave a linear increase in braking effort on the master cylinder as the pedal was pressed. Before ABS, such a mechanism might have led to a greater chance of wheel locking, but working in parallel with the pressure-compensating valve to help maintain optimum brake balance, maximum braking effect could now be achieved without excessive pressure on the pedal.

The new ABS 5 system used new control algorithms to cope with difficult road surfaces, such as partially dried or dirty roads. With faster initial response, ABS 5 offered up to 20 percent shorter braking distances in certain conditions.

The brake discs themselves were larger, increasing in thickness from 28 millimeters (1.10 inches) to 32 millimeters (1.26 inches). The diameter of the front discs increased from 298 millimeters (11.7 inches) to 304 millimeters (12.0 inches), while the rears were unchanged at 299 millimeters (11.8 inches). Larger, four-piston, fixed calipers all around resulted in a 45 percent improvement in the usable surface of the cross-drilled and ventilated discs.

Wheels and Tires

The low-pressure cast-aluminum "Cup Design 93" wheels were designed to suck hot air away from the brake discs when moving fast and also to conduct heat away through the hub and spokes at lower speeds. Sizes on the standard coupe were 7Jx16-inch (front) and 9Jx16-inch (rear), the rims 25 millimeters (1 inch) wider than those of the 964. Tire sizes were 205/55ZR16 (front) and 245/45ZR16 (rear). The approved tires were the Michelin MXX3-WSXX N1, Bridgestone Expedia SO-1 N2, Continental CZ91 NO, and Toyo Proxes F15 NO; Pirelli P Zero N1 and Yokohama A008-P could also be fitted. If the older 17-inch "Cup" wheels were chosen, these achieved a weight saving of 1.5 kilograms (3.3 pounds) per wheel.

For the 1996 model year, the Targa featured a new "concave" five-spoke, two-piece wheel of 17-inch diameter, but rim sizes remained at 7J and 9J. Tires were 205/50ZR17 (front) and 255/ 40ZR 17 (rear).

1995–1996 Carrera RS

Introduced at the start of 1995, the 993 RS was a considerably improved machine compared to the 1993 limited edition 964 RS 3.8 (see page 116). The two cars did share nearly identical maximum power and torque figures, 300-brake horsepower at 6,500 rpm and 355 Nm (262 foot-pounds) at 5,400 rpm, but torque delivery over the entire range was considerably improved by the first use of Porsche's patented Varioram variable length intake stack system. This system is described in the Engine section of this chapter (see page 141).

As with the older RS 3.8, the capacity increase to 3,746cc (228.6 cubic inches) was achieved by enlarging the bore by 2 millimeters (0.08 inch) to 102 millimeters (4.02 inch), the stroke remaining at 76.4 millimeters (3.01 inches). The valve drive mechanism was strengthened to cope with higher maximum revolutions and the intake and exhaust valves increased in diameter, respectively to 51.5 millimeters (2.03inches) and 43 millimeters (1.69 inches).

The RS used the new six-speed 993 transmission with higher ratios on the first three gears. Unlike the earlier RS 3.8, it was equipped with a double mass flywheel to reduce drivetrain vibration.

The 993 RS continued the theme begun by the 964. Although more refined than the earlier models, the new RS was a supremely accomplished performer, particularly on the racetrack. The lowered ride height is evident in this view.

The new Turbo was worth the 12-month wait after the introduction of the 993. The combination of a 408-brake horsepower twin-turbo engine, a six-speed gearbox, and four-wheel drive ensured awesome performance. The top reading on the speedometer increased from 300 to 320 kilometers per hour (from 180 to 200 miles per hour on U.S. and U.K. models).

The 993 Turbo featured the traditional tea-tray rear wing—necessary to accommodate the twin intercoolers in the engine compartment—but with downturned side fences.

While the ride of the earlier RS models was unquestionably harsh for everyday use, the new 993 RS was more refined, helped by the multi-link rear suspension. The big 8Jx18 inches and 10Jx18 inches three-piece wheels, however, led to a rougher ride on normal roads than the regular car's 16-inch wheels. Tires were 225/40ZR18 (front) and 265/35ZR18 (rear).

Because some customers were expected to use their cars for fast track work or competition, the bodyshell was seam-welded and the wheel arches were rolled to clear the big tires. A cross-brace was fitted between the two front strut towers and the spring/damper mountings used ball-joint mountings at their top ends. Stiffer track rods were adopted in the steering linkage (power steering was standard), and ride height was lowered 30 millimeters (1.2 inches) at the front and 40 millimeters (1.6 inches) at the rear. The front anti-roll bar was adjustable through five settings and the rear bar by three. The RS combined the automatic brake differential (ABD) for traction control and a limited slip differential (40 percent lock on acceleration, 65 percent under deceleration). The brakes were the Turbo's 322 millimeters (12.7 inches) cross-drilled and ventilated discs with four-piston calipers. ABS 5 was standard.

Externally the new RS featured a lower splitter on the front valence, shaped sill covers, and a fixed whaletail rear spoiler in body color.

Overall, the RS weighed 1,279 kilograms (2,820 pounds), which was 100 kilograms (220 pounds) lighter than the 1995 993. The savings came from deletion of the usual accessories, such as electric windows and mirrors, central locking, headlamp washers, intermittent wipe control, standard door trims, and loudspeakers. The interior lighting system was replaced by a simple light as used on the earlier Speedster, and even the washer bottle for the windshield held only 1.2 liters instead of its usual 6.5 liters. There were no driver or passenger air bags, and the only sound insulation was in the engine bay. Thin glass was used and the rear window had no demister; the weight saving for the glass alone was

5 kilograms (11 pounds). An aluminum front hood saved 7.5 kilograms (17 pounds) and replacement of the electric seats by Recaro bucket seats saved 30 kilograms (66 pounds). The 92-liter fuel tank was standard.

Top speed for the 1995 RS was said to be 172 miles per hour (277 kilometers per hour), while 0-to-100-kilometer-per-hour (0- to-62.5-miles-per-hour) acceleration was achieved in just 5.0 seconds.

The Club Sport derivative (known as the RSR in the U.K.) could be registered for the road if you were so disposed, but it was aimed at endurance racing (GT2). Costing £71,500 in the U.K., £6250 more than the RS, the Club Sport was immediately recognizable from the outside by its more aggressive front spoiler and characteristic biplane rear spoiler.

1995–1997 Turbo

A Porsche model lineup without a Turbo seems inconceivable, but after the completion of 964 Turbo production in 1994, it was fully 12 months before a 993 with forced induction appeared, in the spring of 1995.

There is an engine under there somewhere! Twin air-to-air intercoolers dominated the engine compartment of the Turbo.

The new 993 Turbo was 60 millimeters (2.36 inches) wider than the normally aspirated 993, this difference continuing the special look that Turbos have always enjoyed. The front and rear valences were squared off to the ground, with the front opening revised to one large central and two side openings, the latter for the front wheel "air" spoilers. On the sides, the sill moldings were given a pronounced flat lower edge and were integrated into the wheel arches. On the engine cover, the moving spoiler of the regular car was replaced by a new interpretation of the tea-tray spoiler with down-turned side fences.

Setting off the overall looks of the new Turbo were 18-inch-diameter cast-alloy wheels called "Technologie-Rad" design by Porsche. Of very lightweight construction, these were a five-spoke design, with each spoke swept back so that that overall impression was of an impeller. The two-piece wheels were friction-welded together during manufacture. The 8J front wheels were fitted with 225/40ZR18 tires and the 10J rears with 285/30 ZR18 tires.

Braking was typically sensational on the new Turbo. The marketing literature noted that its new brakes had a maximum braking power of 1941-brake horsepower, almost five times the engine power. This was calculated in braking from 290 kilometers per hour (180 miles per hour) at curb weight with the driver. In actual terms, this meant the Turbo could brake from 100 kilometers per hour (62.5 miles per hour) to a standstill in just 2.61 seconds. The previous Turbo's giant 322-millimeter (12.7-inch) discs were carried over and used forced-air cooling, while stopping performance at the extremes was enhanced by the next level, ABS 5.

This U.S. model Turbo S interior was a product of the factory's Exclusive customizing program. Special features include the carbon-fiber trim panels, Exclusive steering wheel, matching leather-trimmed Recaro bucket seats, drilled pedals, and reverse-painted instruments.

The new 993 generation 3.6-liter engine was improved with two KKK K16 turbochargers (the 964 version used a single K27 turbocharger), each with integrated wastegates and two-charge air intercoolers. The Bosch M5.2 engine management system controlled airflow in conjunction with the wastegate on the turbochargers. Improved knock control allowed the compression ratio to rise to 8.0:1 from the previous model's 7.5:1 and the engine to run on 95 or 98 RON unleaded fuel. Maximum power was 408-brake horsepower at 5,750 rpm, with maximum torque 540 Nm (398 foot-pounds) at 4,500 rpm. The twin turbo layout gave excellent low-speed torque, a big improvement compared to the 964 Turbo. Even at 2,500 rpm, there was still 450 Nm (332 foot-pounds) available.

The GT2 was a no-compromise racer that was available as a 430-brake horsepower road rocket for those who wanted a little extra in the overtaking department. Track credits included the FIA GT2 championship in 1996 and second place in 1997.

The Turbo used a single spark plug per cylinder, but the heads employed the hydraulic valve adjustment of the new range. Four oxygen sensors (up and downstream of the two catalytic converters) combined with the on-board diagnostic (OBD) system monitored exhaust emissions and ensured the Turbo met new 1996 U.S. regulations for emissions control.

The new six-speed gearbox was fitted with longer ratios and internals strengthened for the increased engine torque. Aside from the 959, the Turbo came with four-wheel drive for the first time. The new Carrera 4's lightweight system was used with maximum power split being 80/20, biased to the rear. A limited slip differential was standard, while the ABD system ensured traction control up to a speed of 70 kilometers per hour (44 miles per hour).

The 993 Turbo had a top speed of 180 miles per hour (290 kilometers per hour) and the 0-to-62.5-miles-per-hour (0-to-100-kilometers-per-hour) acceleration took just 4.5 seconds.

1995–1996 GT2

This is a short indulgence on a car that was built for the track, but of which some 50 were built for the road. The rear-wheel-drive 911 GT2 became the equipment of choice in the lower division of endurance racing from 1995. It was a no-compromise racer, with a level of trim to suit, that was about 200 kilograms (441 pounds) lighter than the 993 Turbo.

The changes compared to the Turbo were extensive in detail. The external changes included large (replaceable) wheel arch flares to accommodate the 235/40ZR18 front (on 9J wheels) and 285/35ZR18 rear (on 11J wheels) tires, revised and more aggressively styled front and rear valences sculpted to match the flares, and an enormous biplane rear spoiler. The suspension was solid bushed, adjustable, and beefed up to meet the demands of racing. The 430-brake horse-power engine for the road-legal version was derived from the standard Turbo version, with a remapped engine control unit and maximum boost pressure raised from 0.8 to 0.9 bar. The racing version offered another 50-brake horsepower.

The 1998 Evolution model further developed the theme, with reduced weight, detailed engine improvements, and revised aerodynamics, including a new front spoiler and an even higher biplane rear wing.

1996–1997 Carrera 4S

For the 1996 model year, the Carrera 4S offered the 993 four-wheel-drive system in the Turbo's chassis and wider body, with ride height reduced by 15 millimeters (0.6 inch). The Turbo's fixed tea-tray spoiler was not used because no intercooler was fitted. Consequently the less ostentatious movable spoiler was retained as the standard fit. Brakes were the Turbo's 322-millimeter (12.7-inch) diameter cross-drilled and ventilated discs with four-piston fixed calipers. The Turbo's 8Jx18-inch and 10Jx18-inch wheels were fitted with 225/40 front and 285/30 rear tires.

A high level of equipment for the Carrera 4S included air conditioning, leather, full electronically adjustable front seats, and the 10-speaker sound package. The factory noted a top speed of 168 miles per hour (270 kilometers per hour) for the 4S compared to the 171 miles per hour (275 kilometers per hour) claimed for the regular Coupe, while 062.5 miles per hour (0 to 100 kilometers per hour) acceleration was 5.3 seconds compared to the two-wheel-drive Carrera's 5.4 seconds.

Production Changes

December 1993 (Start of R-series)

New 911 Carrera (993) introduced in Coupe form only; 1994 models also include Carrera 2 Speedster and Carrera 2 Cabriolet in earlier 964 body style. Engine crankshaft strengthened and 1kg heavier, connecting rods lightened (from 0.632kg to 0.520kg), pistons lightened (from 0.657kg to 0.602kg) and elimination of the vibration damper. Hydraulic valve adjustment. Separate exhaust catalytic converters and pipe exits after central mixing chamber. Bosch M2.10 engine management. Battery 75Ah; 115A/1,610W alternator; new six-speed manual gearbox (Tiptronic optional); multi-link LSA rear-axle suspension system; fuel tank 74.5 liters (92 liters optional). Drag coefficient, Cd = 0.33. Anti-roll bars (Tiptronic in brackets): 21mm front (22mm), 18mm rear (20mm). Service intervals now 12,000 miles (20,000km). New 993 Cabriolet launched in U.K. spring 1994 (as was U.S. 993, as 1995 S series model).

August 1994 (Start of S-series)

Tiptronic S with steering wheel shift buttons introduced. October 1994 new Carrera 4 in 993 bodyshell. The 993 Carrera RS (and Club Sport) introduced February 1995: 3.8-liter engine

A car that fails the drug test! This Carrera 4S has had the Porsche Exclusive custom treatment, including a biplane rear wing and cooling ducts for the front brakes in place of the standard driving lights. The Carrera 4S combined the Turbo's sure-footed handling and exceptional brakes with the much-improved four-wheel-drive system and the responsiveness of the normally aspirated engine.

(bore 102mm, stroke 76.4mm) with 300bhp (uses Varioram, bigger valves). Battery 36Ah. Gearbox ratios (Club Sport in brackets): first, 3.154; second, 2.0; third, 1.522; fourth, 1.242 (1.241); fifth, 1,024 (1.031); sixth, 0.821 (0.829); reverse, 2.857; 240mm clutch, dual mass flywheel. Crown wheel/pinion ratio: 3.444. Reduced shifting effort on first/second compared to 1993 RS3.8. 40 percent/65 percent acceleration/deceleration differential lock; 322mm cross-drilled ventilated disc brakes all round; 360mm steering wheel. Adjustable anti-roll bars (23mm front, 19mm rear). RSR wing adjustable 0 to 12 degrees.

August 1995 (Start of T-series)

Introduction of Targa with new moving roof design. New wheels and tires (also optional for Coupe/Cabriolet): front 7Jx17in with 205/50ZR 17, rear 9Jx17in with 255/40ZR17. Engine in 911 Carrera, Cabriolet, Targa, 4, and 4S upgraded to 285bhp (uses Varioram, bigger valves). Carrera 4S is turbo-bodied Carrera 4. Includes Turbo's brakes, lowered suspension, hollow-spoke wheels. Introduction of 911 GT2 with 430bhp and, from March 1996, 993 Turbo: 408bhp, 3,600cc. Two valves/one plug per cylinder; Bosch M5.2 Engine Management; 2 KKK K16 turbochargers with two intercoolers; OBD2 diagnostic system; six-speed gearbox with 25 percent acceleration/40 percent deceleration locking differential; 18in (8J/1 OJ) aluminum hollow spoke wheels (also Carrera 4S and elsewhere optional) with 225/40ZR 18 front and 285/30ZR 18 rear tires; 322mm cross-drilled ventilated disc brakes all round. Turbo has 22mm/21mm front/rear anti-roll bars.

August 1996 (Start of V-series)

Carrera S uses Turbo bodyshell but with two-wheel drive. Speed-related volume control on standard radio fit (Porsche CR11 RDS).

September 1997 (Start of W-series)

All new 996 replaces two-wheel-drive 993 models. Four-wheel-drive and Turbo production continues until approximately July 1998. Outline 996 specification: water-cooled boxer six-cylinder engine; 3,387cc (bore 96mm, stroke 78mm); compression ratio 11.3:1; four valves per cylinder; four overhead camshafts; max power 300bhp at 6,800rpm; max torque 350 Nm at 4,600rpm; electronic ignition with solid-state distributor (six coils); sequential multi-point injection; variable intake manifold system. Drag coefficient, Cd = 0.33. Data (Tiptronic in brackets): weight, 1,320kg (1,365kg); length, 4,430mm; width, 1,765mm; height, 1,305mm; wheelbase, 2,350mm; track front/rear, 1,455mm/1,500mm on 17in wheels; fuel tank, 64 liters; 0 to 62mph, 5.2sec (6.0sec); top speed, 174mph (171 mph).

Dimensions

Wheelbase: 2,272mm.

Track (front/rear): 1,405mm/1,444mm (RS: 1,413mm/1,452mm; Turbo: 1,411mm/1,504mm).

Length: 4,245mm.

Width: 1,735mm (Carrera S, 4S, and Turbo: 1,795mm).

Height: 1,300mm (RS: 1,270mm; Turbo: 1,285mm).

Turning circle: 11.74m.

Options

Ex-factory—in some countries some of these options may have been fitted as standard. Common options without M numbers are as follows: metallic paint, paint to customer choice, leather seats, leather seats with heating, full leather interior (including seats) in series colors, custom color, and/or soft ruffled leather.

M058 bumpers with impact absorbers; M425 rear wiper (only for Coupe); M498 deletion of model designation; M567 windshield with graduated tint; M650 electric sunroof; M551 automatic wind deflector (Cabriolet only); M545 92-liter fuel tank; MP08 active limited slip differential (manual only); M224 active brake

Identification

Model year	Model	Engine	Gearbox	Chassis numbers	Engine numbers
964 production					
1994	964 Carrera 2/4	M64/01	G50/G64	WPOZZZ96ZRS40001–0505	62R00001 onward
	964 Carrera 2/4 U.S.	M64/01	G50/G64	WPOAB296RS420001–0456	62R00001 onward
	964 RS America U.S.	M64/01	G50/05	WPOAB296RS41900 1–9144	62R00001 onward
	964 Carrera 2/4 Cab	M64/01	G50/G64	WPOZZZ96ZRS450001–0315	62R00001 onward
	964 Carrera 2/4 Cab U.S.	M64/01	G50/G64	WPOCB296RS460001–0283	62R00001 onward
	964 Speedster	M64/01	G50/03	WPOZZZ96ZRS455001–5581	62R00001 onward
	964 Speedster U.S.	M64/01	G50/05	WPOCB296RS465001–5469	62R00001 onward
	964 Turbo	M64/50	G50/52	WPOZZZ96ZRS470001–0471	61R00001 onward
	964 Turbo U.S.	M64/50	G50/52	WPOAC296RS480001–0466	61R00001 onward
993 production					
1994	993 Carrera	M64/05	G50/21	WPOZZZ99ZRS310001–6412	63R00001 onward
	993 Carrera + 718	M64/05	G50/21	WPOZZZ99ZSS310001–1582	63R00001 onward
	993 Carrera Tiptronic	M64/06	A50/04	As Carrera	63R50001 onward
	993 Carrera U.S. + 718	M64/07	G50/20	WPOAA299SS320001–1453	64R00001 onward
	993 Carrera Tiptronic U.S.	M64/08	A50/05	As Carrera U.S.	64R50001 onward
	993 Cab	M64/05	G50/21	WPOZZZ99ZSS330001–5850	63R00001 onward
	993 Cab + 718	M64/05	G50/21	WPOZZZ99ZSS330001–0061	63R00001 onward
	993 Cab U.S.	M64/06	G50/20	WPOCA299SS340001–0061	64R00001 onward
	993 Cab U.S. + 718	M64/06	G50/20	WPOCA299SS340001–1224	64R00001 onward
	993 Cup + M001	M64/70	G50/30	WPOZZZ99ZRS39800 1–8100	63R80001 onward
1995	993 Carrera	M64/05	G50/21	WPOZZZ99SS310001–70 18	63500001 onward
	993 Carrera Tiptronic	M64/06	A50/04	As Carrera	63550001 onward
	993 Cab	M64/05	G50/21	WPOZZZ99SS330001–2878	63500001 onward
	993 Carrera U.S.	M64/07	G50/20	WPOAA299SS320001–4139	64500001 onward
	993 Carrera Tiptronic U.S.	M64/08	A50/05	As Carrera U.S.	64500001 onward
	993 Cab U.S.	M64/07	G50/20	WPOCA299SS340001–3718	64500001 onward
	993 Carrera RS	M64/20	G50/31	WP0ZZZ99SS390001–274	63585001 onward
	993 Cup	M64/70	G50/30	WPOZZZ99SS39800 1–8110	63580001 onward
	993 Turbo	M64/60	G64/51	WPOZZZ99SS370001–0078	61T00001 onward
1996	993 Carrera	M64/21	G50/21	WPOZZZ99TS31000 1–6762	63T00001 onward
	993 Carrera Tiptronic	M64/22	A50/04	As Carrera	63T50001 onward
	993 Carrera Targa	M64/21	G50/21	WPOZZZ99TS38000 1–1980	63T00001 onward
	993 Carrera Cab	M64/21	G50/21	WPOZZZ99TS330000 1– 2066	63T00001 onward
	993 Carrera U.S.	M64/23	G50/20	WPOAA299TS3200 1– 3671	64T00001 onward
	993 Carrera Targa U.S.	M64/23	G50/20	WPOBA299TS385001–5462	64T00001 onward
	993 Carrera Cab U.S.	M64/23	G50/20	WPOCA299TS340001–2152	64T00001 onward
	993 Carrera Tiptronic U.S.	M64/24	A50/05	As Carrera U.S.	64T50001 onward
	993 Turbo	M64/60	G64/51	WPOZZZ99TS370001–2484	61T00001 onward
	993 Turbo U.S.	M64/60	G64/51	WPOAA299TS37500 1–6357	61T00001 onward
	993 GT2	M64/60R	G50/32	WPOZZZ99TS392001–2202	61T00001 onward
1997	993 Carrera	M64/21	G50/21	WPOZZZ99VS310001–5794	63T00001 onward
	993 Carrera Tiptronic	M64/22	A50/04	As Carrera	63T50001 onward
	993 Carrera Targa	M64/21	G50/21	WPOZZZ99VS380001–1276	63T00001 onward
	993 Carrera Cab	M64/21	G50/21	WPOZZZ99VS330001–1679	63T00001 onward
	993 Carrera U.S.	M64/23	G50/20	WPOAA299VS32001–4972	64T00001 onward
	993 Carrera Targa U.S.	M64/23	G50/20	WPOBA299VS385001–567	64T00001 onward
	993 Carrera Cab U.S.	M64/23	G50/20	WPOCA299VS340001– 2157	64T00001 onward
	993 Carrera Tiptronic U.S.	M64/24	A50/05	As Carrera U.S.	64T50001 onward
	993 Turbo	M64/60	G64/51	WPOZZZ99VS370001–97 2	61T00001 onward
	993 Turbo U.S.	M64/60	G64/51	WPOAA299VS375001–6046	61T00001 onward

Notes

Chassis numbers These are 17-character VIN industry standard sequences. Consider this example: WPOCA299RS340001 (a U.S. specification 1994 Cabriolet): WPO is the world make code; CA2 is the U.S. VSD code (first letter is body type, A, C, or D for Coupe, Cabriolet, or Targa; second letter is engine/transmission type, A for two-wheel drive, B for four-wheel drive; third digit is occupant safety system type, 0 for seat belt only, 1 for driver air bag, 2 for driver/passenger air bags; in other markets these three characters were just left ZZZ; 99 is the first two digits of the type; next is the model year letter (R for 1994); S refers to the plant code (Stuttgart); next is the third digit of the type number (3), followed by the body code number.

Engine option From the 1995 model year, a 3,746cc engine was an option for the 3.6-liter cars, this enhanced performance version developing 285-brake horsepower at 6,000rpm. These engines were designated M64/05S (manual) or M64/06S (Tiptronic). For 1996 the enhanced version developed 300bhp at 6,500rpm, and designated M64/21 S (manual) or M64/22S (Tiptronic).

Miscellaneous The above table makes no distinction between rear-wheel-drive and all-wheel-drive models (except for Tiptronic, which was available with rear-wheel drive only). Models for Canada, Switzerland, and Austria were as U.S. model specification. All manual rear-wheel-drive models were available with the optional (M220) limited slip differential. From the U.S. introduction in April 1994, the majority of early models were sold as 1995 models under option M718. Chassis numbers show the letter "S" for the 1995 model year.

differential (Tiptronic only); M398 17in Cup design wheels; MP31 sport suspension with 17in wheels; MP15 full electric adjustable front seats (left and right); M437 same (left only); M438 same (right only); M383/387 sports seats (left/right); M586 lumbar support in seat (left); M513 same (right); MP14 heated seats (left/right); M454 automatic speed control; M573 automatic air conditioning; M659 onboard computer (standard on Tiptronic); M613 Installation for D-Netz cellular (Germany only); M614 Porsche telephone (Motorola) D-Netz (Germany only); M333 Blaupunkt Paris RCR42 radio/cassette (with M490 or M692); Blaupunkt Bremen RCM42 radio cassette; M693 Blaupunkt London RDM42 CD-Radio; M692 CD changer (only with M334 and M490); M490 hi-fi loudspeaker system.

1995 RS: driver and passenger air bags; full climate control; RSR spoilers; RSR front strut support; top tinted windshield.

Color Schemes

1994

Standard body colors

A1 Black, S8 Riviera Blue, G1 Guards Red, 13 Amaranth Violet, P5 Grand Prix White, X4 Speed Yellow

Special order body colors

A8 Polar Silver metallic, D3 Iris Blue metallic*, K6 Aventura Green metallic*, F8 Midnight Blue metallic*, Q9 Slate Gray metallic, Z8 Black metallic.* Also any solid or metallic color to sample (* denotes pearl effect color).

Interior colors

Midnight Blue, Classic Gray, Chestnut Brown, Black.

Fabrics

Leatherette for seats, carpets, dash, knee bar, roofliner, A and B pillars, sun visors, windowsills front and rear, backwall top section, steering wheel (leather), and other color-coded trim. Two-tone interiors with second color for carpets: Midnight Blue/Marble Gray, Black/Marble Gray, Black/Marble Gray. Leather in Midnight Blue, Classic Gray, Chestnut Brown, and Black (except roofliner, A and B pillars, sun visors in leatherette). Special leather in Flamenco Red, Cedar Green, Provence Blue/Midnight Blue*, Provence Blue/Black* (* for dash, knee bar, roofliner, A and B pillars, sun visors, windowsills front and rear, back wall top section in leather, steering wheel). Or leather to customer sample.

Carpets

Midnight Blue, Classic Gray, Chestnut Brown, Black, Marble Gray, Cashmire Beige. Special colors: Flamenco Red, Cedar Green, Provence Blue.

Cabriolet soft-top colors

Classic Gray, Chestnut Brown, Marble Gray, Dark Blue, Black.

1995

Standard body colors

A 1 Black, G 1 Guards Red, P5 Grand Prix White, S8 Riviera Blue, T3 Amaranth Violet, X4 Speed Yellow.

Special order body colors

A8 Polar Silver metallic, D3 Iris Blue metallic, F8 Midnight Blue metallic, K6 Aventura Green metallic, Q9 Slate Gray metallic, Z8 Black metallic. Plus any paint color and material to special order.

Interior colors

Black, Cedar Green, Cashmire Beige, Midnight Blue, Classic Gray, Chestnut, Marble Gray.

Fabrics

Leatherette, leather, "soft ruffled" leather, "Porsche" cloth.

Carpets

Midnight Blue, Classic Gray, Chestnut Brown, Black, Marble Gray, Cashmire Beige. Special colors: Flamenco Red, Cedar Green, Provence Blue, Rubicon Gray.

Cabriolet soft-top colors

Black, Dark Blue, Classic Gray, Chestnut, Marble Gray.

1996

Standard body colors

A1, Black; G1, Guards Red; J1, Blue Turquoise; P5, Grand Prix White; X4, Speed Yellow.

Special order body colors

A8, Polar Silver Metallic; D3, Iris Blue Metallic; F8, Midnight Blue Metallic; H8, Arena Red Metallic; K1, Turquoise Metallic; K6, Aventura Green Metallic; Z8, Black Metallic.

Interior colors

Black, Classic Gray, Midnight Blue, Cashmire Beige, Chestnut. Plus special order colors: Flamenco Red, Cedar Green, Provence Blue, Rubicon Gray.

Fabrics

Leatherette, leather, "soft ruffled" leather, "Porsche" cloth.

Carpets

Midnight Blue, Classic Gray, Chestnut Brown, Black, Marble Gray, Cashmire Beige. Special colors: Flamenco Red, Cedar Green, Provence Blue, Rubicon Gray.

Cabriolet soft-top colors

Black, Classic Gray, Marble Gray, Dark Blue, Chestnut.

1997

Standard body colors

A1, Black; G1, Guards Red; J1, Blue Turquoise; G1, Pastel Yellow; Z1, Glacier White.

Special order body colors

E1, Ocean Blue Metallic; F1, Zenith Blue Metallic; H8, Arena Red Metallic; X1, Arctic Silver Metallic, Z8, Black Metallic.

Interior colors

Black, Classic Gray, Midnight Blue, Cashmire Beige, Chestnut. Plus special leathers in Rubicon Gray, Nephrite (blue/green), Boxster Red (with black Cabriolet soft-tops).

Fabrics

Leatherette, leather, "Porsche" cloth.

Carpets

Midnight Blue, Classic Gray, Chestnut Brown, Black, Cashmire Beige. Special colors: Rubicon Gray, Nephrite (blue/green), Boxster Red.

Cabriolet soft-top colors

Black, Classic Gray, Dark Blue, Chestnut.

Production Data

Model year	Model	Power (bhp DIN@rpm)	Torque (Nm@rpm)	Compression ratio	Weight (kg)	Number built
994 production						
1994	964 Carrera 2/4	250@6,100	310@4,800	11.3:1	1,350/1,450	505
	964 Carrera 2/4 U.S.	250@6,100	310@4,800	11.3:1	1,350/1,450	456
	964 RS America U.S .	250@6,100	310@4,100	11.3:1	1,350/1,450	144
	964 Carrera 2/4 Cab	250@6,100	310@4,800	11.3:1	1,350/1,450	315
	964 Carrera 2/4 Cab U.S.	250@6,100	310@4,800	11.3:1	1,350/1,450	283
	964 Speedster	250@6,100	310@4,800	11.3:1	1,350	581
	964 Speedster U.S.	250@6,100	310@4,800	11.3:1	1,400	469
	964 Turbo	360@5,500	520@4,200	7.5:1	1,470	471
	964 Turbo U.S.	360@5,500	520@4,200	7.5:1	1,470	466
993 production						
1994	993 Carrera	272@6,000	330@5,000	11.3:1	1,370	7,994
	993 Carrera U.S.	272@6,000	330@5,000	11.3:1	1,370	1,453
	993 Carrera Cab	272@6,000	330@5,000	11.3:1	1,370	5,911
	993 Carrera Cab U.S.	272@6,000	330@5,000	11.3:1	1,370	1,285
1995	993 Carrera 2/4	272@6,100	330@5,000	11.3:1	1,370/1,420	7,018
	993 Carrera U.S. 2/4	272@6,100	330@5,000	11.3:1	1,370/1,420	4,139
	993 Carrera Cab 2/4	272@6,100	330@5,000	11.3:1	1,370/1,420	2,878
	993 Carrera Cab U.S.	272@6,100	330@5,000	11.3:1	1,370/1,420	3,718
	993 Carrera RS	300@6,500	355@5,400	11.3:1	1,279	274
	993 Cup	310@6,200	370@5,500	11.5:1	1,100	110
	993 Turbo	408@5,750	540@4,500	8.0:1	1,575	78
1996	993 Carrera 2/4	285@6,100	340@5,250	11.3:1	1,370/1,420	6762
	993 Carrera Targa	285@6,100	340@5,250	11.3:1	1,400	1,980
	993 Carrera Cab 2/4	285@6,100	340@5,250	11.3:1	1,370/1,420	2,066
	993 Carrera U.S.	285@6,100	340@5,250	11.3:1	1,370	3,671
	993 Carrera Targa U.S.	285@6,100	340@5,250	11.3:1	1,400	462
	993 Carrera Cab U.S.	285@6,100	340@5,250	11.3:1	1,370/1,420	2,152
	993 Turbo	408@5,750	540@4,500	8.0:1	1,575	2,484
	993 Turbo U.S.	408@5,750	540@4,500	8.0:1	1,575	1,357
	993 GT2	430@5,750	535@4,500	8.0:1	1,290	202
1997	993 Carrera 2/4	285@6,100	340@5,250	11.3:1	1,370/1,420	5,794
	993 Carrera Targa	285@6,100	340@5,250	11.3:1	1,400	1,276
	993 Carrera Cab 2/4	285@6,100	340@5,250	11.3:1	1,370/1,420	1,679
	993 Carrera U.S.	285@6,100	340@5,250	11.3:1	1,370	2,972
	993 Carrera Targa U.S.	285@6,100	340@5,250	11.3:1	1,400	567
	993 Carrera Cab U.S.	285@6,100	340@5,250	11.3:1	1,370/1,420	2,157
	993 Turbo	408@5,750	540@4,500	8.0:1	1,575	972
	993 Turbo U.S.	408@5,750	540@4,500	8.0:1	1,575	1,048

Notes

Models denoted U.S. include Canada, Austria, and Switzerland. For Tiptronic, add 25 kilograms to weights given for relevant models.

Buying and Driving

The first 911s are now rare but have an elegance all of their own. Wood on the dashboard and lots of chrome recall the spirit of the 1960s.

With more than 50 years of production to choose from and significant differences in performance between the models, buying a 911 is not a straightforward process of matching budget to car and then going out to the dealers to kick tires.

As will be obvious from the large number of models outlined in this book, the Porsche 911 is more a sports car design philosophy than a given assembly of nuts and bolts. It is that philosophy that links the first, the most recent, and all those to come in the future. They are all 911s, and unmistakably so.

Choosing the right air-cooled 911 is also complicated by the significant overlaps in value between some models. Perhaps the first decision to be made is to ask yourself what you want your 911 for. If you need it for everyday use, or to fit in with a particular lifestyle, then the simple advice is go for the latest model you can afford, assuming good condition of course.

If you are looking for something of a present to yourself—a weekend toy—then one of the classic models may

be for you. With these models you can also think a little more in terms of whether you want a project car to work on in your leisure time, or whether you want a car ready to drive and enjoy. Nevertheless, the costs of restoration on an older model should not be underestimated.

The last group to consider is the faster 911s. Typically, these cars are the S, RS, GT, and Turbo models and are suited to both fast road or noncompetitive track use.

Choosing the type of 911 you want should be made easier by this book, but you'll need to spend some time scanning specific classified advertisements understanding what prices are doing. Only then will you be able to match what you would like with what might be possible.

The first rule of buying a used 911 is to appreciate that there are no cheap cars out there (unless you are very lucky indeed). If you see what appears to be a bargain, there's usually good cause. There can be any number of reasons why a Porsche will be advertised below the typical average for a given model, but seller ignorance isn't often one of them. Misrepresentation (whether deliberate or in

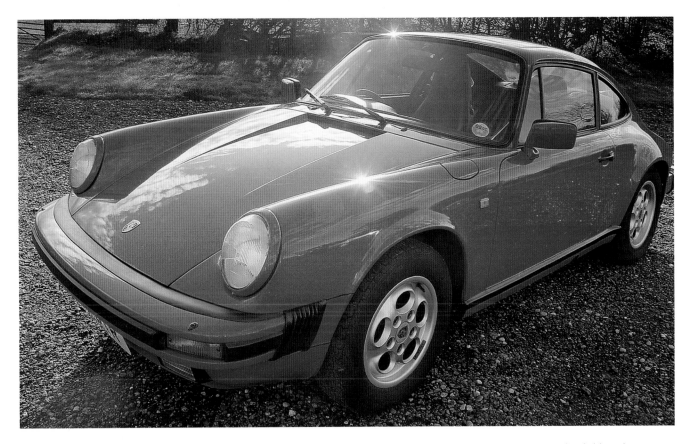

A Carrera 3.2 makes a great deal of sense for anyone new to Porsches because by this time the whole 911 package was supremely reliable and trouble-free.

ignorance) is frequent, both on type and condition. If it appears too good to be true, then it probably is.

For any given authentic model, condition is the single most important component driving the value. Poor condition or an adventurous past is usually the reason why Porsches are advertised cheaply.

Doing the book and Internet research and going to see some cars is all part of the fun, and any prospective owner can make these first steps on their own. Once you have identified a given car that seems to tick all the right boxes, it seems obvious to say that the next steps should involve an expert.

Having somebody on your side who knows your model of 911 inside out, how it should drive, what the current values are, and what inspection checks need to be made will give you peace of mind in what is a substantial personal investment. The cost of such expert involvement will often pay for itself in just the extra negotiating information you'll be given before you do the deal. Such independent Porsche inspection specialists can be found easily on the Internet.

Many buyers assume that sourcing a car from a dealer with a showroom means that the car must have some sort of underwritten quality over a private purchase. It doesn't and unless you have a bulletproof warranty and you live right next door to the dealer, it will be you who pays any immediate bills.

After condition, there follows a list of parameters that will add or reduce the value of the car. These include mileage, service history, and color (exterior and interior). The items that will always reduce the value of a given car are aftermarket customization and accident repairs. Many buyers will also regard the number of owners as important, but remember that it only takes one bad owner to ruin a good car. In my view, having multiple owners doesn't necessarily mean a bad car.

You must also drive your chosen model before you buy. Arrange temporary insurance to drive a given car and you will find it money well spent, particularly if you don't like the experience. The earlier 911s (even the 993s) have a unique driving character that not everybody will like.

Performance at a Glance

Year	Model	Weight (kg)	Power (bhp)	Top speed kph	Top speed mph	0–62mph (sec)	Source
1963	901	1080	130	210	131	8.5*	P.Frère
1964–1967	911 (2.0)	1040	130	210	130	8.3*	Motor
1967–1969	911S (2.0)	1050	160	220	137	8.0*	Autocar
1968–1969	911T (2.0)	1075	110	200	124	8.3	AM&S
1968	911L (2.0)	1075	130	210	131	10.6*	Car
1968	911L US Sporto	1098	130	188	117	10.3*	R&T
1969	911E (2.0)	1020	140	215	134	8.4*	R&T
1969	911E Sporto	1060	140	209	130	9.1*	AMM
1970–1971	911T (2.2)	1020	125	205	127	9.5	AM&S
1970–1971	911E (2.2)	1020	155	220	137	7.6*	Autosport
1970–1971	911S (2.2)	1020	180	220	138	7.0	P.Frère
1972–1973	911T (2.4)	1075	130	204	127	8.1/9.5*	Motor
1972–1973	911E (2.4)	1050	165	220	138	7.9	Factory
1972–1973	911S (2.4)	1050	190	230	144	6.6	P.Frère
1973	Carrera RS M471	975	210	245	152	5.8	P.Frère
1974	Carrera RS 3.0	1063	230	238	148	4.9*	Road Test
1974–1975	911	1075	150	210	131	7.9*	R&T
1976–1977	911	1123	165	217	135	7.8/7.2*	Motor
1974–1977	911S	1105	175	229	142	6.1*	Autocar
1974–1977	911S US	1130	165	232	144	7.5*	R&T
1974–1975	Carrera 2.7	1075	210	240	150	6.3	AM&S
1974–1977	Turbo 3.0	1140	260	250	155	6.0*	Motor
1976–1977	Carrera 3.0	1120	200	235	146	6.1*	AM&S
1978–1979	911SC	1233	180	227	141	6.5*	Autocar
1978–1979	911SC US	1243	180	203	126	6.3*	R&T
1978–1979	911 Turbo (3.3)	1300	300	260	162	5.1*	Motor
1980	911SC	1232	188	225	141	7.0	Factory
1981–1983	911SC	1160	204	235	146	5.7*	Motor
1984–1985	Carrera 3.2	1210	231	245	152	5.6*	Autocar
1984	911SC RS	960	255	255	159	5.0*	AM&S
1987–1989	911 Club Sport	1110	231	251	156	5.6*	Autocar
1989–1993	Carrera 4	1450	250	260	162	5.7	Factory
1990–1993	Carrera 2	1350	250	260	162	5.7	Factory
1990–1993	Carrera 2 Tiptronic	1355	250	253	157	6.6/6.2*	Factory/A&M
1991	Carrera 2 RS	1230	260	260	162	5.3	Factory
1991–1992	Turbo	1470	320	270	168	5.0	Factory
1992	Turbo S	1290	380	290	180	4.6	Factory
1993	Carrera 2 Speedster	1350	250	260	162	5.7	Factory
1993	Carrera RS 3.8	1210	300	269	168	4.9	Factory
1993–1994	Turbo 3.6	1470	360	280	175	4.8	Factory
1994–1997	Carrera 3.6	1370	272	270	168	5.4	Factory
1995–1998	Carrera 4	1420	272	270	168	5.3	Factory
1994–1996	993 Cup	1120	315	280	175	4.7	Factory
1995–1996	Carrera RS	1270	300	275	172	5.0	Factory
1995–1997	Turbo	1500	408	288	180	4.5	Factory
1996–1997	Carrera 3.6	1370	285	274	171	5.4	Factory
1996–1997	Carrera S Tiptronic	1365	285	269	168	6.4	Factory
1996–1997	Carrera 4	1420	285	274	171	5.3	Factory
1996–1997	Carrera 4S	1450	285	269	168	5.3	Factory
1996–1997	Carrera S	1400	285	269	168	5.4	Factory
1998	Carrera 3.4	1320	300	278	174	5.2	Factory

Notes

All power figures are DIN. Weights generally tend to quote a specific publication's curb weight (which usually includes oil and fuel for about 50 miles). Factory figures are the base model with no options, so they are not very realistic! Where 0–62mph time is marked*, this is a 0–60mph time. Magazine source codes: AMM, Australian Motor Manual; A&M, Autocar & Motor (UK); AM&S, Auto Motor & Sport (Germany); R&T, Road & Track (USA).

The last general buying point to remember is to be careful about how you pay for the car. There are many unscrupulous individuals out there only too willing to rip you off. Given that whatever the value, the amount of money involved is always going to be important to you, it pays to buy the seller as well as checking out the car. By this I mean it is important to get a sense of trust established with the person selling the car. Don't buy from a guy in a filling station with only a mobile cell phone as the point of contact. If it's a private purchase, go to the seller's house and match the address with the registration documents. There are no completely safe ways of exchanging money for cars that protect both buyer and seller, so it's important you both establish that sense of trust. Talk to your bank or funds holder about safe ways to transfer cash.

This book covers four clearly defined eras in the 911 story. The early 911s, up to and including the 1973 models, represent the antique segment of the family and are almost without exception rare and highly sought after. Once you have identified this is the type of 911 you want, the importance of learning about what makes the car authentic—so preserving its intrinsic value—is an essential next step before seeing any cars in the metal. You may find some less expensive early 911s advertised, but these cars will be money pits. Such cars need careful restoration cost assessment and a strict ceiling set on purchase price.

The driving experience of these early cars is something from another age. The early models (the short wheelbase cars to 1968) feel light and flighty at speed and are notable for the "wooden" feel in the brakes. They don't particularly handle well and inexperienced use of the throttle will have them swapping ends in a blink. The later long-wheelbase models are better and the 2.2-liter, 2.4-liter, and 2.7 RS cars are the ones everybody wants. Don't believe the fuel-injected cars are the only ones to have. At this stage of the 911's development a nicely tuned and set-up carburetor car can be just as much fun as the mechanically injected models.

The bottom line with the early cars is that you have to be highly motivated to buy one, never underestimate the cost of restoration, and be prepared for maintenance costs that can be similar to running a derelict Scottish castle or teenage children. Nevertheless, these cars are fantastically rewarding. They are fun to work on, and they have a driving character that the newer models would die for. Previous trends also suggest that in good condition, they make good long-term investments.

The second group is what we might term the classic 911s. These are the cars manufactured between 1974 and 1989. They include the 2.7s, the 911SC, the Carrera 3.2, and the 930 Turbos. These models represent the perfect starter group for a new 911 driver, combining realistic reliability with raw 911 driving character.

The 1974 models marked the introduction of the so-called "impact-bumper" cars, but with the first worldwide oil crisis the nature of the 911 began to change. These 911s began to have exhaust emissions equipment and safety equipment that switched the focus from pure performance development to refining the ride, handling, and acceptability of the car. These cars don't command the sky-high values of the early models and as such offer a good choice if you are looking to run your first 911 on a sensible budget. Again, condition is the key.

Full zinc coating (galvanizing) as a comprehensive form of bodywork protection didn't appear on the 911 until the 1976 model year. While the coating protects a car that hasn't been repaired or crashed for about 10 years through the salt-laden Northern hemisphere winters, after that, the bodywork condition becomes something of a lottery. After 20 years, you might as well forget it. You have to look closely at structure condition of any car past that age.

These and the later 911 models to 1989 progressively deteriorate in the sills (rocker panels), with corrosion working its way out from the door posts and jack points. You'll often see cars that may have a few harmless looking paint blisters in the rear of the door opening. These require careful assessment by somebody who has experience with the 911. The same applies to blisters anywhere on the exterior. It is also easy for the unscrupulous to conceal such corrosion with filler and a quick repaint.

The 911SC and Carrera 3.2 represent the best options in the late-classic era 911s. From the start of the 1978 model year, the 911SC has the more reliable Turbo-based 930 engine. Being air-cooled, the engine oil plays a part in cooling as well as lubricating. For longer engine life, there should be evidence that the oil has been changed at the prescribed intervals.

The Carrera 3.2 engine benefits not only from the extra 200cc capacity but also from the first electronic engine management to appear on the 911.

Both the 911SC and the Carrera 3.2 manufactured to the end of the 1986 model year (check out the vehicle identification numbers) use the Porsche-designed type 915 gearbox.

It needs time to warm up and is a relatively slow shift, but it does replicate the shift of every important Porsche racer of the late 1960s and 1970s. It isn't for everyone, and those seeking a more modern feel will prefer the 1987-onward cars fitted with the Getrag G50 gearbox.

The 964–model Carrera 2 and Carrera 4 were supremely refined sports cars—the ultimate grand tourers. Civility was further enhanced when the new "intelligent" Tiptronic automatic transmission was incorporated onto the Carrera 2.

The other point to note about the driving experience of the 911SC and the Carrera 3.2 is that these cars pride themselves in giving the driver a very involving contact with the road. They drive quite differently, perhaps more confidently is the right description, than the early 911s. They are also the first 911s that won the car its reputation for "being hewn from granite," so good was their initial reliability.

The third 911 group are the Type 964 911s: the Carreras, RSs, and Turbos made between 1989 and 1993. The 964 was a major step forward for the 911, enough to warrant a new type number. The new all-wheel-drive version brought considerable stability to the 911 equation. The thoroughly revised 3.6-liter engine also gave the rear-wheel-drive models far livelier performance than before. General improvements included the addition of ABS, coil spring suspension, and power steering. Nevertheless, the cars did suffer from some teething troubles.

It took a while to get the dual mass flywheel right, and oil leaks were a perennial problem. Most cars should have had any issues like that sorted out by now, and the main task will be identifying the improved later models from the earlier cars. Checking the date of first registration lines up with the model year shown on the VIN is an important step, as many cars were stockpiled during the 1991–1992 recession.

The 964-model RS and Turbo are landmark 911s for their sheer performance, the 1993 3.6-liter Turbo being the last of the single-turbo, rear-wheel-drive 911s.

The fourth grouping is the 993 family. This was the "interim" model developed to plug the gap ahead of the new generation cars from 1997. As such, these 911s must be regarded as the best of the air-cooled breed, and good examples are most sought after. As well as a fresh new appearance, their most significant performance improvement was the multi-link rear suspension, which transformed the predictability of the handling.

The all-wheel-drive system was significantly improved from the 964's system. Choosing a model shouldn't be so much about whether it has two- or four-wheel drive but more about its all-important condition. The all-wheel drive was introduced to the Turbo, which also gained twin turbos for smoother power delivery. Like the 964 family, the RS and Turbo variants are the most sought-after 993s. The Targa was also relaunched with a new panoramic glass roof. These cars maintained the strong niche appeal of secure, open-topped 911 life.

What has changed since the ending of the 993's production in 1998 is that every air-cooled 911 has become desirable. No matter how problematic or undesirable a specific air-cooled 911 might have been back in the day, it has been swept forward on a seemingly unstoppable wave of demand for older 911s. In most developed countries today, demand for good air-cooled 911s of any performance level outstrips supply. This demand has been fueled by an increasing desire to park personal savings into hard assets such as artwork and collectible cars. It is a market that has also made starlets out of 911s that were previously completely unloved, simply because of the insatiable demand. However, that doesn't apply to every car. Getting top prices requires either very low mileage and excellent condition or vast expenditure on "make as new" authentic restorations.

Doing your homework before stepping into the marketplace is essential, and today it is so much easier to research car and seller integrity using online resources.

Look for the best condition and mileage, certainly, but don't focus on color or options. There's always a Porsche more expensive than the one you can afford, and in the classic Porsche market, it may not be the most expensive car that offers you the most enjoyment—and, yes, financial return. A top-condition 911SC may make more sense than a scruffy Carrera 3.2.

If you take away only one piece of advice from this Buying and Driving chapter, let it be this: if you don't have the necessary time or experience to find the right 911, enlist an expert to advise you on the condition and value of your proposed car. There are plenty of lemons around, as well as people ready to relieve you of your cash.

Few would disagree that the air-cooled Porsche 911 is a landmark in automotive history. It is a unique car both technically and in its very significant commercial success.

If you drive, or want to drive, just one sports car in your life, it has to be a 911.

Porsche Clubs

There are now officially recognized Porsche clubs in more than 60 countries worldwide with tens of thousands of members.

You can obtain details of your nearest Porsche club by going to the Porsche website (www.porsche.com), going

to your own country's home page, and following the subheadings as follows: Events and racing: Porsche clubs: Porsche club addresses: Find Porsche clubs: Please choose a Porsche club.

Index